Dead Funny

D1556738

Dead Funny

Illustrated by
Bill Tidy

Introduced by Bevis Hillier

ASH & GRANT

Ash & Grant Limited
11 Griffin Road,
London SE18 7QG

First published 1974

Dead Funny
© Ash & Grant Limited 1974
Hardback ISBN 0 904069 02 8
Paperback ISBN 0 904069 01 X

Designed by Janette Palmer

Printed in Great Britain by
Sydney Lee (Exeter) Ltd.

Introduction

Thomas Sherrer Ross Boase, formerly President of Magdalen College, Oxford, who died earlier this year, was famed for his charming and slightly inane smile, and for his genius in coining truisms. When Sir John Betjeman said that the new Waynflete Building of Magdalen was a hideous eyesore that would ruin Oxford for ever, Boase replied mildly,

'Oh, I don't know, John, it's not as ugly as it looks, you know.'

An Indian undergraduate was reported to him for being idle and incompetent. He commented,

'You really shouldn't be *both*, Mr Banerji.'

So when Boase began his book *Death in the Middle Ages* with the sentence 'Death was a grim business in the Middle Ages', there was much sniggering in common rooms over what was taken to be an award-winning new Boasism. Who, wits asked each other, was likely to welcome with screeches of joy the onset of bubonic plague? But as usual there was an edge to the banality. With the long historical perspective which he was able to take, Boase knew that, although we are still suffering the hangover of Victorian mawkishness about death, and therefore take a view almost as gloomy as the medieval, one doesn't have to go far back in history to find an age when death was a riot of fun; when the parson must have gurgled with ill-suppressed mirth as he tossed the proud and angry dust into the pit, while the mourners were shaking with irrepressible guffaws (as in Bill Tidy's cover cartoon) at the pungent epitaph the local carver had hacked on the stone. The recent film about 'Punch' Miller, the jazz trumpeter, showed how jolly a thing a funeral can still be in a not too sophisticated community. The fearfulness of death can be compensated or at least disguised by a little black levity.

'Who cared about the corpse? The funeral made the attraction', wrote Byron in *The Vision of Judgment*.

Writers linger on for a little while in what they have written; others, only in what is written about them; and it's just bad luck if your tombstone happens to be in a Yorkshire churchyard exposed to ferocious wuthering. It is also very hazardous to have a name like Spark or Pease. Humbert Wolfe wrote,

> Not Helen's wonder
> nor Paris stirs,
> but the bright untender
> hexameters.
> And thus, all passion
> is nothing made,
> but a star to flash in
> an Iliad.

All very well, but at least Paris and Helen had Homer to write them up; what if your lot is a jobbing epitaphist who decides that your whole life, loves, dreads and achievements can be encapsulated in one silly rhyming joke? The religious themselves are not above playing this trick. In an old cemetery at Bilbao is an epitaph which reads,

> Aqui Fra Diego reposa
> Jamás hizo otra cosa.

(Here rests Friar James. He never did anything else.)

In many of the epitaphs, while the chisel ceased chipping centuries ago, one can still hear the axe grinding. There is religious propaganda of the 'Reader take heed' type; the reader is 'put in minde of humane frailtie' as William Camden said (quoted by John Weever in his *Ancient Funerall Monuments* of 1631). There are paeans of hate to the departed, as in the itemized denunciation by William Bond of his unprepossessing sister-in-law, quoted in full in this book. Severe practical warnings are given—against inadequate fencing around wells, wrong prescriptions, thin ice, and 'burglarizing', which could still draw down summary justice from a trigger-happy squireen. 'Inconsolable' widows advertised on tombstones that business would continue as usual—though not, perhaps, precisely the business suggested in Bill Tidy's cartoon (p. 54).

In the late 18th and early 19th centuries, epitaph-hunting became a popular sport of the leisured classes. Examples were published in the *London Chronicle* and the *Gentleman's Magazine*, which makes such a telling appearance in the epitaph of Viscountess Downe (p.85). Some of the clergy strongly resented this practice, rather as some today dislike brass-rubbing. The Rev. Legh Richmond wrote in *Annals of the Poor* (1814),

> I have often lamented, when indulging a contemplation among the graves, that some of the inscriptions were coarse and ridiculous; others, absurdly flattering... What can be more disgusting than the too common spectacle of trifling, licentious travellers, wandering about the churchyards of the different places through which they pass, in search of rude, ungrammatical, ill-spelt and absurd verses among the gravestones; and this for the gratification of their unholy scorn and ridicule!

Church-crawlers today are not just looking for laughs, but also for fragments of social history and good amateur verse. I recently went on an epitaph hunt in the west of England. Dorset is Thomas Hardy country, and the church of Bere Regis contains the tombs of the Turbervilles, perhaps kinsmen of that Bryan Turberville of St James's, Westminster, celebrated in the epitaph on p.12. In the church of Queen Camel, Somerset, is a splendid epitaph to Humphry Mildmay, lord of the manor:

> He sustain'd severall Wounds in the Warrs for his
> Loyalty to his Prince King Charles the first
> particularly at Newbury Fight, where he served as
> Major under his Uncle ye Earle of Cleveland, and
> was taken up among the slain. d. 1690 aged 67. . .

A more humble stone, in the graveyard of St Clement's in Moresk, Cornwall, commemorates Elizabeth Gay, a servant:

> Here lye the Remains of Elizabeth Gay who after a service of forty years finding her strength diminished with unparalleled distinterestedness requested that her Wages might be proportionately lessened. d. July 7 1790. As a testimony of their Gratitude for the Care she took of them for their tender years, this Stone is Erected by the Surviving Daughters of her late Master and Mistress Christopher and Elizabeth Warwick of Park in this Parish.

In the churchyard of St Andrew's, Ashburton, Devon, are two stones commemorating John Winsor, Sergemaker (d.1772) and Miriam Adams 'who for Forty four Years discharged the responsible duties of letter-Carrier to the Post Office in this town with uniform cheerfulness and strict fidelity (d.1838 aged 77.)' Truro Cathedral contains a monument to Edwy Arthur West, 'formerly a chorister of this cathedral church who in the wreck of the S.S. Titanic passed through the Great Waters. April 15, 1912.'

Such modern public scolds as Malcolm Muggeridge are fond of telling us that 'Death has replaced sex as the new pornography.' In other words, while everyone chatters freely about sex, death has become a taboo subject—an exact reversal of the Victorian situation, in which an obsessive interest was taken in the minutiae of death and funeral obsequies—every last detail, as it were—but talk of sex was confined to dirty jokes with the port, or to those covert volumes from whose republication the Drs Kronhausen and their publishers have lately made many an honest penny. This book goes far to disprove the scolds. We are talking about death again, even laughing at it. If death is the new pornography, funny epitaphs are its dirty jokes.

Bevis Hillier

My husband
promised me
that my
body should
be cremated
but other
influences
prevailed.

(Emily Spear, d. 1901, aged 64)

Glendale Cemetery, Cardington, Ohio

Donald Robertson
Born 11th January, 1785. Died 4th June, 1848
aged 63 years

He was a peaceable quiet man and to all appearances a sincere
Christian. His death was very much regretted, which was caused by
the stupidity of Laurence Tulloch of Clotherton, who sold him
nitre instead of Epsom salts, by which he was killed in the space of
3 hours after taking a dose of it.

Cross Kirk burial ground, Esha Ness, Shetland

Lord, she is Thin.

(Susannah Ensign, d. 1825)

Presbyterian churchyard, Cooperstown, New York

Here lieth Mary, the wife of John Ford,
We hope her soul is gone to the Lord,
But if for hell she has changed this life
She had better be there than be John Ford's wife.

(Mary Ford, d. 1790)

Potterne, Wiltshire

Mary Randolph Keith Marshall
wife of Thomas Marshall, by whom she had
Fifteen Children
was born in 1737 and died in 1807.
She was good but not brilliant
Useful but not great.

Nr Washington, Kentucky

In memory of
Julius Lee
who was exploded
in a powder
mill
July 13, 1821
AE 21

Old Cemetery, Southwick, Massachusetts

Here lies Juan Cabecca, Chorister of our Lord the King. When he was received into the choir of angels, in augmentation of that happy company, his voice was so distinguished from the rest that even God himself harkened to him with attention, and said, rather severely, to the angels, "Hold your tongues, ye calves, and let Juan Cabecca, Chorister to the King of Spain, sing my praise".

(Translated)

Saragossa, Spain

Sacred to the memory of our 'steamed friend.

(Said to be the epitaph of a New Orleans man who was scalded to death)

Exact location unknown

Philip Row's son died October 8, 1915, age three years, by ardent spirits.

Goshen, Connecticut

In memory of Thomas Theobald, merchant, eldest son of Peter Theobald of Lambeth, who married Martha, daughter of Thomas Turner of Lincoln's Inn Esq., by whom he had issue 7 sons and 2 daughters, who after six voyages to India and ten years residence there, returned 20 Jul. 1727 and amidst ye gratulations of his friends, resigned to death ye 9 Sep following.

St Mary the Virgin, Lambeth, London

Sacred
to the Memory of
Thomas Sheldon
(late of Sheffield)
who died
while on a Journey
at the Golden Lion Inn,
in this Town,
Febry the 5th 1828
Aged 53 years
"In the midst of life we are in death"
This Stone was erected
by a few commercial friends, as
a tribute of respect.

St Matthew's, Ipswich, Suffolk

Devoted Christian mother who whipped Sherman's bummers with scalding water while trying to take her dinner pot which contained a hambone being cooked for her soldier boys.

(Rebecca Jones, d. 1890, aged 78)

Pleasant Grove Cemetery, Raleigh, North Carolina

Bryan Turberville, late of St. James Westminster Gent. deceased, did by his last will and testament bearing date of 20 Oct. 1711 give and bequeath to this parish of Lambeth £100 for ever to be laid out in purchase and the interest thereto for the putting out yearly two poor boys apprentices. His children also have given £100 more for the better putting out the said boys as aforesaid. Provided Rector and churchwardens shall mention this and keep the setting of this place fairly carved in a legible hand setting forth this bequest in default of which the said legacy is to become the right of St Margaret Westminster. N.B. None to be to the chimney-sweepers, watermen or fishermen and no Roman Catholic to enjoy any benefit thereof. A.D. 1719.

St Mary the Virgin, Lambeth, London

This stone is designed
by its durability
to perpetuate the memory
and by its colour
to signify the moral character
of
Miss Abigail Dudley
who died Jan 4, 1812
aged 73

Old Hill Burying Ground, Concord, Massachusetts

Sacred to the memory of Hester Fisher of Waterhouse, also of Anne
Rothery wife of N.P. Rothery, R.N. and of Elizabeth Ann Rothery
their daughter, who were unfortunately drowned at Chepstow on
the evening of Saturday Septr. 20th 1812 after hearing a sermon
from Philippians 1st chapter 21st verse.

Monkton Combe, Somerset

Sacred
To the Memory of
Maria
Widow of Baker John Littlehales Esqre.,
And daughter and sole heiress
Of Bendall Martyn Esqre.
She was a lady of rare endowments,
Both of body and mind,
But eminently distinguished
For her piety, meekness and charity.

(d. Nov 11, 1796)

St Michael's, Highgate, London

This town was settled in 1748 by Germans who emigrated to this place with the promise and expectation of finding a prosperous city, instead of which they found nothing but wilderness.

(Rev. John Starman, d. 1854, aged 72)

Old German Cemetery, Waldorboro, Maine

Here lyeth the bodie of John Middleton the childe, borne 1578 dyede 1623. Nine feet three.

Hale churchyard, Lancashire

Under the sod, under the trees
Lies the body of Jonathan Pease
He is not here
But only his pod:
He shelled out his peas
And went to God.

Nantucket, Massachusetts

Below lyes for sartin
Honest old Harting,
And snug close beside un,
His fat wife, a wide one.
If another you lack,
Look down and see Jack;
And further a yard,
Lyes Charles who drank hard.
And near t'un lies Moggy,
Who never got groggy,
Like Charles and her father,
Too abstemious the rather,
And therefore popp'd off
In a tissickey cough.
Look round now and spy out
The whole family out.

Ditchling, Sussex

Anything for a change.

New Gray Cemetery, Knoxville, Tennessee

The deceased being asked on the evening of his arrival in Waverly
where he was going answered here and no farther.

When your razor is dull
    and you want to shave
Think of the man
    that lays in this grave.

For there was a time
    It might have been whet
You was afeared of a dime
    And now it's too late.

(August Hefner, d. 1856, aged 70)

Evergreen Cemetery, Waverly, Ohio

In Memory of Mr Nath. Parks, aged 19, who on 21st March 1794 being out a hunting and concealed in a ditch was casually shot by Mr Luther Frink.

Elmwood Cemetery, Holyoke, Massachusetts

In Memory of William French
Son of Mr Nathaniel French; Who
Was Shot at Westminster, March ye 13th
1775, by the hands of Cruel Ministereal Tools
of Georg ye 3d; in the Corthouse, at a 11 a Clock at Night,
in the 22d year of his Age.

Here William French his body lies.
For murder his blood for vengeance cries.
King Georg the Third his Tory crew
Tha with a bawl his head shot threw.
For liberty and his country's good
He lost his life his dearest blood.

Westminster, Vermont

Here lies Esther, the wife of James Roberts Forty-six years. She was
a loving wife, a tender Mother, a good Housekeeper — and Stayed
at Home.

Ollerton, Nottinghamshire

She was very Excellent for Reading and Soberness

(Mary Brooks, d. 1736, aged 11)

Hill Burying Ground, Concord, Massachusetts

Asad Experience Wilson
1895   1946

(Given this name because he was illegitimate)

Idlewild Cemetery, Hood River, Oregon

Here lies poor Charlotte,
Who was no harlot,
But in her virginity
Though just turned nineteen—
Which within this vicinity,
Is hard to be found and seen.

Somerset

Here lies Joseph, Anthony Myonet's son;
Abigail his sister to him is come.
Elemental fire this virgin killed,
As she sat on a cock in Stanway's field.

Winchcombe, Gloucestershire

Jonathan Richardson, 1872, aged 82,
Who never sacrificed his reason at the altar of
superstition's God, who never believed that
Jonah swallowed the whale.

East Thompson, Connecticut

Let the wind go free
Where'er thou be
For 'twas the wind
That killed me.

Leyland churchyard, Lancashire

Solomon Towslee Jr. who was killed in Pownal Vt. July 15, 1846,
while repairing to grind a scythe on a stone attached to the gearing
in the Woollen Factory. He was entangled. His death was sudden
and awful.

Pownal, Vermont

Sacred to the memory of Mrs Sarah Wall, the old and faithful but
ill-requited servant of Lord Carrington who departed this life
June 1832 aged 70 years.

Langley Marish, Buckinghamshire

To the memory of William Bacon of the Salt Office, London, Gent., who was killed by thunder and lightning at his window 12 Jul. 1787 aged 34 years.

St Mary the Virgin, Lambeth, London

The wedding day decided was,
The wedding wine provided;
But ere the day did come along
He drunk it up and died did.
    Ah Sidney!   Ah Sidney!

(*Sidney Snyder, d. 1823, aged 20*)

Providence, Rhode Island

In Memory of Thomas Thetcher a Grenadier in the North Regt. of Hants Militia, who died of a violent Fever contracted by drinking Small Beer when hot the 12th of May 1764. Aged 26 Years. In grateful remembrance of whose universal goodwill towards his Comrades, this stone is placed here at their expence, as a small testimony of their regard and esteem.

    Here sleeps in peace a Hampshire Grenadier
    Who caught his death by drinking cold small Beer,
    Soldiers be wise from his untimely fall
    And when ye're hot drink Strong or none at all.

This memorial being decay'd was restor'd by the Officers of the Garrison A.D. 1781.

    An honest soldier never is forgot
    Whether he die by Musket or by Pot.

This stone was replaced by the North Hants Militia when disembodied at Winchester on 26th April 1802, in consequence of the original Stone being destroyed.

Winchester Cathedral graveyard, Hampshire

To the Memory
of
Abraham Beaulieu
Born 15 September
1822
Accidentally shot
4th April 1844
As a mark of affection
from his brother.

Catholic Cemetery, La Pointe, Wisconsin

The Unfortunate Miranda
Daughter of John and Ruth Bridgeman Whose Remains
are here interred, fell a prey to the flames that
consumed her Father's Hoose on ye 11th of June
1791, aged 28.

The room below flamed like a stove
Anxious for those who slept above
She ventured on ye trembling floor
It fell, she sank and rose no more.

Vernon, Vermont

Here lies John Ross
Kicked by a hoss.

Jersey, Channel Islands

He rests in pieces.

(*Allegedly an epitaph to a man blown up with gunpowder*)

Exact location unknown

Here lies John Higgs,
A famous man for killing pigs,
For killing pigs was his delight
Both morning, afternoon and night.
Both heats and cold he did endure,
Which no physician could ere cure.
His knife is laid, his work is done;
I hope to Heaven his soul has gone.

(*John Higgs, pig-killer, d. 26 November, 1825, aged 55 years*)

St Mary's, Cheltenham, Gloucestershire

Erected to the Memory of
John McFarlane
Drown'd in the Water of Leith
By a few affectionate friends

Edinburgh, Midlothian

Lizzie Angell
d. 1932
I don't know how to die.

John Angell
In God's Workshop

East Derry, New Hampshire

Henry Harris d. 1837 aet. 15
Killed
by the kick of a colt
in his bowels

Peaceable and quiet, a friend to his father
and mother, and respected by all who knew
him, and went to the world where horses don't
kick, where sorrows and weeping is no more.

Ross Park Cemetery, Williamsport, Pennsylvania

Sacred to the memory of inestimable worth of unrivalled excellence
and virtue, N. R., whose ethereal parts became seraphic May 25th
1767.

Litchfield, Connecticut

In Mem. of Joseph, son of Joseph and Mary Meek, who was
accidentally drowned in the cistern of the day school adjoining this
church, April 30th 1845, aged 8 years. This distressing event is
recorded by the minister, as an expression of sympathy with the
parents and caution to the children of the school—a reproof to the
proprietors of the open wells, pits and landslips; the want of fencing
about which is the frequent cause of similar disaster in these districts;
and as a memento to all of the uncertainty of life, and the consequent
necessity of immediate and continued preparation for death.

Bilton, Warwickshire

Ruth S. Kibbe
wife of
Alvin J. Stanton
May 5, 1861
Apr 5, 1904
The Lord don't make any mistakes

South Plymouth, New York

Office up stairs

(Dr Fred Roberts, d. 1931, aged 56)

Pine Log Cemetery, Brookland, Arkansas

Caroline H.
Wife of Calvin Cutter, M.D.
Murdered by the Baptist Min-
istry and Baptist Churches as fol-
lows:— Sept. 28, 1838. Aet. 33.
She was accused of Lying in
Church Meeting, by the Rev. D.D.
Pratt and Deac. Albert Adams—was
condemned by the church un-
heard. She was reduced to pov-
erty by Deac. William Wallace.
When an expert council was
asked of the Milford Baptist
Church, by the advice of their committee, George Raymond, Calvin
Averill and Andrew Hutchinson,
they voted not to receive any com-
munication upon the subject:
The Rev. Mark Carpenter said
he thought as the good old Deac.
Pearson said "we have got Cutter
down and it is best to keep him
down". The intentional and
malicious destruction of her
character and happiness, as above
described, destroyed her life.
Her last words upon the subject were "tell the truth & the
iniquity will come out".

Elm St Cemetery, Milford, New Hampshire

Here lies the body of Mary Ann Lowder
Who burst while drinking a Seidlitz powder.
Called from this world to her heavenly rest.
She should have waited till it effervesced.

Burlington, New Jersey

Richard Kendrick was buried August 29th, 1785 by the desire of his wife, Margaret Kendrick.

Wroxham, Norfolk

Dear Friends and companions all
Pray warning take by me;
Don't venture on the ice too far
As 'twas the death of me.

(John Rose, d. 27 January 1810, aged 10)

Reigate, Surrey

This is what I expected but
not so soon

(William Reese, d. 1872, aged 21)

Westernville, New York

Going, going, GONE!

(Epitaph to an auctioneer)

Greenwood, Hampshire

Dorothy Cecil. Unmarried as yet.

Wimbledon, London

Underneath this pile of stones
Lie the remains of Mary Jones;
Her name was Lloyd, it was not Jones
But Jones was put to rhyme with stones.

Launceston, Tasmania

Capt Thomas Stetson
who was killed by the fall of a tree
d. 1820 a. 68
Nearly 30 years he was master
of a vessel & left that
employment at the age
of 48 for the less hazardous
one of cultivating his farm.
Reader remember man
is never secure from the
arrest of death.

Old Cemetery, Harvard, Massachusetts

He left his hose, his Hannah, and his love
To sing Hosannahs in the world above.

(Epitaph to a hosier)

St Michael's, Aberystwyth, Cardiganshire

Here lays John Tyrwitt,
   A learned divine;
He died in a fit,
   Through drinking port wine.
Died 3rd April, 1828, aged 59 years.

Malta

'Twas as she tript from Cask to Cask,
In at a bung-hole quickly fell,
Suffocation was her task,
She had no time to say farewell.

(Ann Collins, d. 1804)

Kings Stanley, Gloucestershire

God is Omnipotent, Omniscient, Omnipresent Electric Fluid in his life principle man which ceased to act through the organization of Dr George W. Gale of Exeter, N.H. Aug. 5 1873 aged 80 years, son of Capt. Jacob Gale of East Kingston, N.H.

The breath of life is the breath of life. After it ceased to act in the formation of dust, which returned to earth from which it was taken. Man has no power independent of any other power.

Exeter, New Hampshire

In life a jovial sot was he
He died from inebriete
A cup of burnt canary sack
To Earth from Heaven would bring him back

(John Webb, an inkeeper)

Cheshire

For the other fellow

(Aaron J. Beattie Sr., d. 1950, aged 50)

Elm Lawn Cemetery, Bay City, Michigan

Poor Martha Snell, her's gone away,
Her would if her could but her couldn't stay,
Her had two bad legs and a badish cough,
But her legs it was that carried her off.

Bangor, Caernarvonshire

Elizabeth,
the wife of Richard Barkland,
passed to eternity on Sunday, 21st May, 1797,
in the 71st year of her age.
Richard Barkland,
the ante-spouse uxorious,
was interred here 27th January, 1806,
in his 84th year.
William Barkland
brother to the preceding, Sept. 5th 1779,
aged 68 years.

When terrestrial all, in chaos shall exhibit effervescence
Then celestial virtues, in their most refulgent brilliant essence
Shall with beaming beautious radiance thro' the ebullition shine;
Transcending to glorious regions beatifical sublime;
Human power absorbed defficient to delineate such effulgent
    lasting spirits;
Where honest plebians ever will have precedence over
Ambiguous great monarchs.

(Richard & Elizabeth Barkland, 1779)

Ercall Magna, Shropshire

Here lies Jane Smith, wife of Thomas Smith, marble cutter. This monument was erected by her husband as a tribute to her memory and a specimen of his work. Monuments of the same style 350 dollars.

Springdale, Ohio

Know posterity, that on the 8th of April, in the year of grace 1757, the rambling remains of the above John Dale were in the 86th yeare of his pilgrimage, laid upon his two wives.

Bakewell, Derbyshire

Here lies I
Jonathan Frye
Killed by a sky
Rocket in my eye-socket.

Frodsham, Cheshire

This gallant young man gave his life in the attempt to save a perishing lady.

Bodmin, Cornwall

Sudden and unexpected was the end
Of our esteemed and beloved friend.
He gave to all his friends a sudden shock
By one day falling into Sunderland Dock.

Whitby, Yorkshire

Though shot and shell around flew fast
On Balaclava's plain,
Unscathed he passed to fall at last,
Run over by a train.

Martham, Norfolk

Killed by means of a Rockett.

(Simon Gilkes, d. 5 November, 1696)

Milton Regis, Kent

Papa — did you wind your watch?

(Charles B. Gunn, d. 1935, aged 88)

Evergreen Cemetery, Colorado Springs, California

Elijah Bardwell d. 1780

Having but a few days survived ye fatal night, when he was flung from his horse; and drawn by ye stirrups, 26 rods along ye path, as appeared by the place where his hat was found and here he had spent ye whole of the following severe cold night treading down the snow in a small circle. The family he left was an aged father, a wife and three small children.

Montague, Massachusetts

Here lieth Martin Elphinston,
Who with his sword did cut in sun-
der the daughter of Sir Harry
Crispe, who did his daughter marry.
She was fat and fulsome;
But men will some-
times eat bacon with their bean,
And love the fat as well as lean.

Alnwick, Northumberland

He called
Bill Smith
a Liar

(Alleged to be inscribed on a boulder near Mount Pisgah Cemetery,
Cripple Creek, Colorado)

Rosa,
My first Jersey Cow
Record 2lbs 15oz Butter
From 18qts 1 day milk

Central Village, Connecticut

Here lies the body of Alexander Macpherson
He was a very extraordinary person.
He was two yards high in his stocking-feet,
And kept his accoutrements clean and neat.
He was slew
At the battle of Waterloo:
He was shot by a bullet
Plumb through his gullet:
It went in at his throat
And came out at the back of his coat.

Exact location unknown, Scotland

Asenath
widow of
Simeon Soule
Died
Feb 25, 1865
Aged
89 years 11 mo.
& 19 days.
The Chisel can't help
her any.

Mayflower Cemetery, Duxbury, Massachusetts

Let this small monument record the name
Of Cadman, and to future times proclaim
How, by an attempt to fly from this high spire,
Across the Sabrine stream, he did acquire
His fatal end. 'Twas not for want of skill,
Or courage to perform the task, he fell;
No, no! A faulty cord drawn too tight
Hurried his soul on high to take her flight
Which bid the body here beneath, good night.

(Epitaph to a tightropewalker, killed 1739)

St Mary Friars, Shrewsbury, Shropshire

Anne Harrison well known by the name of Nanna Ran Dan, who was chaste but no prude; and tho' free yet no harlot. By principle virtuous, by education a Protestant; her freedom made her liable to censure, while her extensive charities made her esteemed. Her tongue she was unable to control, but the rest of her members she kept in subjection. After a life of 80 years thus spent, she died 1745.

Easingwold, Yorkshire

Here lies John Racket
In his wooden jacket
He kept neither horses nor mules;
He lived like a hog,
And died like a dog,
And left all his money to fools.

Woodton, Norfolk

Here lies buried in the tomb,
A constant sufferer from salt rheum,
Which finally in truth did pass
To spotted erysipelas.
A husband brave, a father true,
Here he lies; and so must you.

Baton Rouge, Louisiana

In memory of Charles H. Salmon, who was born September 10th, 1858. He grew, waxed strong, and developed into a noble son and loving brother. He came to his death on the 12th of October, 1884, by the hand of a careless drug clerk and two excited doctors, at 12 o'clock at night in Kansas City.

Morristown, New Jersey

The mortal remains of
　John Brindle;
After an evil life of 64 years
　Died June 18th, 1822,
And lies at rest beneath
　This stone.

St Giles' Cemetery, King's Road, London

They lived and they laugh'd while they were able
And at last was obliged to knock under the table.

Newbury, Berkshire

Of such is the kingdom of Heaven
Here lie the remains of Thomas Chambers
Dancing Master
Whose genteel address and assiduity in teaching
Recommended him to all that had the
Pleasure of his acquaintance.
He died June 13, 1765, Aged 31.

Llanbedlig, Carnarvonshire

Here lies the body of Mary Ellis daughter of Thomas Ellis & Lydia, his wife, of this parish. She was a virgin of virtuous character & most promising hopes. She died on the 3rd of June 1609 aged one hundred and nineteen.

Leigh, Essex

This tomb was erected by William Picket, of the City of London, goldsmith, on the melancholy death of his daughter, Elizabeth. A testimony of respect from greatly afflicted parents.

In memory of Elizabeth Picket, spinster, who died December 11, 1781. Aged 23 years. This much lamented young person expired in consequence of her clothes taking fire the preceding evening. Reader — if ever you should witness such an affecting scene; recollect that the only method to extinguish the flame is to stifle it by an immediate covering.

Stoke Newington, London

She was a lady of Spiritual and cultivated mind, and her death was instantaneous, arising from fright occasioned by a violent attack made upon her house door by three or four men in a state of intoxication with a view to disturb the peaceful inmates in the dead of night.

Long Buckby, Northamptonshire

Asa Whitcomb, a Pillow of the Settlement

Barnard, Vermont

In memory of **Mr. Neh. Hobart**, who died Jan. 5, 1789
in the 72 yr. of his age
whose death was caused by falling backwards, on a
Stick, as he was loading wood. Nobody present but his
grandson, who lived with him.
A kind husband, a tender parent, a
trusty friend, respectable in his
day, his death remarcable!

Pepperell Center, Harvard, Massachusetts

In memory of _____ who died of cholera morbus caused by
eating green fruit. In the certain hope of a blessed immortality.
Reader, go thou and do likewise.

Grantham, Lincolnshire

How shocking to the human mind
The log did him to powder grind.
God did command his soul away
His summings we must all obey.

(Elisha Woodruff, d. 1816, aged 70)

Old Burial Ground, Pittsford, Vermont

Some called him Garrett, but that was too high,
His name was Jarrett that here doth lie:
Who in his life was tost on many a wave,
And now he lies anchored here in his own grave.
The Church he did frequent while he had breath
He desired to lie therein after his death.
To heaven he is gone, the way before
Where of Grocers there is many more.

St Saviour's, Southwark, London

Here lie the bodies
of Thomas Bond and Mary his wife.
She was temperate, chaste and charitable
But
She was proud, peevish and passionate.
She was an affectionate wife and tender mother
But
her husband and child, whom she loved,
Seldom saw her countenance without a disgusting frown,
Whilst she received visitors, whom she despised,
With an endearing smile.
Her behaviour was discreet towards strangers;
But
Independent in her family.
Abroad, her conduct was influenced by good breeding;
But
At home, by ill temper.
She was a professed enemy to flattery,
and was seldom known to praise or commend;
But
The talents in which she principally excelled
Were differences of opinion, and discovering
flaws and imperfections.
She was an admirable economist,
And, without prodigality,
Dispensed plenty to every person in her family
But
Would sacrifice their eyes to a farthing candle.
She sometimes made her husband happy
With her good qualities;
But
Much more frequently miserable—with
her many failings
Insomuch that in 30 years cohabitation he
often lamented
That maugre all her virtues,
He had not, in the whole, enjoyed two years
of matrimonial comfort.
At length
Finding that she had lost the affections of her husband,
As well as the regard of her neighbours,
Family disputes having been divulged by servants,
She died of vexation, July 20, 1768,
Aged 48 years.

Her worn-out husband survived her
four months and two days
And departed this life, November 28, 1768
in the 54th year of his age.
William Bond, brother to the deceased, erected
this stone, as a *weekly monitor* to the
Surviving wives of this parish,
That they may avoid the infamy
Of having their memories handed to posterity
With a Patch-work Character.

Horsley-Down Church, Cumberland

Let her R.I.P.

Exact location unknown

Trumpets shall sound,
And archangels cry,
"Come forth, Isabel Mitchell,
And meet William Mattheson in the sky".

West Churchyard, Tranent, East Lothian

Here lies Jemmy Little, a carpenter industrious,
A very good-natured man, but somewhat blusterous.
When that his little wife his authority withstood,
He took a little stick and bang'd her as he would.
His wife, now left alone, her loss does so deplore,
She wishes Jemmy back to bang her a little more;
For now he's dead and gone this fault appears so small,
A little thing would make her think it was no fault at all.

Portsmouth, Hampshire

Sacred to the memory of Mr John Stevenson, late of this parish, who was unfortunately killed by a stag at Astley's Amphitheatre, 6 Dec. 1814 aged 49 years.

St Mary the Virgin, Lambeth, London

My good lads, do not sit upon this stone on account you do disfigure
it with your heels; lean on it if you please.
        Yours, &c.
          R. Pocock.

North Curry, Somerset

Here lie the bones of Richard Lawton,
Whose death, alas, was strangely brought on:
Trying one day his corns to mow off,
His razor slipped and cut his toe off;
His toe, or rather what it grew to,
An inflammation quickly flew to,
Which took, alas, to mortifying,
Which was the cause of Richard's dying.

Moreton-in-Marsh, Gloucestershire

Here lies one wh
os life thrads
cut asunder she
was stroke dead
by a clap of thunder

(Mary Hale, d. 1719, aged 38)

Green Cemetery, Glastonbury, Connecticut

In memory of J_____
Aged 787 years

Malmesbury Abbey, Wiltshire

His inconsolable widow dedicated this monument to his memory and continues the same business at the old stand, 167 rue Mouffetard.

(Pierre Cabochard)

Père la Chaise, Paris

Stop here, ye Gay
& ponder what ye doeth
Blue lightnings flew &
Swiftly seized my Breath
A more tremendous
flash will fill the skies
When I and all that sleep in death shall rise

(Simon Willard, d. 1766, aged 60)

Bow Wow Cemetery, Sheffield, Massachusetts

Here lies the man Richard,
And Mary his wife;
Their surname was Pritchard,
They lived without strife;
And the reason was plain, —
They abounded in riches,
They had no care or pain,
And his wife *wore the breeches*.

Chelmsford, Essex

Sacred to the memory
Of Miss Martha Gwynne
Who was so very pure within,
She burst the outward shell of sin
And hatched herself a cherubim.

St Peter's churchyard, St Albans, Hertfordshire

Sacred to the memory of Jared Bates who died August the 6th, 1800.
His widow, aged 24, lives at 7 Elm Street, has every qualification for
a good wife, and yearns to be comforted.

Lincoln, Maine

In memory of Mary Ann, a Native Woman aged 38 years, built by John Macleod.

Dum-Dum burial ground, West Bengal, India

Thomas Wood. Formerly a bather at this place.

St John's Church, Margate, Kent

Richard Basset, the old sexton of this parish, who had continued in the office of clerk and sexton for the space of forty-three years, whose melody was warbled forth as if he had been thumped between the shoulders with a pair of bellows, was buried on 20th September, 1866.

Sussex

Here lies the body of John Mound
Lost at sea and never found.

Winslow, Maine

Sacred to the Memory of
Miss
Elizabeth Tucker
Who died
July 29, 1834
aged 47 years
Like a good steward what the Lord gave her
she left in the bosom of the church.
$1200.

Massachusetts

Sacred to the memory of Andrew Craig, late spirit merchant in Edinburgh, who, by persevering industry and strict integrity in all his dealings, raised himself to a respectable station in society. In the relative duties of domestic life, kindness of heart was his distinguishing characteristic. He was an affectionate husband, a tender parent, a kind master and a faithful friend; while his frank, unreserved, and affable manner, combined with fascinating social qualities, endeared him to all his acquaintances. Died 24th March, 1830, aged 45 years.

Greyfriars churchyard, Edinburgh

She drank good ale, good punch and wine
And lived to the age of 99.

(Rebecca Freeland, d. 1741)

Edwalton, Nottinghamshire

Here lies the body of Richard Hind,
Who was neither ingenious, sober or kind.

Cheshunt, Hertfordshire

Joseph Palmer. Died Oct. 30, 1873, aged 84 yrs. and 5 mos. Persecuted
for wearing the beard.

Leominster, Massachusetts

Julia Adams. Died of thin shoes, April 17th, 1839, aged 19 years.

New Jersey

Here lie the bones of one, poor Louch,
A cricketer so staunch,
That vexed his hands should miss the ball,
He caught it in his paunch.

(Louch was killed by a blow in the stomach from a cricket ball, in the 1880s)

Rochester, Kent

Died of Grief
Caused by a Neighbour
Now Rests in Peace

(Louisa Adler, d. 1933, aged 60)

Palm Springs, California

Here lies the body of Thomas Vernon,
The only surviving son of Admiral Vernon.

(d. 23 July, 1753)

Plymouth, Devonshire

This Blooming Youth in Health Most Fair
To His Uncle's Mill-pond did repair
Undressed himself and so plunged in
But never did come out again.

(Abial Perkins, d. 1826, aged 13)

Center Cemetery, Plainsfield, Vermont

In memory of Mr.
Joseph Grapp — ship
wright who died ye 26th of
Novbr 1770 Aged 43 years

Alas Frend Joseph
His End was Allmost Sudden
As though the mandate came
Express from heaven
his foot it slip, And he did fall
help help he cried & that was all.

Mylor Creek churchyard, Cornwall

Save me O God, the mighty waters role
With near Approaches, even to my soul:
Far from dry ground, mistaken in my course
I stick in mire, brought hither by my horse.
Thus vain I cry'd to God, who only saves:
In death's cold pit I lay ore whelm'd with waves.

(1730)

Wick St Lawrence Church, Somerset

Those that knew him best deplored him most

(John Young, d. 1836)

St Andrew's churchyard, Staten Island, New York

Here lies Rufus Sweet and wife
They fed the hungry and
clothed the naked
and fought secret societies
And here may they rest until
Gabriel blows his horn

(Rufus Sweet, d. 1884)

Hope Cemetery, Perry, New York

Under this stone lieth the Broken
Remains of Stephen Jones who had
his leg cut off without the Consent of
Wife or Friends on the 23rd October
1842 in which day he died. Aged 31 years.
Reader I bid you farewell. May
the Lord have mercy on you in the
day of trouble.

St John's churchyard, Chester, Cheshire

Here lies ye Precious Dust of
Thomas Bailey

A painfull Preacher
An Exemplary liver
A Tender Husband
A careful Father
A brother for Adversity
A faithful Friend

A most desirable neighbor
A pleasant companion
A common good
A cheerful doer
A patient Sufferer
Lived much in a little time

A good copy for all Survivors

(Thomas Bailey, d.1688, aged 35)

Old Burying Ground, Watertown, Massachusetts

In memory of the old fish:
Under the soil the old fish do lie
20 year he lived and then did die
He was so tame you understand
He would come and eat out of your hand.
Died April the 20th 1855.

Blockley, Gloucestershire

Here lies the body of William Gordon,
He'd a mouth almighty and teeth accordin';
Stranger, tread lightly on this sod
For if he gapes you're gone, by God.

Reading, Berkshire

His illness laid not in one spot,
But through his frame it spread,
The fatal disease was in his heart,
And water in his head.

Whitby, Yorkshire

Here lyes the Body of Lewis Galdy Esqr. who departed this life at Port Royal the 22nd December 1739. Aged 80. He was born at Montpelier in France but left that Country for his Religion and came to settle in this Island where He was swallowed in the Great Earthquake in the Year 1692 and by the Providence of God was by another shock thrown into the Sea and Miraculously saved by swimming until a Boat took him up. He Lived many Years after in Great Reputation. Beloved by all that knew him and much Lamented at his Death.

St Peter's churchyard, Port Royal, Jamaica

Sacred
To the Memory of
Edward Fitzgibbon Esq.,
who died the
19th of November, 1857, aged 54.
Author of numerous works on angling
and was better known as
Ephemera
This
monument
is erected by a few of his friends
in admiration of
his piscatory writings

Highgate Cemetery, London

Been Here
and Gone
Had a Good Time

(Dr J. J. Subers, d. 1916, aged 78)

Rosehill Cemetery, Macon, Georgia

Here lies Phebe, wife of David Ames, who was a succorer of many and of Brother Osgood also. She died October 20, 1838.

Osgoodite Cemetery, Canterbury, Connecticut

In memorie of the Clerk's son
Bless my iiiiii
Here I lies
In a sad pickle
Killed by an icicle

(Unnamed, 1776)

St Michael & All Angels, Bampton, Devonshire

Buried in this churchyard, Hugh Mackenzie, born 4 July 1783, died 27 Aug. 1814, shortly after he had begun to distinguish himself at the Bar of England; of excellent talents; of character pure, sincere, placid, diligent, just, benevolent, religious; blameless as far as it can be said of human nature.

Greyfriars churchyard, Edinburgh, Midlothian

Here lie the bones
Of Joseph Jones
Who ate whilst he was able;
But once o'er fed
He dropt down dead,
And fell beneath the table.
When from the tomb
To meet his doom
He rises amidst sinners:
Since he must dwell
In heav'n or hell
Take him — which gives best dinners.

Wolverhampton, Staffordshire

Capt Samuel
Jones' Leg which
was amputated
July 7 1804

Old Cemetery, Washington, New Hampshire

Here lies the body of Robert More,
What signifys more words?
Who kill'd himself by eating of curds:
But if he had been rul'd by Sarah his wife,
He might have lived all the days of his life.

Dundalk, Louth, Ireland

Near this place lies Charles Claudius Philips, whose absolute con-
tempt of riches, and inimitable performances on the Violin, made
him the admiration of all who knew him. He was born in Wales,
made the tour of Europe, and, after the experience of both kinds of
fortune, died in 1732.

Wolverhampton, Staffordshire

Against his will
Here lies George Hill
Who from a cliff
Fell down quite stiff;
When it happen'd is not known,
Therefore not mention'd on this stone.

St Peter's, Isle of Thanet

In memory of Anna Hopewell:
    Here lies the body of our Anna
    Done to death by a banana
    It wasn't the fruit that laid her low
    But the skin of the thing that made her go.

Enosburg Falls, Vermont

To Lem S. Frame, who during his life shot 89 Indians, whom the Lord delivered into his hands, and who was looking forward to making up his hundred before the end of the year, when he fell asleep in Jesus at his house at Hawk's Ferry, March 27, 1843.

Exact location unknown (USA)

Suddenly fell asleep in Jesus at the Pinner Railway Station, while waiting for a train to return to London.

Brompton Cemetery, London

Weep, stranger, for a father spilled
From a stage coach, and thereby killed;
His name was John Sykes, a maker of sassengers,
Slain with three other outside passengers.

Wimborne Minster, Dorset

In Memory of Mr Peter Daniels
Born August 7, 1688. Died May 20, 1746.

Beneath this stone, a lump of clay,
Lies Uncle Peter Daniels,
Who too early in the month of May
Took off his winter flannels.

Medway, Massachusetts

Gone to be an angle.

(Gertrude Walker, d. 1893)

Lt. John Walker Cemetery, White Horn, Tennessee

The private sleeping chamber of
Richard Hislop, Islington.

Highgate Cemetery, London

In Memory of William Bingham,
Surgeon to the Fever Hospital, Pancras Road,
Who departed this life May 31st, 1821, aged 28 years
His death was occasioned by the puncturing his finger,
While sewing up a dead body.

St Giles Cemetery, Kings Road, London

In memory of
Abraham Rice
who departed this life
in a sudden and Awful
manner and as we trust
enter'd a better June ye 3, Anno D, 1777
in ye 81st year of his age.

(Rice was killed by lightning)

Framingham, Massachusetts

In the garden here below
Water me that I may grow;
When all grace to me is given,
Then transplant me into heaven.

Charlton Kings, Gloucestershire

Our little Jacob has been taken from this earthly garden to bloom in a superior flower-pot above.

Maine

Neglected by his doctor,
   Ill treated by his nurse,
His brother robbed the widow,
   Which made it all the worse.

Dulverton, Somerset

Now Aint
That Too Bad

(Charles DuPlessis, d. 1907, aged 53)

Rosehill Cemetery, Chicago, Illinois

Here lies poor, but honest Bryan Tunstall; he was a most expert angler, until Death, envious of his Merit, threw out his line, hook'd him, and landed him here the 21st day of April 1790.

Ripon Cathedral graveyard, Yorkshire

Ransom Beardsley
Died Jan. 24 1850
Aged 56 yrs. 7 mo. 21 days
A vol. in the war of 1812
No pension

Mottville, Michigan

Here lies Mrs. Buff, who had money enough;
   She laid it up in store:
And when she died she shut her eyes
   And never spoke no more.

(She was a fortune teller)

St Mary's, Nottingham, Nottinghamshire

Beneath this stone our Baby lies
   He neither cries nor hollars:
He lived just one-and-twenty days,
   And cost us forty dollars.

Burlington, Iowa

Died on the 11th inst., at his shop, No. 20, Greenwich Street, Mr. Edward Jones, much respected by all who knew and dealt with him. As a man he was amiable; as a hatter upright and moderate. His virtues were beyond all price, and his beaver hats were only three dollars each. He has left a widow to deplore his loss, and a large stock to be sold cheap, for the benefit of his family. He was snatched to the other world in the prime of life, just as he had concluded an extensive purchase of felt, which he got so cheap that his widow can supply hats at a more reasonable rate than any house in the city. His disconsolate family will carry on business with punctuality.

Exact location unknown (USA)

Unknown man shot in
the Jennison & Gallup Co's store
while in the act of burglarizing
the safe Oct. 13, 1905
(Stone bought with money
found on his person)

Sheldon, Vermont

Once ruddy and plump
But now a pale lump,
Here lies Johnny Crump
Who wished his neighbour no evil;
What tho' by death's thump,
He is laid on his rump,
Yet up he shall jump,
When he hears the last trump,
And triumph o'er death and the devil.

Worcestershire

This disease you ne'er heard tell on —
I died of eating too much mellon.
Be careful, then, all you that feed — I
Died because I was too greedy.

Chigwell, Essex

Here lie I, and no wonder I'm dead
For the wheel of the waggon went over my head.

Pembrokeshire

Here lies the carcase
Of honest Charles Parkhurst,
Who ne'er could dance, sing,
But always was true to
His Sovereign Lord the King
Charles the First

(d. December 20th, 1704, aged 86)

Epsom, Surrey

Here lies the body of Samuel Young who came here and died for the benefit of his health.

Ventnor, Isle of Wight

In memory ov
John Smith, gold digger, who met
weirlent death neer this spot
18 hundred and 40 too. He was shot
by his own pistill.
It was not one of the new kind
but a old fashioned
brass barrel, and of such is the
Kingdom of Heaven

(Exact location unknown. Said to be near Sparta, California)

John Blair
Died of Smallpox
Cowboy Throwed Rope
over Feet and dragged him
To his Grave

Boothill Graveyard, Tombstone, Arizona

In Memory of Mr Ebenezer Tinney
who died March 12, 1813, aged 81 yrs.

My virtue liv's beyond the grave
My glass is rum.

Grafton, Vermont

Here lyes the Body of William Speke, aged 18, Son of Hy. Speke
Esq. Captain of His Majesty's Ship Kent; He lost his Leg and Life
in that Ship at the capture of Fort Orleans the 24th of March Anno.
1757

St John's Church, Calcutta

Williston Winchester
Son of Antipas and Lois Winchester. Born 1822, Died 1902. He
never married.
"Uncle Wid"
One of nature's noblemen, a quaint old-fashioned, honest and
reliable man. An ideal companion for men and boys. Delighted in
hunting foxes and lining bees.

Marlboro, Vermont

Her neighbors and friends stood weeping and showing the coats and garments which she made while she was with them.

(Rebecca Corey, d. 1810)

Middle Cemetery, Lancaster, Massachusetts

In honoured memory of
Sarah J. Rooke
Telephone Operator
Who perished in the flood waters
of the Dry Cimmaron at Folsom
New Mexico, August 27, 1908
while at the switchboard warning
others of the danger. With heroic
devotion she glorified her calling
by sacrificing her own life that
others might live.

Folsom, New Mexico

Joshua
Son of Mr Joshua
& Mrs Anna Miller
who was killed with a
Sawmill May 26th
AD 1781 in the 15th
year of his age

Old Farm Hill Cemetery, Middletown, Connecticut

Through Christ, I'm not inferior
To William the Conqueror.
    (Rom. viii. 37.)

Cupar, Fife

A real unpretending and almost unconscious good sense and a firm desire to act right on all occasions to the best of her judgement were her most distinguished characteristics, hereditary personal grace of both form and face which even in age had not disappeared completes her picture. For her character and other particulars see the Gentleman's Magazine for May, 1812.

(Viscountess Downe, d. 1812)

York Minster, York

Sacred
to the memory of
Edward Hunt
late of Islington
who died a Martyr to the Gout
August 18th, 1848, aged 53 years.

Highgate Cemetery, London

To the Memory
Of the late Mr John Stevens,
Celebrated corn operator,
And many years resident
Of this parish, who departed
This life February 21st, 1813
Aged 81 years

St Andrew's Cemetery, Grays Inn Road, London

Hail!
This stone marks the spot
Where a notorious sot
Doth lie;
Whether at rest or not
It matters not
To you or I.
Oft to the "Lion" he went to fill his horn,
Now to the "Grave" he's gone to get it warm.

Beered by public subscription by his hale and stout
companions, who deeply lament his absence.

Tonbridge, Kent

Here lies a man of good repute
Who wore a No. 16 boot.
'Tis not recorded how he died,
But sure it is, that open wide,
The gates of heaven must have been
To let such monstrous feet within.

Keeseville, New York

Warren Gibbs
died by arsenic poisoning
Mar. 23, 1860
Ae. 36 yrs. 5 mos. 23 d'ys.

Think, my friends, when this you see
How my wife hath dealt by me
She in some oysters did prepare
Some poison for my lot and share
Then of the same I did partake
And Nature yielded to its fate
Before she my wife became
Mary Felton was her name.
Erected by his brother, Wm. Gibbs

Pelham, Massachusetts

Prof. Joseph W. Holden.
Born Otisfield Me. Aug. 24, 1816,
Died Mar. 30, 1900.

Prof. Holden the old Astronomer
discovered that the Earth is flat
and stationary, and that the sun
and moon do move.

Elmwood Cemetery, East Otisfield, Maine

Capt. John Cleves Symmes was a Philosopher and the originator of "Symmes' Theory of Concentric Spheres and Polar Voids". He concluded that the Earth was hollow and habitable within.

(John Cleves Symmes, d. 1829, aged 49)

Hamilton, Ohio

Here lies Dame Mary Page, relict of Sir Gregory Page, Bart. She departed this life March 4th, 1728, in the 56th year of her age. In 67 months she was tapped 66 times. Had taken away 240 gallons of water, without ever repining at her case, or ever fearing the operation.

Bunhill Fields, London

In memory of Ellen Shannon, aged 26 years, who was fatally burned March 21st 1870 by the explosion of a lamp filled with 'R. E. Danforth's Non-Explosive Burning Fluid'.

Girard, Pennsylvania

Aaron S. Burbank
1818   1883

Bury me not when I am dead
Lay me not down in a dusty bed
I could not bear the life down there
With earth worms creeping through my hair

Winsted, Connecticut

A sacred truth! now learn our awful fate!
Dear Friends, we were first cousins, and what not —
To toil as masons was our humble lot;
As just returning from a house of call,
The parson bade us set about his wall;
Flushed with good liquor cheerfully we strove
To place big stones below and big above;
We made too quick work — down the fabric came,
It crush'd our vitals — people bawled out, shame!
But we heard nothing — mute as fish we lay
And shall lie sprawling till the judgement-day.
From our misfortune this good moral know,
Never to work too fast or drink too slow.

(Thomas & Richard Fry, d. August 25th, 1776, aged 19 & 21)

Nr Bath, Somerset

Grieve not for me father dear
Nither my mother while you'r hear
Though sudden death on me did call
Which happened by a falling wall
Weep not therefore it is in vain
Weep for your sins and them refrain.

(1720)

Clapton-in-Gordano, Somerset

Here lies in a state of perfect oblivion John Adams who died Sept. 2 1811 aged 79. Death has decomposed him and at the great resurrection Christ will recompose him.

Newbury, Massachusetts

Rothwell
William P. Rothwell M.D.
1866–1939
This is on me.

R.

Oak Grove Cemetery, Pawtucket, Rhode Island

Here lie the remains of honest Joe Miller, who was a tender husband, a sincere friend, a facetious companion, and an excellent comedian. He departed this life the 15th day of August, 1738, aged 54 years.

(On the comedian, Joseph Miller)

King's College Hospital, London

Gone home.

Grafton, Vermont

P. S.
The Old Nuisance

(Philip Sydney Bennett; erected at his own direction, to perpetuate the insulting description of him by his son-in-law, who reportedly asked his wife how long the old nuisance would be around).

East Calais, Vermont

While every effort has been taken to assure the authenticity of these epitaphs, we cannot guarantee that all of them are genuine, or that the tombstones on which they were inscribed have survived the ravages of time.

The publishers would be grateful for any comments, corrections or further examples of amusing or curious epitaphs.

Dead Funny

with 40 original cartoons by
Bill Tidy

IN 67 MONTHS SHE WAS TAP'D 66 TIMES
HAD TAKEN AWAY 240 GALLONS OF WATER
WITHOUT EVER REPINING AT HER CASE
OR EVER FEARING THE OPERATION

Brian Shuel

Irritating neighbours and fond husbands, hot-blooded
housewives and religious maidens, intrepid cavalrymen and
Rosa the cow—all are commemorated in DEAD FUNNY,
a rambling collection of epitaphs from four continents and
four centuries. Bill Tidy's original cartoons add a hilarious new
dimension to the sentiment, wit, absurdity or plain ill-humour
of our forefathers' final remarks to their passing fellow men
and women.

£1·25
UK price only

Australia $3.75*
New Zealand $3.75
Not for sale in Canada or the U
*Recommended

ISBN 0 904069 01 X

To Hatter, Theo and Loki

Acknowledgements

FIRSTLY, A huge thank you to Jane Camillin and the team at Pitch Publishing for agreeing to take my book on. Also, thank you to Duncan Olner for designing a cover that surpassed any expectations that I had.

Secondly, a thank you must also go to Karan Tejwani for being the person that first gave me a chance to write for someone other than myself when he agreed to let me work with him in the early stages of *Football Chronicle*. Without Karan, this would not have been possible. The same is true for the team at *These Football Times* who published my work, guided me towards becoming a better writer and whose own authors inspired me to take this challenge on as well.

I also have to thank my parents, family and friends for always encouraging me to never give up and let my dreams slip away. Their support has always been at the forefront of my mind and a motivating factor to continue to strive for excellence.

Lastly, the biggest thank you to my wonderful partner Sophie, who, despite an apathy for anything football-related, has patiently listened to my endless discussion about this tournament and even tried to engage meaningfully. You are the reason that any of this has been possible and this book would never have come to fruition without your support, patience and love.

Introduction

WHAT IS it about a World Cup that captures the imagination of the footballing world? Long gone are the days where it was the pinnacle of the game, with money and the Champions League taking the European game to the summit of world football. There is not even that same joy of witnessing players from the other side of the globe for the first time. That feeling of watching the next Brazilian magician in the iconic yellow shirt with no prior knowledge has disappeared because those previously unknown footballing geniuses are all primarily playing in Europe and the vast majority of football is available to watch in some format along with the rise of video games bringing lesser-known players to attention. The simple joy of football has also faded. As more details emerge in relation to FIFA's corrupt dealings and the shady nature in which they operated, it has become clear that if the money is right, nothing else really matters. This has led to more people taking an introspective look at their relationship with the beautiful game. It has led to a greater feeling of disconnect as fans are priced out of following their team. In a game that is supposed to be for everyone, the last World Cup was held in a country where it is illegal to be homosexual. Hardly open to all, then.

The answer, therefore, is probably as simple as nostalgia. Everyone remembers the first World Cup that they watched, the race home from school to catch a kick-off or a late-night/early-morning viewing of a tournament held in a different time zone. The free-to-air nature of the tournament makes it accessible and watchable for all, especially in countries where the majority of football is behind a pay wall. We forget the morally challenging nature that modern sports present us with as we remember that excitement that followed an entire four weeks of easily accessible football content. We remember our childhoods. The innocence and carefree nature that those times afforded us. It is an old cliché, but football is always described as being better a certain number of years ago. That statement is rarely meant to mean the actual game itself but rather everything that accompanies it. It is easier to connect when there are limited responsibilities. Following a club or country is not an arduous task when there is nothing else to focus on. As we age, we also become increasingly aware of the world around us and the problematic nature of it, making it easier to see the flaws in the game we have been conditioned to love.

Away from nostalgia it is important to see the flaws that existed in the past. The decision to have Germany as the host nation was certainly not without its controversy. There were four bids still active at the time of the vote in 2000, with Brazil dropping out just a few days before. Alongside Germany in contention were England, Morocco and South Africa. The Moroccan bid was eliminated after the first round with just three votes, followed by the English bid in the second with just two. The German bid received 12 votes, narrowly pipping the South African bid, which had 11 votes, with one abstainer. That person was Charlie Dempsey, the delegate from Oceania. Having voted for the English bid in the second round, he said he was pressurised into switching his vote to back the South African bid. Had he switched his vote, the final outcome would have been a tie and the tiebreaker was Sepp Blatter. The FIFA president was publicly in favour of a World Cup hosted by an African nation and it is highly likely that he would have cast his vote that way, meaning Germany would not have hosted another World Cup and we would have been treated to a World Cup on the African continent four years earlier than we were.

The pressure and peculiarities were not limited to the push from the South African bid. In the build-up to the vote, there was an increased German interest in activities in countries that would ultimately cast their vote in Germany's favour. DaimlerChrysler, Volkswagen and Bayer all announced investments into Hyundai and companies in Thailand and South Korea, respectively. The allegations became even louder in 2015 when German newspaper *Der Spiegel* released an article suggesting that the World Cup had been bought by Germany through the use of a slush fund to bribe officials into voting for their bid. The fund, consisting of €6.2m, was created by the CEO of Adidas at the time, Robert Louis-Dreyfus. The money was ultimately paid back, through FIFA, with no record of the payments ever appearing in the tournament budgets. The money was allegedly used by German footballing legend Franz Beckenbauer and Wolfgang Niersbach, who was executive vice-president and press officer of the 2006 FIFA World Cup Organizing Committee. The purpose of the fund was to bribe four officials of the Asian representatives on the FIFA Executive Committee. When combined with the European votes for Germany, the Asian votes that had been allegedly bought saw the outcome fall in Germany's favour.

The German football federation's response was peculiar to say the least. After initially saying they could not comment straightaway, they released a statement the following morning after the breaking of the story. Rather than deny that any money was ever paid, they admitted that it was possible that that amount of money was paid to FIFA but not for the reason that it was stated it had been for. They also said that the payment had nothing to do with the awarding of the tournament. If the money had not been used in its initially stated purpose, then what was the fund for? The story seemed to be less than airtight and certainly brought a closer inspection on just how Germany came to be the hosts in 2006.

Away from the awarding of the tournament, there was another controversy clouding its build-up. The Italian national team had arrived in Germany at the start of June amid calls from some in the media to have them removed from the competition entirely. The summer of 2006 began with an investigation into alleged match-fixing that had been rampant throughout Italian football, with Reggina, Milan, Lazio, Fiorentina and Juventus all being investigated. The accusation was that there was pressure being applied on officials to favour the bigger teams in their matches and help tailor the outcome in their direction. Juventus's executive Luciano Moggi was at the very centre of the storm, with his phone being wiretapped by Italian authorities and the pressure he was exerting on referees being laid bare.

The scandal was still in full flow when the World Cup got underway, with the Italian players having to focus on their preparations while wondering about the state their domestic game was going to be in when they returned. However, it was more than just the Italy squad that would have been keeping one eye on the news channels, as 60 of the 736 players selected for the tournament were playing for clubs based in Italy, with only England and Germany having more. The punishments were not handed out until August and, when they came, they caused serious ramifications.

Those punishments came in three categories. Firstly, Lazio, Fiorentina and Juventus were all demoted a division, meaning that they would begin the 2006/07 season in Serie B. There were points deductions, 7 points for Lazio, 12 for Fiorentina, 15 for both Milan and Reggina, and a massive 30 points for Juventus. Lazio, Milan and Fiorentina were all banned from European competition for the following season, while Milan and Juventus also had retrospective points deductions for the previous season, or two in the case of the Turin club. Those deductions meant that the 2004/05 Serie A title remains vacant in the history books, while the 2005/06 one was awarded to Internazionale. Naturally, the clubs appealed and the punishments were reduced. Only Juventus were ultimately relegated, with just a nine-point deduction. Fiorentina and Lazio were both reinstated to Serie A but with a 15-point and three-point deduction respectively, while Milan started the season on minus eight points.

A major European club in a second-tier league seems more like a *Football Manager* challenge than a reality but that was the case for Juventus in 2006/07. Some players stayed, notably Gianluigi Buffon, Alessandro Del Piero and Pavel Nedvěd, but many others left, including Zlatan Ibrahimović, Patrick Vieira, Fabio Cannavaro, Lilian Thuram and Gianluca Zambrotta, who would all appear in Germany over the preceding summer. Juve stormed back through the league, winning it comfortably and returning to their position of power in Italy as they won nine consecutive titles between 2011/12 and 2019/20.

On the pitch, however, the anticipation was very much building. The major international nations seemed to be entering at the perfect time. England, France, Italy, Brazil and Argentina all could realistically claim to be in possession of the best squad at the tournament, reflected by those five being among the top six favourites to win, only infiltrated by an emerging Germany. Yet those nations not as highly ranked certainly would have fancied their chances of causing an upset. Spain, Portugal and the Netherlands are always highly rated and their squads were at varying stages of development but definitely had the potential to beat everyone else.

A fun tradition before any international tournament is the picking of the dark horse nation that will cause a surprise. There are the typical nations, Switzerland, Mexico and Croatia, that are always listed as the dark horses for any tournament they compete in, but this year had seemingly more than ever. The Czech Republic, entering for the first time as a sovereign nation and off the back of a brilliant run to the semi-finals of the European Championships two years earlier. Ukraine and Serbia and Montenegro were also both competing for the first time in their new guise and both had qualified extremely well. These three nations represented the new European hopefuls. Away from Europe, both the Ivory Coast and Ghana highlighted burgeoning African optimism. After Senegal's outstanding debut in 2002, the hopes were high that either of these two African nations could at least match that effort as they were both littered with star players, although they had been drawn in arguably the two toughest groups. By qualifying for the World Cup, the Ivory Coast had helped bring an end to the brutal civil war that had been raging through their country, with Didier Drogba giving an impassioned speech about uniting behind their successes. There was a genuine belief that they could further unite their people and become the first African nation to ever reach the semi-finals of the World Cup.

At the other end of the spectrum and the storylines did not dry up. There were more debutants, with both Togo and Angola facing opponents during the group stage that had once been their colonisers. Trinidad and Tobago made up the new nations, entering amid a cloud of controversy with the failure of their federation to pay them bonuses they were owed, something that would play out further with the corruption scandal that rocked FIFA in the years after. Even the supposed smaller nations had star players. Togo were led by Arsenal's Emmanuel Adebayor, Manchester United legend Dwight Yorke was captaining Trinidad and Tobago, and Bayern Munich's Ali Karimi was leading the line for Iran.

This was a tournament of stars. It was the last World Cup before football became dominated by two players on a different planet to the rest. The squads at this tournament were on a level that has maybe never been seen before. Every nation seemingly had a degree of talent that they had never boasted previously. For some of the smaller nations that talent was on a lesser scale than that of the traditional international powers, but they had still qualified for the finals for the first time. The term has become a cliché in recent years, as any talented squad is labelled a 'golden generation', but if any period can lay claim to that moniker, then it might well be this tournament. Perhaps never before had it been so equal at the sharp end of international football. Heading to Germany during that summer was a collection of the greatest footballers to ever play the game. This is the story of the 2006 FIFA Men's World Cup. This is the story of those Golden Generations.

Group A

RATHER THAN the opening match being contested by the current holders, as had been standard practice since 1974, it was the now the turn of the host nation to get the tournament under way. For Germany it represented an ideal opportunity to get their tournament started on the right note. An opening match against Costa Rica, arguably the weakest team in their group, was a chance for Jürgen Klinsmann to show that this team had progressed in the right direction since the debacle of the European Championships in 2004 and that he was indeed the right man to lead them into the new era. The selection choice was not exactly straightforward though. Captain and talisman Michael Ballack was nursing a calf injury heading into the tournament and had been ruled out of participating in the opener. Bernd Schneider, the right-winger from Bayer Leverkusen and fellow veteran from the 2002 World Cup squad, took the captain's armband, while Tim Borowski, a Bundesliga winner with Werder Bremen in 2003/04, replaced Ballack in the starting line-up.

For the Costa Ricans, the tactical acumen of Brazilian coach Alexandre Guimarães, who had turned around their fortunes during the qualification campaign, was likely to be their determining factor. They were a team that could create chances but would also give away just as many, a 3-2 friendly defeat to France, where they had been 2-0 ahead at half-time, highlighting their attacking potential and defensive vulnerabilities. Strikers Paulo Wanchope, once of Derby County and Manchester City, and Rónald Gómez, the only Costa Rican with more than one goal in World Cup history, were the main players and the ones most likely to cause the hosts problems in the opening fixture.

A young, attack-minded team playing against a defensively vulnerable one was always likely to lead to a fast start, but few would have predicted how the opening 20 minutes of the match would play out. The Germans started on the front foot, controlling possession and taking the game to their opponents, and it only took six minutes for them to make the breakthrough. Phillip Lahm, playing at left-back rather than the right-back or central midfield positions he would become more predominantly known for, received the ball out wide on the left. Rather than driving to the byline and sending in a cross, he cut back inside on to his favoured right foot, creating a favourable angle. Aided by a slip from Costa Rica midfielder Danny Fonseca, Lahm curled a beautiful effort into the far side of the goal, the ball clipping the post as it found the back of the net. It was a goal-of-the-tournament contender already and it was just the first goal. Having taken the early lead, Germany looked to push on and increase their advantage, with Bastian Schweinsteiger following his Bayern Munich team-mate's lead and drifting in from the left-hand side, slipping the ball through for Miroslav Klose, whose effort was well smothered by goalkeeper José Porras. The Germans seemed to be sending most of their attacks down the left-hand side, with the link-up play between Lahm and Schweinsteiger causing the Costa Rican players problems.

Despite the early dominance, Costa Rica showed that they were in Munich to do more than just make up the numbers. Wanchope managed to win a header near halfway, the ball falling to his partner Gómez, who dinked it beyond the German defence.

Arne Friedrich, the German right-back, did not manage to match the aggressive offside line his defensive colleagues had played and Wanchope suddenly found himself one-on-one with Jens Lehmann. Managing to keep his composure, something English fans will not remember him primarily for, he took a couple of touches before slotting the ball beyond Lehmann. With their first chance, Costa Rica had stunned Germany and drawn level at 1-1. It was a goal completely against the run of play, but an early warning sign for the Germans.

Rather than trying to settle the game down, Germany came immediately back on the offensive, seemingly determined to regain the lead as soon as possible. That only took five minutes. Making use of the right flank this time, stand-in captain Schneider managed to beat Luis Marín to the byline and played an intelligent pull-back into the area, where Schweinsteiger, having drifted all the way over from the left, was free in space on the edge of the area. His first touch drove him into the box and his clever low ball to the back post found Klose waiting for the simplest of tap-ins. It was a typical poacher's effort from the striker, and it saw the Germans retake the lead. Germany 2, Costa Rica 1, a scoreline that would not have looked out of place at the end of the match, yet it had taken just 17 minutes for the opening three goals of the tournament.

Finally, after the frantic opening 20 minutes, the match began to settle down into a steady rhythm. The Germans were dominating the ball, moving it around well but falling short when it came to the final third. To their credit, Costa Rica were defensively well organised, belying their pre-tournament characterisation as a team weak at the back. Even with the Germans controlling the majority of the ball, it was the Central American team that created the next clear-cut chance, Wanchope again breaking the attempted offside trap, although this time Germany coped with perfectly.

Then it was Costa Rica with the best chance once more, as just after half-time a cleverly worked corner found Fonseca free in the penalty area, but he could only guide his header wide.

It was a miss that would prove costly, as just after the hour Germany added a third. Once more it was Phillip Lahm causing problems with his overlapping runs down the left. His cross was deflected by Costa Rican defender Martínez, only to find Klose free at the back post. His header was well saved by Porras, but he was the quickest to react to the loose ball, slamming it into the roof of the net to give Germany a two-goal cushion for the first time. Just eight minutes later and it was Lahm again who had burst beyond the defenders, this time finding himself through on goal but he could only fire a tame effort at Porras.

It was a chance that should have been taken, and a few minutes later was made to look an even worse miss. Costa Rican midfielder Walter Centeno found space in the middle of the German half, was able to chip the ball through to Wanchope, who again flicked the ball beyond the outrushing Lehmann to bring the score to 3-2. The German defenders immediately called for offside and the Costa Rican attackers looked straight towards the assistant to make sure the goal counted, but the flag stayed down. Replays showed that the goal should have been disallowed as Wanchope had strayed just beyond the central defenders, but it stood. Both central defenders, Per Mertesacker and Christoph Metzelder had tried to close down Centeno rather than having one drop with the runner. Although the goal should not have counted, it showed that the German defence could be breached with runners in behind.

As often happens in the second half of close matches, the introduction of substitutes disrupted the flow of play. Costa Rica sent on Christian Bolaños to try to inject extra pace into their attack, while Germany replaced Klose with Oliver Neuville, with the departing striker getting a deserved standing ovation from the home crowd in Munich. The Central Americans were unable to create any extra momentum to push on for an unlikely equaliser and, just three minutes before the end, any hopes of snatching a point were over. Schweinsteiger took a quick free kick from the left-hand side, rolling the ball into the path of Torsten Frings in the centre of the pitch. Letting the ball roll across his body, Frings unleashed an effort from 40 yards that perhaps caught everyone by surprise. His effort was unstoppable, swerving viciously into the top right corner beyond the despairing dive of Porras. If Lahm's goal was a goal-of-the-tournament contender, his team-mate may have ended that specific competition just 80 minutes later.

A couple of late substitutions aside, Frings's goal was the last meaningful moment of a truly legendary World Cup match. Germany 4, Costa Rica 2. For the Central Americans it was a performance of real heart and spirit, defending well and finishing their chances on the counter, although there were few actual chances, with many attacks breaking down before the final third. For the hosts it was a mixed performance. In an attacking sense they had scored four goals, including two stunning strikes. They had played on the front foot and dominated in the way that Klinsmann had been trying to promote since his appointment. However, there were question marks raised by the defensive performance. Their attempt at a high defensive line was too easily exposed by the pace of the Costa Rican forwards, and the goalkeeping selection of Lehmann over Kahn could be called into question as the Arsenal stopper was beaten by the only two chances Costa Rica created. Ultimately, an opening match win is still a win, and a positive result against neighbours Poland would all but secure Germany's passage into the knockout rounds. For Costa Rica to have any chance of reaching the latter stages for a second time, they would almost certainly need to beat fellow inexperienced team Ecuador, but a defeat would almost certainly see them out of the tournament after just two matches. The expectations had been set by this classic encounter, and the 2006 World Cup had kicked off in true style.

After the opening-match victory for the hosts, it was the turn of their neighbours to the east. Poland entered the tournament as comfortable second favourites in the group, although expectations beyond that were incredibly limited. Led by experienced captain Jacek Bąk in central defence and striker Maciej Żurawski, whose 16 goals had just helped Celtic win the Scottish Premier League by a comfortable 17 points, the Poles certainly would have fancied their chances against their South American opponents.

Fresh from a first World Cup appearance in 2002, Ecuador had once again successfully navigated the battle that is CONMEBOL (the South American football confederation) qualifying, finishing fourth and impressing with victories over both Brazil and Argentina. *La Tri* were perhaps expected to be solid at the back, with defenders Iván Hurtado, Ulises de la Cruz and Giovanny Espinoza all featuring in a defence that combined experience and skill. It was more than just a defensive team that Ecuador brought to Germany, however, with Carlos Tenorio and Agustín Delgado leading the line, and future Manchester United star Luis Antonio Valencia providing the youthful dynamism down the right-hand side.

With this match perhaps representing the decisive factor in who qualified alongside Germany, it was unsurprising that it started in a cagey fashion. The opening 20 minutes presented little action aside from a speculative shot from Segundo Castillo that was easily caught by Poland goalkeeper Artur Boruc. Ecuador settled the quicker of the two, and it was the South Americans who took the lead in the 24th minute. De la Cruz took a throw-in from an advanced position on the right. Delgado was the first to the ball and flicked a header towards the middle of the penalty area for his strike partner Tenorio. The striker was sharper than his marker Marcin Baszczyński and glanced his header into the far corner, beyond Boruc's dive. It was a simple goal that Poland would have been disappointed to have conceded and it should have been a wake-up call.

Yet, just five minutes later, Ecuador should have doubled their lead. In a similar fashion to the goal, De la Cruz fired a throw-in into the area for Delgado to win, and the ball again reached Tenorio. This time he was tightly marked by two defenders but wriggled his way free on the byline and managed to pull the ball back to Delgado, who had found a little bit of space. For a player of Delgado's quality, it should have been a simple finish, but perhaps the occasion got the better of him and he wastefully fired his shot over the bar. A couple of minutes later and the left side of Poland's defence was breached again, with De la Cruz allowed to run into the box unchallenged before his shot was eventually cleared behind for a corner. With Ecuador beginning to turn the heat up, Poland would have been relieved to hear the whistle blow for half-time with the score still just 1-0.

The break seemed to settle Poland down and they began to regain some composure and take control of the match. Despite their possession, though, they were unable to break down the resolute back line of Ecuador. Hurtado and Espinoza seemed almost unbeatable but they were dealt a major setback when Hurtado stayed down after colliding with Euzebiusz Smolarek. Although the captain tried to carry on, he was ultimately forced off and there was renewed hope in the Polish camp.

While Poland began to exert pressure on Ecuador, there was always a threat on the counter-attack and the shaky Polish defence from the first half was still open to being exposed. When Édison Méndez received the ball in between the defence and midfield, he was given time to slide a through ball in for substitute Iván

Kaviedes. The forward was clear on goal, having timed his run beyond the attempted offside trap, and played a simple square ball for Delgado to tap home into an empty net – 2-0 Ecuador and seemingly game over.

For the Poles, it was desperation time. Smolarek created their first real chance with a shot straight at Cristián Mora in the Ecuador goal. Ireneusz Jeleń, on as a substitute, hit the crossbar and saw the ball bounce clear, and fellow substitute Paweł Brożek curled an effort against the post, all within the last six minutes of the match. Ultimately, Poland were unable to break down the stubborn South American defence. In truth, they did not deserve anything from the match. They had struggled to create any chances until the final minutes, when they were desperate, and looked vulnerable at the back to almost every Ecuador attack. For *La Tri* it was a superb result and performance. After they took the lead, they should have added more in a first half they controlled. The second period saw them relinquish the control but they still never looked like conceding. The injury to Hurtado was the big disappointment from the match, although they still looked strong defensively without their leader. With Poland facing a now buoyant Germany and Ecuador facing off against a Costa Rica side who had struggled to cope defensively in the opening match, the South Americans had given themselves an excellent chance of qualifying for the knockout stages in just their second appearance at the World Cup finals.

* * *

Having won their opening fixture against Costa Rica, Germany knew that they could book their place in the knockout phase with a victory in their second match. It would not be an easy path to qualification, however, as standing in their way were long-time rivals Poland. German-Polish tensions existed beyond the sphere of football and had been a continuous problem between the two nations for centuries. As a recognised nation, Poland had effectively ceased to exist in 1795, having been partitioned for a third time by Prussia, the Habsburg Monarchy and the Russian Empire in the aftermath of the failed Kościuszko Uprising. What little was left of Poland was further divided between the three ruling powers and Polish identity was slowly but surely pushed into the background. This eradication of Poland existed for over 100 years until the end of the First World War, when the victorious Allied powers finalised the Treaty of Versailles, the peace treaty that saw the official end of the war. As a part of the treaty, Germany had to renounce all rights and title over the territory and recognise the independence of Poland.

While the Second Polish Republic was rebuilding its nation, Germany was undergoing its own transformation, with the initial implementation of a democratic system of government followed by the rise of the National Socialist Party, Adolf Hitler and Nazism. The German government had been unhappy at the terms of the treaty, and once Hitler had reached power he began to ignore the terms imposed on his nation. He increased the size of the armed forces and started laying down plans for taking over Europe and removing those he and his party viewed as 'subhuman'. The actions of Hitler and Nazi Germany can and have been discussed in many books and articles, but one of their actions was agreeing with the Soviet Union to divide Poland up between themselves in the Molotov-Ribbentrop Pact. It has since been estimated that around six million Polish citizens were killed during the Second World War, with the majority of those being murdered by the oppressive regimes that had divided the country up among themselves at the start of the conflict. After the war had come to an end, the leaders of Great Britain, the United States of America and the Soviet Union decided at the Yalta Conference to allow a Communist government to be established in the re-formed Poland, a nation that was also significantly smaller than it had been pre-war, with the eastern section of the country being annexed to Soviet rule. As Ryan Hubbard wrote in his book exploring Polish football in the 20th century, 'The Poland that emerged from the ashes of World War Two bore few similarities with the country which had been forced into the conflict.'

While Poland had to recover physically, politically and economically after the war, it also had to recover in a footballing sense. Polish football had been banned by their German occupiers during the war and many of their internationals prior to the conflict were among the victims of the brutality. Poland was not considered a leading international team before the war and that trend continued afterwards, although as the 70s began there were clear signs of the tide turning. Led by Kazimierz Górski, a striker whose own career had been halted by the war, the Poles entered their best-ever period, winning Olympic gold in 1972, silver in 1976 and two third-place finishes at World Cups in 1974 and 1982.

The 1974 tournament held in West Germany was perhaps when the Polish team was at the height of its power as they progressed comfortably through the first group stage, including beating Argentina, who would win their first World Cup four years later. The second group stage saw them placed in a group with Sweden, Yugoslavia and the hosts, with the match-up between the neighbours the last fixture of the group. Both nations won their first two matches, meaning the head-to-head in Frankfurt was the clincher for who would be going to the final to face the Netherlands. Poland knew they had to win as a draw would favour the Germans. As always, the Polish plan was to utilise their pacy forwards and cause problems for the opposition in behind their defensive line. Mother Nature, however, had other plans. The match was played amid a torrential thunderstorm, neutralising the Polish threat, and a solitary Gerd Müller goal was enough to send the Germans through to the final that they would ultimately emerge victorious from. The Polish delegation had asked for the match to be postponed, but their request was refused by the Austrian referee. Had the match been played under different conditions, then the result may have turned out differently and Poland's golden generation may have had an unlikely World Cup triumph to always look back on.

The meeting in 1974 had been the last competitive meeting between the two, but the Poles had never been able to get one over their nextdoor neighbour even in friendly matches. With the troubled political history between the two nations, there was an ever-existing tension that often played itself out on proxy grounds, including the football pitch. For many Poles, beating Germany was the ultimate goal. A chance to get one over their former oppressors. A chance to avenge the 1974 defeat that could have been Polish football's crowning moment. Prior to the meeting at this tournament, both nations were experiencing battles to control the hooliganism that was prevalent within their domestic game. The fear was that the Polish hooligans would be crossing the border and heading to Dortmund looking to create trouble rather than soak up the match atmosphere. There had been violence between Polish and German fans on the border in November 2005, in a fight that was openly declared as just being for practice ahead of the World Cup the following summer. Fortunately, the match ultimately passed by with little trouble from the crowd, with the German police detaining known Polish hooligans beforehand and any violence being limited to drunken clashes in Dortmund city centre that led to around 300 arrests, which was considered a positive number, given the pre-tournament concerns.

With the animosity off the pitch fizzling out into small skirmishes, the hope was that the action on it would match the preamble the game had been given by the media. It certainly had all the ingredients for a memorable one. The hosts knew that a win would guarantee them a place in the knockout stage with a match to spare, while Poland had to win to avoid being all but eliminated after losing their opening match to Ecuador. A grudge match with everything on the line definitely fitted the bill for a classic World Cup encounter. Another positive for everyone bar the Poles was the return of Germany captain Michael Ballack, who was declared fit to make his first appearance of the tournament, having watched the opener from the bench. Paweł Janas also made changes ahead of the match, with Ireneusz Jeleń and Bartosz Bosacki starting in place of Mirosław Szymkowiak and Mariusz Jop as Poland switched from a 4-4-2 to a 4-2-3-1.

As can often be the case in derby matches, the opening exchanges were cagey as both teams tried to feel their way into the match, with the first chance arriving after ten minutes as Ballack worked some space on the left-hand side, played Miroslav Klose in, but his low effort was easily saved by Artur Boruc. It was Klose again who was provided with the best opportunity of the half, allowed to drift into space in the penalty area to meet a clever Philipp Lahm cross. From a German perspective, there are few other strikers you would want the ball to fall to just six yards out, yet Klose could only glance his header past the post. Perhaps it was the outrushing Boruc that caused his attention to be momentarily distracted, but it was a chance that the ultimate penalty-box poacher would have been disappointed to miss. There were few true openings during the rest of the first half until just five minutes before half-time when Podolski was almost played through behind the Polish defence by Klose, but the ball deflected off his heel and halted his progress. Then in added time he received the ball in space in the area after good link-up play between himself and Lahm. He managed to stab his shot beyond Boruc, but it also rolled beyond the far post. Despite the German dominance of the ball throughout the half, it remained 0-0 at half-time, with the hosts creating very few chances of note.

The second half continued in much the same vein, with Germany controlling the tempo and Poland defending efficiently. Also, like the first half, although Germany had control of the ball, they could not create any clear chances, with a snapshot from Klose forcing a smart save from Boruc the only real action early in the half. With 75 minutes gone, Poland looked to be edging their way towards a point that would keep their qualification hopes alive, until Radosław Sobolewski clipped the heels of Klose as he was cutting inside in the Polish half and earned himself a second yellow card, having been booked in the first half. It was not a bad challenge, but a clear cynical foul to stop the counter-attack that deserved a yellow card.

With the extra player, Germany further cemented their dominance but it still did not feel like the luck was falling in their favour. As the clock entered the 89th minute, a Lahm cross was met by a looping Klose header that bounced off the crossbar, and Ballack on the follow-up saw his effort rebound off the bar as well. Although substitute David Odonkor did ultimately smash the ball into the net, Ballack had been offside and the flag correctly went up. It appeared as though the Polish goal was living a charmed life, and Boruc certainly deserved that bit of luck, given how well he had played in keeping the Germans at bay.

But like all elite teams, the Germans never stopped pushing for the late winner and it finally arrived in the first minute of added time, and it was a goal made by their bench. Bernd Schneider picked up the ball on the right and dinked a pass over the head of the Polish left-back for Odonkor to race on to. Letting the ball bounce, he hit a first-time volleyed cross into the penalty area for fellow substitute Oliver Neuville to slide on to and fire past Boruc to give Germany the winner. A far from prolific striker, Neuville had a habit of scoring vital late goals for his adopted nation (he was born in Switzerland but opted to represent Germany), having netted an 88th-minute winner against Paraguay in the Round of 16 at the previous World Cup. More than just a winning goal to seal qualification, it was one that brought full optimism back into the German camp. As Thomas Hitzlsperger describes in Raphael Honigstein's *Das Reboot*, all the remaining negativity surrounding the German team prior to the tournament fully disappeared in that moment. Germany had embraced its status as host nation and created a party-like atmosphere across the country.

The game barely had a chance to restart before the final whistle was blowing and then the party could really get started. Strangely, it was Germany's first competitive victory against European opposition since the European Championship Final against the Czech Republic in 1996, a run that included nine matches across the World Cups in 1998 and 2002 and European Championships in 2000 and 2004. Neuville's goal had confirmed Germany's qualification with a match to spare and had left Poland in need of a miracle. The Poles had to hope that Costa Rica could somehow beat Ecuador and they then needed to beat the Costa Ricans, while hoping Germany could beat Ecuador and that the goal difference swing would be enough to counter Poland's minus three after the opening two matches.

Having watched Germany beat Poland the previous evening, the task for Ecuador was simple. For *La Tri*, all they had to do was beat Costa Rica and they would secure their passage into the second round. The Central Americans knew they needed a win to keep their hopes alive, but a draw would not eliminate them from contention entirely. All signs pointed towards a comfortable victory for the South American nation, as they had looked impressive in all facets of their game against Poland in the opening match, while Costa Rica, despite threatening on the counter-attack, looked defensively suspect against Germany. With the confidence flowing, Luis Fernando Suárez opted to name an unchanged line-up, while his counterpart Alexandre Guimarães brought in the vastly experienced Harold Wallace for Gilberto Martínez, as he pushed his full-backs up towards more traditional wide midfielders in an effort to try to take the game to their opponents.

If Costa Rica's gameplan was to come out firing as suggested pre-match, then they could not have wished for a worse start. Agustín Delgado, Ecuador's first-ever World Cup finals scorer, battled his way through some weak challenges in the final third and, although his shot was blocked, he had drawn three defenders towards him and could play a simple ball out wide right for Antonio Valencia. He whipped in an inch-perfect cross on to the head of Carlos Tenorio, who could not miss from the edge of the six-yard box. Taking an early lead for a team that boasted Ulises de la Cruz, Iván Hurtado and Giovanny Espinoza, who would finish their careers with 101, 168 and 90 caps respectively, was a huge boost to their chances of success. Hurtado's career at international level was so successful that he holds the record as Ecuador's youngest-ever player, has 46 more caps than any other male Ecuadorian footballer and was the most-capped male international from any South American nation until recently, when he was overtaken by Argentina's Lionel Messi.

For the rest of the half, Costa Rica dictated the play, retained the ball well and showed some of the intent that had perhaps surprisingly marked their opening match. Despite all the possession though, they were unable to fashion any real chances, although Douglas Sequeira really should have at least hit the

31

target when provided a with a free header at the back post just before half-time.

Guimarães must have been relatively pleased with his team's performance and the half-time message would probably have been about encouraging his players to keep playing in the same fashion but to not allow Ecuador any easy opportunities to take the match further away from them. As translated from Robert Burns's poem 'To a Mouse', 'the best-laid schemes of mice and men go oft awry', and this was certainly true for Costa Rica at the start of the second half. De la Cruz, having been booked for time-wasting just eight minutes into the second half, launched a throw-in beyond the defensive line. Édison Méndez won his header and flicked the ball over the head of Luis Marín for the onrushing Delgado, who took a touch to drive deeper into the right-hand side of the penalty area, before hitting a fierce shot beyond José Francisco Porras in goal. The old adage of the goalkeeper needing to do better at the near post may have been brought out for this one, but the sheer power on the shot from Delgado would have made it difficult for any keeper to get a hand to.

Having secured their lead, Ecuador were content to allow their opponents to keep the ball, confident in their ability to prevent them from mustering any proper goalscoring opportunities. And so it proved, with *Los Ticos* failing to cause any problems for the Ecuadorian defence, barely looking like scoring one goal, let alone the two that they needed to give themselves a fighting chance of qualification. They did nearly create a grandstand finish with just three minutes remaining, as Kurt Bernard held the ball up well on the left-hand side of the penalty area and laid it off for Álvaro Saborío, who dinked a first-time effort over the head of Cristian Mora, only to see the ball bounce off the underside of the crossbar and bounce clear. Had the ball bounced slightly differently, there could have been a chance for Costa Rica to create an incredible ending to a match that had been petering out, but ultimately it was Ecuador who would add the third goal of the match. Agustín Delgado, receiving the ball on the halfway line, produced a sublime back-heeled chip to flick the ball over Sequeira, who had come to challenge him, and laid a simple pass into the space on the right flank for Méndez. With the freedom of the half, he played an excellent cross to the far post for Iván Kaviedes, who had been brought on at half-time. He had the simple task of knocking the ball first-time beyond Porras and putting the finishing touches to a brilliant win for Ecuador.

Having qualified for the group stage four years earlier but struggling to make a tangible impact, the fact that they had qualified with a match to spare this time around was the cause for a party atmosphere among the travelling Ecuadorians. The most important thing that any football club or nation wants to see is progress. This was certainly the case for this crop of Ecuadorian footballers and, having a plus-five goal difference meant that they only needed a draw against Germany and they would top the group, potentially avoiding a tricky match-up against England in the second round.

* * *

As has been the case since the 1986 World Cup, the final group fixtures were played simultaneously. It was not always the case that the final matches ran side by side, and it was only thanks to an outrageous act of gamesmanship that the rules were changed. At the World Cup in Spain in 1982, Algeria had shocked the world by beating West Germany 2-1 in their opening match of the tournament. With Austria winning both their opening matches and West Germany and Algeria winning one and losing one each, they entered the final round of fixtures with any two from three qualifying. Algeria beat Chile 3-2 to move themselves level on four points with Austria but, crucially, with a neutral goal difference. Austria had a plus-three goal difference and four points, and West Germany had two points and a plus-two goal difference. Having watched Algeria play the previous day, both nations knew that a one or two-goal margin of victory for the West Germans would mean they topped the group and Austria would qualify second. Although both teams have denied any allegations of collusion, after West Germany took the lead ten minutes into the match, the contest faded and neither team seemed to muster any attacking intent. It ended 1-0 and Algeria were eliminated amid fury from the players and staff from the nation and those in attendance in Gijón. In response, FIFA changed their rules, meaning that the final two matches of any future group would take place concurrently to minimise the ability of teams to manufacture a result that would work in both their favours.

For Group A, this was a non-factor as the matches were simply to decide the final positioning of the group rather than who could qualify. Ecuador knew that avoiding defeat to their hosts in Munich would mean that they went through as group winners. However, rather than going all-out to try to maximise their chances of winning the group, they made five changes, resting key players such as Hurtado, Delgado and Carlos Tenorio to keep them as fresh as possible for the second round. Klinsmann was perhaps trying to avoid a potentially tricky match-up against England and only made the single change, bringing Chelsea's Premier League-winning defender Robert Huth into the centre of defence in place of Christoph Metzelder.

In keeping with the new attacking mentality being instilled into the German national team, *Die Mannschaft* began on the front foot and scored after just four minutes. Having remained up from a corner, Per Mertesacker controlled the ball in the penalty area and played a hopeful cross too far across the box. Bastian

Schweinsteiger did brilliantly to keep the ball alive, knocking it back into the path of Klose, who, having been left completely unmarked, drilled a low shot into the far corner.

Much like in 1982, both teams were seemingly content to see the match out from this point. Germany had the lead that would see them top the group and Ecuador had already secured their passage to the knockout phase, so the intensity all but disappeared from the match. Played amid sweltering temperatures during the heatwave that was enveloping Germany during the summer, both teams taking it easy ahead of the key fixtures they had coming up was understandable. While Germany mainly kept the ball among themselves, shortly before half-time Ballack collected it in space in the attacking third, dinking a delightful ball over the top of the defence for Klose, who took the ball round the outrushing keeper and had the simple task of tapping home a second and clinching goal. It was the first truly outstanding moment from Ballack during the tournament, as he was slowly working his way back to full fitness, a worrying sign for any future opponents.

The second half continued in the same vein, although Antonio Valencia was perhaps a bit fortunate to escape with just a yellow card for a lunging challenge on Ballack. In the days of VAR, it is likely that it would have been a red card rather than yellow. As Ecuador began to show some positive intent, with Méndez testing Lehmann from distance, the Germans hit on the counter. From the corner resulting from Méndez's effort, Schweinsteiger picked the ball up in midfield, freed Schneider down the right, and his cross was gratefully converted by Lukas Podolski for his first of the tournament. The youngster had impressed with his work-rate in the opening matches but had yet to get the goal that his performances deserved. The unity within the German camp was clear to see as he celebrated with the substitutes on the bench and with assistant coach Joachim Löw.

Aside from a few long-range efforts, the match was played out at the pace of an exhibition, with neither team wanting to risk picking up any injuries, so it ended with a comfortable 3-0 German victory, one that ensured they won the group and would play the runners-up from Group B, while Ecuador would be taking on the winners from the same group.

While those two nations were deciding who would win the group in Munich, 176 miles away in Hanover, Costa Rica and Poland were facing off for nothing more than the pride of not losing every match at the tournament. Quite often, when the pressure is off as both teams have already been eliminated, it produces a higher-quality contest, as all the expectations have been lifted from the shoulders of the players. As they had been threatening to all tournament, the Costa Ricans began on the front foot and took the lead halfway through the opening half, courtesy of a Gómez free kick. Lining up the effort from just outside the penalty area, he opted to go for power, driving the ball through the wall and through the legs of Boruc. There were understandable question marks about the Celtic keeper's efforts in failing to keep the ball out but the shot was hit with power and through the section of the wall that was lined by Costa Rican players, limiting the keeper's sight until the ball was already nearly upon him.

It should have got better for Costa Rica just a few minutes later, after good play down the right saw Paulo Wanchope receive the ball in space at the top of the penalty area, but rather than taking a touch and getting his shot away, he slipped as he attempted a first-time shot and the ball rolled harmlessly into Boruc's clutches. It was a miss that Costa Rica were immediately made to pay for.

Less than two minutes later, a Polish corner was floated in by Maciej Żurawski, Porras came to punch clear but completely missed the ball, and central defender Bartosz Bosacki met the ball on the volley to fire it into the back of the net via the crossbar.

It had taken 213 minutes but Poland had finally managed to get themselves on the scoresheet. With the pressure lifted, they were now showing more attacking intent than they had managed during their previous matches but were still lacking any cutting edge. The match was played in an open manner, both teams willing to push forward, but there was a clear lack of quality at the top end of the pitch and it was obvious why both were departing the tournament early.

The second period continued in the same manner, good endeavour from both teams but little in the way of goalscoring chances. Finally, a long-range Jacek Krzynówek effort brought a fine save from Porras, and from the resulting corner his cross was met at the back post by Bosacki, who climbed higher than Wanchope and powered a header past the goalkeeper. Bosacki was someone who ultimately had a short-lived international career, only finishing with 20 caps for his nation, but this was no doubt his finest day in a Poland shirt, with these two goals being the only ones he would score for his country.

Despite some nearly moments, Costa Rica were unable to create a chance for themselves to take a point from the match and Poland managed to take a victory that meant their tournament was not a total disaster. More was expected of them heading into the competition, with many predicting that they would qualify alongside Germany, but their tournament was over before it had properly begun. It was the last appearance they would make in the World Cup until 2018, when they again struggled, losing their opening two matches before winning their consolation third. With talented players at their disposal, but not quite a golden generation, Poland would certainly be disappointed with their outcome.

Costa Rica, however, used their experience to propel them forwards on to the international stage. Narrowly missing out on a place at the 2010 World Cup, losing to Uruguay in the inter-confederation play-off, the Central Americans were undoubtedly the surprise package of the 2014 edition. Having been drawn in a group with Italy, Uruguay and England, little was expected, but they topped the group unbeaten and beat Greece in the Round of 16, before losing on penalties to the Netherlands. Although their time would come to be international successes, this version of the tournament came perhaps too early in their development and they could not manage a single point despite playing some nice football and not being afraid of trying to take the game to their more illustrious opponents.

6pm, 9 June 2006
FIFA World Cup Stadium, Munich
Attendance: 66,000
Referee: Horacio Elizondo (Argentina)

Germany 4 (Lahm 6, Klose 17, 61, Frings 87)
Costa Rica 2 (Wanchope 12, 73)

Germany: Jens Lehmann, Arne Friedrich, Per Mertesacker, Christoph Metzelder, Philipp Lahm, Bernd Schneider (c) (David Odonkor 90+1), Torsten Frings, Tim Borowski (Sebastian Kehl 72), Bastian Schweinsteiger, Miroslav Klose (Oliver Neuville 79), Lukas Podolski. **Manager:** Jürgen Klinsmann.

Costa Rica: José Francisco Porras, Gilberto Martínez (Jervis Drummond 66), Michael Umaña, Douglas Sequeira, Luis Marín (c), Leonardo González, Danny Fonseca, Walter Centeno, Mauricio Solís (Christian Bolaños 78), Rónald Gómez (Randall Azofeifa 90+1), Paulo Wanchope. **Manager:** Alexandre Guimarães.

Booked: Fonseca (30)

9pm, 9 June 2006
Arena AufSchalke, Gelsenkirchen
Attendance: 52,000
Referee: Toru Kamikawa (Japan)

Poland 0
Ecuador 2 (C. Tenorio 24, Delgado 80)

Poland: Artur Boruc, Marcin Baszczyński, Mariusz Jop, Jacek Bąk (c), Michał Żewłakow, Euzebiusz Smolarek, Arkadiusz Radomski, Radosław Sobolewski (Ireneusz Jeleń 67), Mirosław Szymkowiak, Jacek Krzynówek (Kamil Kosowski 78), Maciej Żurawski (Paweł Brożek 83). **Manager:** Paweł Janas.

Ecuador: Cristian Mora, Ulises de la Cruz, Iván Hurtado (c) (Jorge Guagua 69), Giovanny Espinoza, Néicer Reasco, Antonio Valencia, Segundo Castillo, Edwin Tenorio, Édison Méndez, Agustín Delgado (Patricio Urrutia 83), Carlos Tenorio (Iván Kaviedes 65). **Manager:** Luis Fernando Suárez.

Booked: Smolarek (37); Hurtado (31), Méndez (70)

9pm, 14 June 2006
Westfalenstadion, Dortmund
Attendance: 65,000
Referee: Luis Medina Cantalejo (Spain)

Germany 1 (Neuville 90+1)
Poland 0

Germany: Jens Lehmann, Arne Friedrich (David Odonkor 64), Per Mertesacker, Christoph Metzelder, Philipp Lahm, Bernd Schneider, Torsten Frings, Michael Ballack (c), Bastian Schweinsteiger (Tim Borowski 77), Miroslav Klose, Lukas Podolski (Oliver Neuville 71). **Manager:** Jürgen Klinsmann.

Poland: Artur Boruc, Marcin Baszczyński, Bartosz Bosacki, Jacek Bąk (c), Michał Żewłakow (Dariusz Dudka 83), Radosław Sobolewski, Arkadiusz Radomski, Ireneusz Jeleń (Paweł Brożek 90+1), Maciej Żurawski, Jacek Krzynówek (Mariusz Lewandowski 77), Euzebiusz Smolarek. **Manager:** Paweł Janas.

Booked: Ballack (58), Odonkor (68), Metzelder (70); Krzynówek (3), Sobolewski (28), Boruc (89)
Sent off: Sobolewski (75)

3pm, 15 June 2006
Volksparkstadion, Hamburg
Attendance: 50,000
Referee: Coffi Codjia (Benin)

Ecuador 3 (C. Tenorio 8, Delgado 54, Kaviedes 90+2)
Costa Rica 0

Ecuador: Cristian Mora, Ulises de la Cruz, Iván Hurtado (c), Giovanny Espinoza (Jorge Guagua 69), Néicer Reasco, Antonio Valencia (Patricio Urrutia 73), Segundo Castillo, Edwin Tenorio, Édison Méndez, Agustín Delgado, Carlos Tenorio (Iván Kaviedes 46). **Manager:** Luis Fernando Suárez.

Costa Rica: José Francisco Porras, Michael Umaña, Luis Marín (c), Douglas Sequeira, Harold Wallace, Mauricio Solís, Danny Fonseca (Álvaro Saborío 29), Leonardo González (Carlos Hernández 56), Walter Centeno (Kurt Bernard 84), Rónald Gómez, Paulo Wanchope. **Manager:** Alexandre Guimarães.

Booked: Castillo (44), De la Cruz (54), Mora (60); Marín (10), Solís (28)

4pm, 20 June 2006
Olympiastadion, Berlin
Attendance: 72,000
Referee: Valentin Ivanov (Russia)

Ecuador 0
Germany 3 (Klose 4, 44, Podolski 57)

Ecuador: Cristian Mora, Ulises de la Cruz, Jorge Guagua, Giovanny Espinoza, Paúl Ambrosi, Antonio Valencia (Christian Lara 63), Marlon Ayoví (c) (Patricio Urrutia 68), Edwin Tenorio, Édison Méndez, Iván Kaviedes, Félix Borja (Christian Benitez 46). **Manager:** Luis Fernando Suárez.

Germany: Jens Lehmann, Arne Friedrich, Robert Huth, Phillipp Lahm, Per Mertesacker, Bastian Schweinsteiger, Torsten Frings (Tim Borowski 66), Michael Ballack (c), Bernd Schneider (Gerald Asamoah 73), Miroslav Klose (Oliver Neuville 66), Lukas Podolski. Manager: Jurgen Klinsmann.

Booked: Valencia (52); Borowski (75)

4pm, 20 June 2006
Niedersachsenstadion, Hanover
Attendance: 43,000
Referee: Shamsul Maidin (Singapore)

Costa Rica 1 (Gómez 25)
Poland 2 (Bosacki 33, 65)

Costa Rica: José Francisco Porras, Michael Umaña, Luis Marín (c), Gabriel Badilla, Jervis Drummond (Harold Wallace 70), Mauricio Solís, Christian Bolaños (Álvaro Saborío 78), Walter Centeno, Leonardo González, Paulo Wanchope, Rónald Gómez (Carlos Hernández 82). **Manager:** Alexandre Guimarães.

Poland: Artur Boruc, Marcin Baszczyński, Bartosz Bosacki, Jacek Bąk (c), Michał Żewłakow, Euzebiusz Smolarek (Grzegorz Rasiak 85), Arkadiusz Radomski (Mariusz Lewandowski 64), Mirosław Szymkowiak, Jacek Krzynówek, Ireneusz Jeleń, Maciej Żurawski (Paweł Brożek 46). **Manager:** Paweł Janas.

Booked: Umaña (12), Marín (45+2), Gómez (45+2), Badilla (56), González (76); Radomski (18), Bąk (24), Żewłakow (29), Baszczyński (60), Boruc (90+1)

Group A	P	W	D	L	GF	GA	GD	PTS
GERMANY	3	3	0	0	8	2	+6	9
ECUADOR	3	2	0	1	5	3	+2	6
POLAND	3	1	0	2	2	4	-2	3
COSTA RICA	3	0	0	3	3	9	-6	0

Germany and Ecuador qualified

Group B

WITH GROUP A starting the tournament off in style, Group B saw one of the pre-tournament favourites beginning their journey. As always, much was expected of England heading into the tournament, yet this year definitely felt different. The English entered as the second favourites to lift the trophy, only behind defending champions Brazil, and they certainly had a squad that could match any of the other main contenders. Although they certainly fancied their chances of making it through the group, they began their campaign against a sneakily strong Paraguay team. *Los Guaraníes* had navigated the notoriously difficult CONMEBOL qualifying campaign, finishing third behind Brazil and Argentina, and were entering the tournament aiming to reach the knockout stages for the third consecutive World Cup, with aspirations of going further than the Round of 16 this time around. Paraguay had also achieved a silver medal in the Olympic Games in Athens two years earlier, narrowly losing 1-0 in the final to an Argentina team led by Marcelo Bielsa and containing the likes of Carlos Tevez, Javier Mascherano, Javier Saviola and a total of seven players who would feature in the final squad for this tournament.

Whatever confidence the South Americans had prior to kick-off was quickly evaporated as England began with serious intent. With just three minutes on the clock, a David Beckham free kick from just inside the Paraguayan half was glanced on by Carlos Gamarra, with his header taking the ball beyond his keeper Justo Villar and giving England the dream start. Things immediately went from bad to worse, as Villar, when rushing out to prevent Michael Owen reaching a through ball, appeared to pull his calf muscle. He immediately grimaced in pain and signalled to the bench that he would be unable to continue. Villar's replacement, Aldo Bobadilla, was inexperienced on the international stage, having earned just five caps despite turning 30 prior to the tournament, perhaps providing England with the perfect opportunity to lay down an early statement to the rest of the contenders.

Unsurprisingly, England remained on top but, as many fans had come to expect at this point, were unable to fashion any clear-cut chances. Half-chances came primarily from the long-range shooting of Lampard, who drilled a free kick against the wall and then wastefully fired the rebound high and wide. He also took aim from 20 yards with an effort that was easily caught by Bobadilla, but there was little for the replacement keeper to be worried about.

As the first half wore on, England's positivity gradually began to disappear, with a more pragmatic and measured approach taking its place. As the Three Lions settled down, the Paraguayans started to gain optimism and a proper foothold in the match. England's withdrawal into their defensive shell was the opportunity Paraguay needed and they began to control the tempo, almost finding an equaliser right on half-time when Nelson Haedo Valdez fired a snapshot narrowly wide of the post after capitalising on hesitant English defending.

The second half carried on in the same manner that the first ended, with the South Americans retaining the majority of control. They had two good chances to equalise just after the hour mark. Firstly, Carlos Paredes fired wastefully over after

Paul Robinson fumbled his attempt to gather a cross, followed by Valdez dribbling the entire length of the England half, cutting inside on to his left foot but sending his shot straight at Robinson. Paraguay had been unable to capitalise on their chances, and England probably created the better ones as the match ticked over, both from Lampard taking aim from outside the area, with Bobadilla producing smart saves to deflect the ball behind for a corner on both occasions.

As the final whistle blew and England gained their victory, their fans could have been forgiven for feeling a sense of disappointment. Having scored inside three minutes and causing the Paraguay defence plenty of early problems, they had retreated into a shell and offered very little attacking intent beyond the first 20 minutes other than long shots from Lampard. There has since been open admission that England struggled to click into gear in the opening match, as both Gary Neville and Sven-Göran Eriksson stated in their autobiographies, but a win was a win. A key factor in England's progress would be the ability of their coach to get the best out of Lampard and Steven Gerrard. Having finished second and third respectively in the most recent Ballon d'Or voting, they represented arguably the best midfield pairing in the world. Yet, the old cliché was that the two were unable to feature successfully in the same midfield. However, the best players are able to adapt to any system, their talent helping them settle quicker into a different team or style, but, for whatever reason, Lampard and Gerrard just never gelled together on the international stage.

As England opened with a win in Frankfurt, fellow Europeans Sweden got underway against the minnows from Trinidad and Tobago. Sweden were favoured to progress alongside England, and this opening match was seemingly the perfect opportunity to warm themselves into the tournament before the opponents got tougher. For the small Caribbean nation, keeping the scoreline close would have been the aim, with their hopes hanging on the shoulders of Manchester United legend Dwight Yorke, who would be captaining the team from central midfield rather than his more customary striking position.

As the teams warmed up, Trinidad and Tobago coach Leo Beenhakker was presented with a problem when a calf injury to his first-choice goalkeeper Kelvin Jack forced a last-minute change to the line-up, with West Ham United's Shaka Hislop coming in. Hislop was not an unknown, having been the goalkeeper for the Hammers in the FA Cup Final against Liverpool just a month earlier, and he was now presented the honour of being the keeper for his nation's first-ever match at the World Cup finals.

As expected, the Swedes started on the front foot, earning two early corners and a free kick that Henrik Larsson sent narrowly wide. Larsson and Zlatan Ibrahimović were creating all the problems for the Trinidadian defence early on, drifting into wider areas and finding space in behind the back line. While Sweden were probing to try to find the early breakthrough, Trinidad and Tobago were giving everything, with full-blooded challenges being dealt out by Yorke, Brent Sancho and Avery John, who would receive the match's first caution just 15 minutes in. Although Sweden had full control, they were unable to take advantage, with Larsson, Anders Svensson and Arsenal legend Freddie Ljungberg all missing chances.

Having held their opponents at arm's length for the opening half an hour, Trinidad and Tobago had the best opportunity of the match so far, with Carlos Edwards firing an effort on target from 35 yards that the Swedish goalkeeper did well to keep hold of. The underdogs were defending well but did offer a threat on the counter-attack, and when Edwards got the ball down the right-hand side and floated a cross to the back post, Stern John should have done better than simply heading the ball high over the bar. In between these two chances, Sweden came close to opening the scoring themselves, with Larsson heading narrowly over and both Ibrahimović and Christian Wilhelmsson forcing smart saves from Hislop. As the half-time whistle blew, the newcomers were good value for their point against their more experienced opponents, with Hislop impressing in his deputy role and Yorke being surprisingly effective in the central role he was operating in.

As the match restarted, more of the same was needed from the Trinidadians to continue their impressive efforts and gain at least a draw. What couldn't be accounted for was, in the name of making sure the Swedes could not get comfortable on the ball for fear of a strong challenge, Avery John would receive a second yellow card just 20 seconds into the second half. It was the definition of a needless challenge as, with the ball rolling into the path of Wilhelmsson on the right edge of the penalty area, John dived in to win the ball and made contact with both ball and the shin of the Swede. It was a clear booking and made the task infinitely harder for his nation.

Despite this, it was actually the Caribbean outfit who created the next chance in the match, just before the hour mark. A simple long ball upfield was flicked into the path of Cornell Glen, who took it forward to a narrow angle on the edge of the area before striking his shot beyond the outstretched arm of the Swedish keeper but against the top of the crossbar, with the ball travelling behind for a goal kick.

With a man advantage, Sweden's odds of victory increased but they still laboured their way through the remainder of the match. They struggled to create clear-cut chances, a problem that had not been evident during qualifying when they managed to score 30 goals in their ten matches. Ibrahimović, Larsson and Ljungberg scored 20 goals between them during that campaign and were joined on the pitch by Marcus Allbäck, fresh from scoring 15 goals in 30 matches for Copenhagen in the Danish Superliga, meaning *The Blue and Yellow* had four top-quality goalscorers on the pitch for the final half an hour against the ten men of Trinidad and Tobago. All four had chances that they would have fancied themselves to finish but a mixture of profligacy and inspired goalkeeping by Hislop kept them at bay.

It was with just ten minutes remaining that the best Swedish chance came. After good link-up play between Larsson and Ibrahimović on the edge of the area, Allbäck was played in behind the back line of the Trinidadians. With just the goalkeeper in his way, the opportunity was on a plate for the striker to finish off the match. Unable to keep his composure, Allbäck stabbed an effort straight into the body of Hislop, who had come off his line well to make himself as big as possible. It summed up the attacking play of the Swedes throughout the match. Nice build-up play but a lack of cutting edge.

Unable to fashion any further noteworthy chances, the final whistle blew and, with it, a first World Cup point for Trinidad and Tobago. It was a monumental effort, especially having gone down to ten men straight after half-time, but they were good value for the draw, keeping Sweden at arm's length for the majority of the contest. Sweden would need to find their scoring touch, and quickly, if they were to qualify. With the tough Paraguayans next up, Sweden's hopes were already looking a little precarious.

* * *

Having won their opening match, England knew that a victory over Trinidad and Tobago would secure their passage into the knockout stages, with Sweden's draw with the same opponents meaning a win would give the Three Lions an excellent chance at topping the group. Trinidad and Tobago, however, had proven that they were in Germany for more than just a holiday and would make sure that their counterparts knew that they had been in a competitive match. With eight players based in England, including Stern John, Kenwyne Jones, Carlos Edwards and Shaka Hislop, who would all feature in the Premier League to varying degrees of success, and the experienced Dwight Yorke controlling the midfield, it was never going to be an easy match for England.

Hislop retained his place, with Kelvin Jack still out injured, and it represented a full-circle moment in Hislop's career. The West Ham stopper was born in England, moving to Trinidad aged two, and had been a part of an England squad back in 1998 for a friendly against Chile, a match most notable for Michael Owen making his full England debut, and had featured for the England Under-21s as an overage player against Switzerland. Yet here he was, in what would prove to be the penultimate match of his 26-cap career for his adopted nation, providing the last line of defence against the country of his birth, the one where he had spent the majority of his playing career.

As to be expected, Hislop was to be the busier of the two keepers, facing two long-range efforts early, spilling a Lampard strike to Owen, who could not react in time to tap home the rebound. England were predictably in control of possession but seemingly had decided that their best path to scoring the opening goal was to come from either a speculative long-range effort or floating a cross on to the head of Peter Crouch. The lanky Liverpool striker did manage to find himself free at the back post from a Joe Cole cross, but his effort on the stretch was parried behind by Hislop, scrambling across his goal. Having struggled to make an impact against Paraguay in the opening match, this contest presented the perfect chance for Crouch to kickstart his campaign and prove his doubters wrong. Had Wayne Rooney been fully fit, the striker is unlikely to have started, with Owen and Rooney the preferred partnership. Crouch had only recently become a fixture in the England squad, making his debut just a year before the tournament in Germany. In his second competitive appearance, as a substitute against Poland in World Cup qualifying at Old Trafford, he was booed by the home fans as he was brought on for Shaun Wright-Phillips. Whether the booing was aimed at the decision to take Wright-Phillips off, Crouch himself or simply the effect of the tribal nature of football, it hardly represented the ideal start to international life for him. In a pre-tournament friendly against Jamaica, designed to prepare England for the match against Trinidad and Tobago, Crouch bagged himself a hat-trick, as well as missing a penalty, perhaps showing that he was an effective option for England without the services of Rooney.

Despite being in total control, much like against Paraguay, England could not find a rhythm and struggled to fashion any real chances to test Hislop and the Trinidadian defence. Brent Sancho and Dennis Lawrence were in complete control at the centre of defence and Cyd Gray and Dwight Yorke were causing problems in the middle of the park, forcing England, most notably Lampard, into wasteful shots from distance. In fact, it was Trinidad who arguably came closest to opening the scoring. Yorke fired a corner into the England penalty area that Robinson came to collect and completely missed, allowing the ball to reach Stern John at the back post, but he could only glance his header wide. Future Stoke City team-mates Kenwyne Jones and Crouch traded half-chances, with Jones heading over from a free kick and Crouch spectacularly miscuing an acrobatic volley when unmarked in the six-yard box. The underdogs came close once again on the stroke of half-time, after a hopeful cross by Edwards was met by Lawrence ahead of Robinson, who was unconvincing once more. The ball fell to John, who managed to direct his header on target this time, only to see John Terry react quickly to clear off the line just in the nick of time.

The second half carried on in the same manner as the first, with England dominating possession but lacking any creativity in the final third. Crouch missed two more chances and Owen headed over from a Beckham free kick, but it was all tentative jabs from England, although the introduction of Aaron Lennon and Rooney did open the match up, especially on the right-hand side where Lennon's pace and intelligent movement freed up space for Beckham to send those crosses into the area. England did have a penalty appeal turned away after a Lennon cross hit Yorke on the arm, but the experienced Trinidadian captain was only a couple of yards away and would not have been able to move out of the way.

As the match faded into the final 15 minutes, Trinidad became slightly more adventurous, perhaps sensing the chance to steal an unlikely and historic victory. Cornell Glen, brought on to replace Jones, had a shot well blocked by Ashley Cole, and then the left-back did well to recover and make a challenge after Glen had turned him on the edge of the area and was bearing down on Robinson's goal.

Trinidad's ventures forward offered a little more space at the back for England to exploit, and Lampard managed to get free on the edge of the six-yard box but could only shoot straight at Hislop. It was another chance that the Chelsea midfielder would expect to score, particularly on the back of a season where he had scored 20 goals for his club. In his autobiography, *Totally Frank*, he admits that he was not at his best, partly due to his lack of goals, and there are missed chances from the tournament that haunt him, although those were to come later. Had he taken one of the numerous chances he had in this match, the outcome in the knockout stages may have been different.

This time, however, Lampard's misses were not to prove costly. With just seven minutes remaining, Beckham whipped a cross to the back post for Crouch, who rose above Sancho and powered a header beyond Hislop. It was a simple goal created by Beckham being afforded extra space on the right-hand side through the introduction of Lennon, but, as simple as it was, it was also controversial. Replays showed that Crouch, to gain leverage over his marker, had pulled down on the defender's dreadlocks, thus stopping him from being able to jump and challenge for the ball. In the game today, it is likely that the goal would have been disallowed, but unfortunately for Trinidad it stood and their resistance had been broken.

There was still time for England to add a little gloss to the final score, with Gerrard firing an excellent left-footed strike into the top corner from 20 yards out in the first minute of added time. Although England had the win that secured their passage through to the knockout stages, there was deserved disgruntlement at their performance. It was a match that they should have comfortably won, as one of the tournament favourites, yet they had laboured their way to a narrow victory that could easily have been different. The hope was that they would gradually find their form, peaking as the tournament progressed, but it was certainly not the ideal start for the Three Lions.

For the Soca Warriors, it was a heart-breaking result that was undeserved, as they had battled bravely and even created the clearer opportunities, but their prospects of progressing had taken a major blow. They were left needing a draw between Sweden and Paraguay to have the best chance, but their hopes were hanging by a thread.

With England's win securing their qualification, Sweden knew that a win against Paraguay would nearly secure their position alongside their fellow Europeans, whereas the South Americans knew that a defeat would end their tournament after just two matches. However, a point or better would put them in pole position for the second qualification spot. The two nations had actually met once before in the World Cup finals, playing out an entertaining 2-2 draw back in 1950, when Sweden ultimately finished third behind Uruguay and Brazil, although the outcome may have been different had the Swedes been able to call on their three best players, the Milan trio 'Gre-No-Li', Gunnar Gren, Gunnar Nordahl and Nils Liedholm. However, Sweden's international team had rules prohibiting the selection of professional players and, as the trio were earning their living playing football in Milan, they were unable to be called up in 1950.

Eight years later, however, Sweden were hosts of the tournament, and the rulers of Swedish football decided to change their minds, allowing Gren and Liedholm to be selected, Nordahl having retired. Although getting on in age, Gren at 37 and Liedholm 35, they helped lead Sweden to their first and only World Cup Final, where Liedholm gave them the lead against Brazil just four minutes in. Led by Vavá and Pelé, Brazil stormed back to win 5-2 and claim their first World Cup title, relegating an incredible era of Swedish football to little more than a footnote in history. While not on the level of the famed Milan trio, having the attacking talents of Larsson, Ibrahimović and Ljungberg to call upon offered hope that Sweden would be able to cause a surprise and perhaps make a deeper run into the tournament than predicted.

Wanting to lay down an early marker, Sweden began on the front foot. Kim Källström, brought into the starting line-up in favour of Anders Svensson, brought a good save from Bobadilla with a fierce shot from 30 yards, Wilhelmsson firing wide from similar range and Larsson narrowly missing getting on the edge of a cross by Ibrahimović, all within the opening 15 minutes. It was not one-way traffic, though, with Santa Cruz narrowly turning the ball past the post from a clever knock-down by Carlos Paredes, although the offside flag would have meant it would not have counted even had it bounced the right side of the post for Paraguay.

The match was a tentative back and forth between the two, with both teams seemingly afraid to make the mistake that could see their hopes of progressing hanging by a thread. The Anderlecht winger Wilhelmsson was regularly finding space in which to operate, drifting well away from his right-hand-side position, finding himself free on the left of the Paraguayan penalty area, but a poor touch allowed the keeper to gather the ball easily.

For Paraguay, getting Nelson Valdez on the ball was their best hope for unlocking the Swedish back line. Valdez, who would move from SV Werder Bremen to Borussia Dortmund once the tournament was over, was a clever forward more akin to a No. 10 than a No. 9 and was the chief creator for Paraguay, forming an effective partnership with fellow Bundesliga player Roque Santa Cruz. It was Valdez who had the South Americans' best chances in the first half, first seeing a header deflected wide and then volleying over from the edge of the penalty area.

Having started slowly, the momentum had drifted back towards Paraguay as the first half drew to a close, and a similar pattern seemed to be emerging for Sweden. Much like in their opening match, they had been in control of possession and had created the better chances but were unable to finish a single one. For a team that boasted the attacking talents that Sweden had and having scored so freely during qualifying, their struggles in front of goal came as a complete shock. It was almost as if they had expected to breeze through the opening two matches and then play England for top spot. As things stood at half-time in their second match, they would have only two points and were at risk of missing the knockout stages altogether.

Sweden coach Lars Lagerbäck was forced into shuffling his pack at the interval, bringing on Allbäck in place of Ibrahimović, with the Juventus striker having picked up a groin strain. Paraguay started the second half on the attack, with Valdez firing into the side-netting just 30 seconds after the restart. Both teams traded long shots, Larsson seeing a free kick parried away by Bobadilla and Roberto Acuña shooting straight at Andreas Isaksson, who had returned in goal for Sweden.

If the Swedes were worried about a drop in quality with Allbäck in place of Ibrahimović then they need not have worried, as the Copenhagen striker had two wonderful opportunities inside a minute. First, he broke through in behind the Paraguayan defence from a through ball by Källström, only for the assistant to flag for offside before he could apply the finish. It was a tight call and the replay clearly showed that he had been played onside by Jorge Núñez. A minute later and Allbäck was through one-on-one with Bobadilla, with the flag staying down. With the keeper rushing out to meet him, he opted to chip the ball over him but did not quite get enough on it. It became a straight race between himself and Denis Caniza, with the Paraguayan defender reacting quickly enough to clear the ball before the striker could tap into an empty net. Wasteful finishing or excellent defending, whichever way you look at it, it was symptomatic of Sweden's problems all tournament.

The flurry of chances to open the second half aside, the match settled into a familiar pattern with both teams offering little in the way of true openings. Both had half-chances, Henrik Larsson once again heading over and Valdez shooting straight at the keeper from distance, but the match seemed destined to fade out into a 0-0 draw that would mean England were group winners and the final qualifying spot was completely up for grabs between the other three nations. But, just as the match seemed finished, Sweden finally found their scoring touch. Having brought on another striker, the future Bolton Wanderers striker

Johan Elmander in place of the impressive Källström, the Swedes were clearly pushing for the winner. And it was Elmander who played a crucial role in providing that winner, floating an inch-perfect cross to the back post for Allbäck to meet. Cleverly aware of the difficulty he would have in scoring from the position he was in, he headed the ball back across the six-yard box. With all the Paraguayan defenders focusing on Allbäck and Larsson, no one noticed Ljungberg arriving at the back post to power a free header beyond the scrambling keeper. Sweden had perhaps had the better of things but it was hard to say that either team deserved to grab a winner. Yet Sweden had found a way, finally breaking their goalscoring drought and winning an international for the first time since beating Iceland 3-1 the previous October, a run stretching back seven matches.

The last-gasp winner meant that Sweden were sitting on four points from their two matches and in an excellent position to qualify. They could still win the group if they managed to beat England in their final match. For Paraguay, the Ljungberg goal meant that their tournament was over after just two matches. Defensively well organised but lacking a clinical nature going forwards, it was perhaps a harsh early exit for a team that would have fancied themselves to go a lot further than just the group stages. And for Trinidad and Tobago, the Sweden victory meant that they could still reach the knockout stage, with a Swedish defeat to England and victory for themselves over Paraguay. Unexpectedly, after two matches, for the vast majority of the watching world the Soca Warriors were still alive heading into the final group fixtures.

* * *

An opportunity of qualifying heading into the final fixtures was maybe even beyond the dreams of the fans from the smallest nation to have ever qualified for the World Cup at this point (their record would be surpassed by Iceland in 2018), but Trinidad and Tobago had a shot against Paraguay. Despite an early header from Santa Cruz being superbly saved by the returning goalkeeper Kelvin Jack, the Soca Warriors started on the front foot in search of a goal. Cornell Glen forced a smart save from Bobadilla with a powerful header and Aurtis Whitley drove a volley over from just outside the penalty box.

All the good play being produced by Trinidad and Tobago was orchestrated by their captain Dwight Yorke, who, despite being 34 and playing a central midfield role, was reminding the world of his abilities as an elite footballer. Yorke and fellow squad member Russell Latapy had nearly helped the island nation qualify for the World Cup back in 1990, losing 1-0 to the USA when a draw would have seen them competing in Italy rather than their conquerors. It was a disappointment that lingered, especially as they never managed to come as close again until 2006. Both Yorke and Latapy had retired from international duty in 2001, with Yorke returning in 2004 and Latapy a year later following intervention from his team-mate and FIFA Vice-President and CONCACAF President Jack Warner, a Trinidadian who was later indicted alongside other FIFA officials during the 2015 corruption scandal that rocked the governing body, to help their nation finally get over the finish line in qualifying for the biggest moment of their little island's footballing history.

It was not completely plain sailing, however. Warner had brokered a deal with the federation and players to share the money made from qualifying for the tournament and provide those who helped in the qualifying effort with financial bonuses. Yet those payments were not forthcoming. The players who represented their nation for the first time at a World Cup finals did not see a cent of the money that their efforts brought in. They chased

Warner for the money they were owed but the businessman remained elusive and coy on when that would be. Ultimately, he accused the squad of being 'greedy', despite the fact that tickets under his name from FIFA were being resold by a travel company owned by him. Sponsorship deals were doctored to make it seem like they were worth less and the players were made to pay for their own travel and accommodation for the tournament, so the final amount each player received was under £1,000. It was a small tale in the corruption that was rampant throughout FIFA, but for those who gave everything for their nation, it was an injustice that lingered and was never resolved.

Back on the pitch, unfortunately for Trinidad their positivity was undone after 25 minutes when a free kick from Acuña was floated into the area and flicked on by Julio dos Santos. His header may have been going wide but the ball deflected off the back of Sancho's head as he reacted to try to clear it, and the ball flew beyond Jack. There was little that could have been done to avoid the goal, but it was a moment that seemingly knocked the wind out of the sails of Beenhakker's team. Paraguay began to wrestle control of the match, with Valdez once again showing his class when pulling the strings. He had Paraguay's best opportunities when seeing a one-on-one and a header well stopped by Jack either side of Caniza poking the ball underneath the Trinidadian keeper only to see the flag belatedly raised to disallow it for an offside after a slight touch from Édgar Barreto in the build-up.

Opting for an early tactical switch, Beenhakker brought on striker Kenwyne Jones for defender Avery John after just half an hour, but when the dangerous Glen was stretchered off after 40 minutes with a nasty-looking knee injury, everything seemed to be turning against the Caribbean nation. There was still time for Paraguay to nearly grab a second before half-time, with Paredes steering a bobbling ball in the box goalward, only for Densill Theobald to clear off the line.

If Trinidad were going to mount the improbable comeback, they would need to start the second half quickly and they certainly came out with intent. A wicked cross from Edwards after just two minutes narrowly evaded two attackers when even the slightest of touches would have sent the ball into the back of the net. For all the endeavour of the Trinidadians, however, they struggled to create any real openings as the second half progressed. Their South American opponents had settled into a steady defensive rhythm and were successfully keeping them at arm's length. The introduction of Latapy for his tournament debut with a little over 20 minutes remaining did offer a little hope, with both he and Yorke narrowly shooting wide from distance.

Throwing everything forwards in the hope of getting their first World Cup goal and potentially creating the possibility for the most extraordinary of comebacks, Trinidad and Tobago were leaving gaps at the back for Paraguay to try to exploit on the counter, and with just four minutes left they doubled their lead. Nelson Cuevas, having replaced Valdez, collected the ball in the inside-left position. Drifting inside, he played a simple one-two with Santa Cruz that saw him driving into the penalty area, where he calmly slotted the ball beyond Jack.

Both teams accepted the match was over from this point and the final few minutes of the tournament fizzled out for both nations. For Paraguay it was a positive end to a disappointing tournament. Having reached the knockout stages at the previous two World Cups, they would have fancied their chances of progressing beyond the groups, but a failure to score against England or Sweden meant that they were hanging by a thread almost immediately, with the late defeat to Sweden ending their tournament after just two matches. With Gerard Martino taking the helm after the tournament, Paraguay qualified for the 2010 World Cup in South Africa, a record fourth consecutive tournament for *Los Guaraníes*, ultimately winning their group and reaching the quarter-finals, narrowly losing 1-0 to eventual champions Spain. This was the best spell in Paraguayan footballing history, although the 2006 squad will be considered the weakest in that run, having not managed to get out of their group.

As for Trinidad and Tobago, the tournament can only be considered a huge success, even with their disappointment of finishing bottom of the group without a single goal scored. Little was expected of the tiny Caribbean island, with most pundits predicting defeat in every match. Their performances each time were magnificent, holding a fearsome Swedish attacking line to a goalless draw and keeping England at bay for just over 80 minutes, only finally being breached through nefarious means. The Paraguay match was perhaps a step too far, with the pressure on the Soca Warriors to get the win, and their tournament ended with little more than a whimper; however, they could all still be proud of their efforts. As a reward, the entire playing and coaching staff were awarded the Chaconia Medal, Gold, the second-highest honour in Trinidad and Tobago, as well as financial bonuses. The tournament was also a great showcase for the talents within the squad, especially for Kenwyne Jones and Carlos Edwards, who would both move to Premier League Sunderland in the summer following the tournament. It may have been a sad end for the country, but the journey had been remarkable and their small island nation had been firmly placed on the footballing map.

With Paraguay's win, Sweden had secured qualification to the knockout stages regardless of the result against England, and after their first-half display, it must have come as a relief. Having already qualified, England were hoping to escape from the match with at least the point they needed to secure top spot and avoid a second-round match-up against Germany. England had no injury concerns, and this included Rooney and Owen, who had entered the tournament as injury doubts. However, for the latter the match was over after just two minutes. In his 80th cap for his country, Owen had turned awkwardly when collecting the ball in the Sweden half and tore his anterior cruciate ligament, ending his participation in the tournament. The loss of Owen again raised questions of Sven-Göran Eriksson's squad selection. He had only named four forwards in the squad, one of those being 17-year-old Theo Walcott and another being Rooney, who was working his way back from a broken metatarsal. There had been calls for Tottenham's Jermain Defoe, who had scored nine goals the previous season, or Crystal Palace's Andy Johnson, who was the second-highest scorer in the Premier League in 2004/05, but Sven had opted for Walcott as the wildcard option. With Owen being ruled out for the knockout stages, Sven's decision was perhaps going to come back to haunt him.

Spurred on by the loss of Owen, England controlled the first half, with Lampard heading wide, Joe Cole firing over from the edge of the area and Rooney seeing his effort blocked by Teddy Lučić after a wonderful piece of control. Cole and Rooney, in his first start of the competition, were running the show for England, both demonstrating their undoubted ability and enjoying playing in a freer system that was anchored by Owen Hargreaves taking on a holding role in place of the rested Gerrard. The biggest shock of the half was that it took England until the 34th minute to opening the scoring, but it was certainly worth the wait. A simple cross from Beckham was unconvincingly dealt with by the Swedes, with the clearing header only reaching Cole 30 yards out. The immediate danger seemed to have passed but the Chelsea man had other ideas, controlling the ball on his chest before unleashing a swerving, dipping volley that flew into the far top corner beyond the stretch of Isaksson in the Swedish goal. It was a goal of the highest quality and proof of just how good a player he could be when freed from the shackles of José Mourinho's defensively minded set-up at Chelsea.

Despite the total dominance of the first half, England once again emerged for the second period a different team. Whether due to the heat they were playing in, arrogance in thinking that the matches were won or any other factor, England never managed to continue their positive starts to produce a statement performance. It took Sweden just six minutes of the second half to draw themselves level, an outcome that never looked likely at the interval. It was a simple goal as well, with a Tobias Linderoth corner being glanced on at the near post by Allbäck, with his header lopping over the desperate jump of Ashley Cole on the goal line.

Sweden were playing with a higher intensity in the second half, perhaps fearing a Trinidadian comeback against Paraguay that never materialised, but England were masters of their own downfall, sleepwalking their way through the opening exchanges of the second half. And it nearly got worse just three minutes later. In much the same manner as the equalising goal, this time it was a Larsson header from the corner but Robinson was able to react, producing a brilliant save to turn the ball on to the crossbar, with Terry completing the clearance. Set pieces were clearly an effective weapon for Sweden, as just a few minutes later Aston Villa captain Olof Mellberg hooked a shot that rebounded off the crossbar. In the space of just eight minutes Sweden had scored and hit the crossbar twice, all from corners.

After Sweden's flurry of chances to start the second half, things settled down into a less frenetic pace with the chances drying up. Gerrard was brought on in place of Rooney to give the Manchester United striker a breather ahead of the knockout phase, and the Liverpool midfielder was in the right place to clear a goalbound volley from Källström off the line as Sweden again threatened from a corner.

It came against the run of play when England grabbed what seemed to be the winner with just five minutes remaining. A hopeful punt upfield by Robinson was won by Crouch and collected by Joe Cole. He brought the ball under control and calmly dinked a ball to the back post, where Gerrard had drifted into space and was unmarked to drive a header into the back of the net. It was a goal that was as effective as it was simple. It was the option that having Crouch as the lone striker with a creative player behind him presented.

Yet it would not be England at a major tournament without them throwing away the opportunity of a victory. With the clock ticking down into added time, Erik Edman launched a throw-in from the left into the England box. With Terry and Sol Campbell on the pitch, England should have easily dealt with the ball, but Terry missed his header, the ball bounced over Campbell, and Larsson crept in ahead of Ashley Cole and got a toe to the ball to send it nestling into the far corner. It was a poor goal to concede from an English perspective but a deserved one for Sweden, as their second-half efforts meant that they did not deserve to be on the losing side.

It was relief for England as the final whistle blew as they had managed to leave Cologne with the point they needed to top the group. Having lost Owen to a serious injury after just two minutes, securing top spot was crucial but England had yet to click into top gear in any match, which was the lingering worry. The old adage is that teams that go far in international tournaments often click as the rounds progress, and that was clearly the hope for this English team, but there were still warning signs despite qualifying unbeaten. The Swedes would have been disappointed as the opportunity was there for them to pinch top spot, even after an unimpressive campaign so far. Their second-half performance against England would have served as a hopeful reminder to Lagerbäck's team of the quality they possessed and offered hope that they could spring a shock against hosts Germany in the second round.

3pm, 10 June 2006
Waldstadion, Frankfurt
Attendance: 48,000
Referee: Marco Rodríguez (Mexico)

England 1 (Gamarra 3 o.g.)
Paraguay 0

England: Paul Robinson, Gary Neville, Rio Ferdinand, John Terry, Ashley Cole, David Beckham (c), Steven Gerrard, Frank Lampard, Joe Cole (Owen Hargreaves 83), Michael Owen (Stewart Downing 56), Peter Crouch. **Manager:** Sven-Göran Eriksson.

Paraguay: Justo Villar (Aldo Bobadilla 8), Denis Caniza, Julio César Cáceres, Carlos Gamarra (c), Delio Toledo (Jorge Núñez 82), Carlos Bonet (Nelson Cuevas 68), Roberto Acuña, Carlos Paredes, Cristian Riveros, Roque Santa Cruz, Nelson Valdez. **Manager:** Aníbal Ruiz.

Booked: Gerrard (19), Crouch (63); Valdez (22)

6pm, 10 June 2006
Westfalenstadion, Dortmund
Attendance: 62,959
Referee: Shamsul Maidin (Singapore)

Trinidad and Tobago 0
Sweden 0

Trinidad and Tobago: Shaka Hislop, Cyd Gray, Brent Sancho, Dennis Lawrence, Avery John, Carlos Edwards, Chris Birchall, Dwight Yorke (c), Densill Theobald (Aurtis Whitley 66), Stern John, Collin Samuel (Cornell Glen 52). **Manager:** Leo Beenhakker.

Sweden: Rami Shaaban, Niclas Alexandersson, Olof Mellberg (c), Teddy Lučić, Erik Edman, Christian Wilhelmsson (Mattias Jonson 78), Tobias Linderoth (Kim Källström 78), Anders Svensson (Marcus Allbäck 62), Freddie Ljungberg, Zlatan Ibrahimović, Henrik Larsson. **Manager:** Lars Lagerbäck.

Booked: John (15), Yorke (74); Larsson (90),
Sent off: John (46)

6pm, 15 June 2006
Frankenstadion, Nuremburg
Attendance: 41,000
Referee: Toru Kamikawa (Japan)

England 2 (Crouch 83, Gerrard 90+1)
Trinidad and Tobago 0

England: Paul Robinson, Jamie Carragher (Aaron Lennon 58), Rio Ferdinand, John Terry, Ashley Cole, David Beckham (c), Steven Gerrard, Frank Lampard, Joe Cole (Stewart Downing 74), Michael Owen (Wayne Rooney 58), Peter Crouch. **Manager:** Sven-Göran Eriksson.

Trinidad and Tobago: Shaka Hislop, Carlos Edwards, Brent Sancho, Dennis Lawrence, Cyd Gray, Chris Birchall, Aurtis Whitley, Dwight Yorke (c), Densill Theobald (Evans Wise 85), Kenwyne Jones (Cornell Glen 70), Stern John. **Manager:** Leo Beenhakker.

Booked: Lampard (64); Theobald (18), Whitley (19), Jones (45+1), Hislop (47), Gray (55)

9pm, 15 June 2006
Olympiastadion, Berlin
Attendance: 72,000
Referee: Ľuboš Micheľ (Slovakia)

Sweden 1 (Ljungberg 89)
Paraguay 0
Sweden: Andreas Isaksson, Niclas Alexandersson, Olof Mellberg (c), Teddy Lučić, Erik Edman, Christian Wilhelmsson (Mattias Jonson 68), Kim Källström (Johan Elmander 86), Tobias Linderoth, Freddie Ljungberg, Zlatan Ibrahimović (Marcus Allbäck 46), Henrik Larsson. **Manager:** Lars Lagerbäck.

Paraguay: Aldo Bobadilla, Denis Caniza, Julio César Cáceres, Carlos Gamarra (c), Jorge Núñez, Carlos Bonet (Édgar Barreto 81), Roberto Acuña, Carlos Paredes, Cristian Riveros (Julio dos Santos 62), Nelson Valdez, Roque Santa Cruz (Dante López 63). **Manager:** Aníbal Ruiz.

Booked: Linderoth (14), Lučić (48), Allbäck (60); Caniza (3), Acuña (51), Núñez (54), Paredes (74), Barreto (85)

9pm, 20 June 2006
RheinEnergieStadion, Cologne
Attendance: 45,000
Referee: Massimo Busacca (Switzerland)

Sweden 2 (Allbäck 51, Larsson 90)
England 2 (J. Cole 34, Gerrard 85)

Sweden: Andreas Isaksson, Niclas Alexandersson, Olof Mellberg (c), Teddy Lučić, Erik Edman, Mattias Jonson (Christian Wilhelmsson 54), Kim Källström, Tobias Linderoth (Daniel Andersson 90+1), Freddie Ljungberg, Marcus Allbäck (Johan Elmander 75), Henrik Larsson. **Manager:** Lars Lagerbäck.

England: Paul Robinson, Jamie Carragher, Rio Ferdinand (Sol Campbell 56), John Terry, Ashley Cole, David Beckham (c), Owen

Hargreaves, Frank Lampard, Joe Cole, Wayne Rooney (Steven Gerrard 69), Michael Owen (Peter Crouch 4). **Manager:** Sven-Göran Eriksson.

Booked: Alexandersson (83), Ljungberg (87); Hargreaves (76)

9pm, 20 June 2006
Fritz-Walter-Stadion, Kaiserslautern
Attendance: 46,000
Referee: Roberto Rosetti (Italy)

Paraguay 2 (Sancho 25 o.g., Cuevas 86)
Trinidad and Tobago 0

Paraguay: Aldo Bobadilla, Denis Caniza (Paulo da Silva 89), Julio César Cáceres (Julio Manzur 77), Carlos Gamarra (c), Jorge Núñez, Édgar Barreto, Roberto Acuña, Carlos Paredes, Julio dos Santos, Nelson Valdez (Nelson Cuevas 66), Roque Santa Cruz. **Manager:** Aníbal Ruiz.

Trinidad and Tobago: Kelvin Jack, Carlos Edwards, Brent Sancho, Dennis Lawrence, Avery John (Kenwyne Jones 31), Chris Birchall, Aurtis Whitley (Russell Latapy 67), Dwight Yorke (c), Densill Theobald, Cornell Glen (Evans Wise 41), Stern John. **Manager:** Leo Beenhakker.

Booked: Paredes (30), dos Santos (54); Sancho (45), Whitley (48)

Group B	P	W	D	L	GF	GA	GD	PTS
ENGLAND	3	2	1	0	5	2	+3	7
SWEDEN	3	1	2	0	3	2	+1	5
PARAGUAY	3	1	0	2	2	2	0	3
TRINIDAD AND TOBAGO	3	0	1	2	0	4	-4	1

England and Sweden qualified

Group C

NOT ALL groups in a World Cup are created equal, often with one being labelled by the media as the 'Group of Death' as there are usually two tournament contenders, a dark horse and a plucky underdog capable of causing a shock. At this edition of the competition, two groups could lay a strong claim to that title and one of those was Group C. Containing two international powerhouses who had aspirations of victory, in Argentina and the Netherlands, a debutant nation riding the crest of a wave and having household names littered throughout their squad, Côte d'Ivoire, and a qualifying star who had gone unbeaten and upset the apple cart by reaching the tournament directly ahead of Spain in their qualification group, Serbia and Montenegro, Group C had all the ingredients for an incredible series of matches and the potential for a major early shock.

The group kicked off with third favourites to win the tournament Argentina facing off against the debutant African nation of Ivory Coast. Despite having only qualified for the World Cup for the first time, Ivory Coast had higher hopes than just turning up in Germany and savouring the experience. Led by captain Didier Drogba, their squad contained numerous top-level talents, including Arsenal pair Emmanuel Eboué and Kolo Touré, future Barcelona and Manchester City legend Yaya Touré and Paris Saint-Germain (PSG) striker Bonaventure Kalou. Hope and expectation may have been high for *Les Éléphants* but their tournament could hardly have been given a tougher start against two-time World Cup champions and footballing powerhouse Argentina. *La Albiceleste* entered the tournament with deserved expectations of winning the entire thing, having not progressed past the quarter-finals since 1990 when they finished runners-up to West Germany. It had been 20 years, five tournaments, since they had won the title, triumphing against the same opposition in Mexico 1986. With a squad containing Juan Román Riquelme, Javier Saviola, Hernán Crespo, Maxi Rodríguez and a precocious 18-year-old Barcelona talent named Lionel Messi, to name just five, not winning the entire competition may be seen as a failure to capitalise on perhaps the most-talented Argentina squad since 1986.

The match started in a cagey fashion with neither team being able to gain a stranglehold over the contest, but there were no signs that the West African nation had been overawed by the occasion of their first World Cup match. Both sets of strikers had early chances, with Drogba heading over and Crespo narrowly missing turning a cross goalbound, the ball deflecting behind for a corner. From the resulting set piece, Roberto Ayala's powerful header was caught by Jean-Jacques Tizié in the Ivorian goal, but the goalkeeper fumbled the ball, potentially carrying it over the goal line. The Argentines were convinced that the ball had crossed the line to give them the lead but the initial replay was inconclusive, although a later replay suggested that Tizié had recovered in the nick of time to prevent the goal. In the days before goal-line technology made these decisions black and white, it was down to the discretion of the referee and their assistants, and it seems that the Belgian officiating team came to the right decision on this occasion.

The opening goal was not far away though, and when it did come it was one that the Ivorians will have been extremely disappointed to concede. Another set piece, this time a free kick from Riquelme, was floated into the box. Central defender Gabriel Heinze was the first to reach the ball, although his header was blocked by a combination of Ivorian defenders. As the loose ball bounced in the area, Crespo was the quickest to react and pounced on the bouncing ball to fire home and give his country the lead. It was a typical Crespo goal, a true poacher's effort from a striker often in the right place at the right time, but from an Ivorian perspective, they will have been frustrated at not having anyone marking the most dangerous finisher on the opposition team.

The goal seemed to inspire Ivory Coast into finding another level, as they spent the next ten minutes on the front foot, causing problems for the Argentina defence. Kalou had two good chances, firing wide on both occasions, Drogba saw an effort deflected behind, but the best chance fell to Kader Keïta. A Kanga Akalé cross from the left to the far post was squared by Drogba into the path of the Lille midfielder just seven yards from goal. Had he placed his effort anywhere else it would have nestled into the back of the net but he could only nod the ball down towards the feet of Argentina's keeper, Roberto Abbondanzieri, who managed to bring the ball under control.

This profligacy was punished just seven minutes before half-time when Argentina doubled their advantage, and once again it was too simple a goal to concede. Riquelme picked up the ball in the Ivory Coast half and was criminally given the freedom in which to raise his head and play a delightful through ball beyond the back line for Saviola to race on to and deftly poke the ball beyond the onrushing keeper. The defenders immediately appealed for offside, and while Crespo had been in an offside position, Saviola's run was perfectly timed.

The match had been an open and entertaining affair, with Ivory Coast playing as equals to their more storied counterparts, but they had spurned their best chances while the Argentine strikers had taken theirs. It was a ruthless lesson in taking your opportunities when they presented themselves that would haunt the West Africans.

The more experienced Argentina squad managed to take control of the match in the second half, with play being dictated by Riquelme. One of the most-talented players in the world on his day, Riquelme was often criticised for failing to show up in the important matches. A true No. 10, a link between the midfield and attack, his performance against Ivory Coast showed that, when he was on it, he was a very difficult player to stop. He almost added his own name to the scoresheet when Tizié came out and flapped at an inswinging free kick that only narrowly evaded the far post.

As often happens as matches progress into the latter stages, the introduction of substitutes for both teams slowed the tempo, making it harder for either to keep the rhythm of the opening exchanges, but Ivory Coast were still impressively pushing forward, led by their star man and captain. Fresh from winning a second consecutive Premier League with Chelsea, Drogba was almost single-handedly mounting his team's fightback, having shots blocked by defenders, dragging an effort just wide and firing a free kick into the Argentina wall. It was no surprise that when the breakthrough did finally come it was Drogba who provided it. A hopeful cross reached Aruna Dindane on the left-hand side. He pulled the ball back into the centre of the penalty area, where Drogba was waiting, calmly slotting the ball beyond the keeper. With eight minutes remaining, the match was set for a tense finish for Argentina.

Yet it was the South Americans who had the ball in the back of the net next. Riquelme, again at the heart of Argentina's good play, struck an effort on goal from the edge of the area that Tizié was unable to gather, although he really should have. The loose ball fell to Maxi, who dinked the ball over the stranded keeper and tapped home into the empty net. However, his celebrations were cut short, as the assistant was waving his flag. Maxi had been in an offside position when Riquelme took his shot, with the replay proving it was an excellent decision. Neither team were able to carve out another opening and Argentina came away with a hard-fought but slightly deserved victory.

The other opening fixture in Group C also presented an interesting match-up. Serbia and Montenegro were competing in their first, and last, World Cup under this official name, having been present in 1998 as the Federal Republic of Yugoslavia, when they reached the knockout stages, losing to their opponents in this match in the Round of 16, the Netherlands. Having missed the 2002 World Cup, they were back after an impressive qualifying campaign that saw them go unbeaten, finishing above Spain and conceding only once in ten matches. The Eastern Europeans were beginning their campaign without their star man, Manchester United defender Nemanja Vidić, but they were starting with four of the back five that had been so secure during their qualification.

Their opponents, the Netherlands, were also returning to the tournament, having missed out on qualification four years earlier, and were hoping to surpass expectations, recapturing the glory days of the 1970s to make a deep run to the latter stages of the competition. Although this was not a vintage Dutch team of the ilk of those fabulous squads, the emergence of Chelsea's Arjen Robben, Arsenal's Robin van Persie, and Ajax's Wesley Sneijder as fixtures in the starting line-up brought a renewed hope that they were heading towards the sharp end of the international game once more, especially after reaching the semi-finals of Euro 2004.

Although the Dutch started the match with the first chance, Robben flicking a header straight into the arms of Jevrić, it was

Serbia and Montenegro who created the best two early openings. Firstly, Predrag Djordjevic produced a clever run down the left-hand side before crossing, where Savo Milošević and Mateja Kežman hindered each other's attempt to convert, followed by Milošević being free in the box but only managing to shoot into the arms of Edwin van der Sar.

In a similar fashion to the other match in the group, despite the early chances of the underdog, the more established team took the lead. A simple punt upfield from the back was flicked on by Van Persie for Robben, who had breached the high line employed by Serbia and Montenegro and had the freedom of the half. Driving towards goal, the Chelsea winger was one-on-one with Jevrić and calmly slotted the ball underneath the keeper to give the Netherlands the lead.

With the Dutch having taken the advantage, the match settled into a steady flow, with both teams managing to create opportunities. Milošević fired over the bar from an enviable position, while Van Persie's diving header was caught by Jevrić, and Robben had one shot palmed away and sent one just wide when unusually cutting in from the left on to his right foot, a reverse of the move that he would become famous for.

As the half-time interval came and went, the Serb and Montenegrin's made two changes, bringing Koroman and Žigić on, attempting to switch to a more direct style to take advantage of the fact that Žigić was 6ft 8in tall.

The future Valencia and Birmingham City striker provided the ultimate target to aim for and the hope was that Kežman would be able to feed off the knockdowns and rediscover his poacher's touch, having struggled to make a serious impact for either Chelsea or Atlético Madrid after leaving PSV Eindhoven, where he scored a remarkable 129 goals in just 176 appearances across all competitions.

Aside from a half-hearted appeal for a penalty after the ball struck John Heitinga on the chest, there were few real chances fashioned for either team. Koroman was looking the liveliest player on the pitch, causing the Dutch defenders problems with his direct running. He created the best opportunity for Serbia and Montenegro with just 20 minutes remaining when he drilled a low shot that was well saved by Edwin van der Sar. The Netherlands did come close when Van Persie sent a free kick narrowly wide of the post, but apart from a smattering of yellow cards for both nations, the game fizzled out to a drab end. It was a winning start for the *Oranje* but they would need to produce a more confident display if they were seriously attempting to push on and capture their first-ever World Cup title.

* * *

Having won their opening match against Ivory Coast, Argentina knew that victory over Serbia and Montenegro would secure their place in the knockout stages, but they certainly were not heading into the match with any ounce of complacency. Despite losing their opener, the Serbian and Montenegrins were a well-organised defensive unit, rarely conceding and being adept at grinding out results when they needed them. The loss of Nemanja Vidić, who was suspended for the opening match, was bad enough, so losing him to a serious knee injury that ruled him out of contention for the remainder of the tournament was a devastating blow. Even with the loss of the Manchester United defender, nobody would have foreseen what was about to unfold under the afternoon sun in Gelsenkirchen.

It only took six minutes for the two-time world champions to take the lead. Argentina captain Juan Pablo Sorin picked up the ball on the left touchline and flicked it beyond his marker to find Saviola in space. He drove towards the penalty area and played a simple pass into space in the area for Maxi Rodríguez, who had the simple task of firing the ball home, perfectly placing the ball in the top corner. It was the second goal that Serbia and Montenegro had conceded and it was again far too simple, one that may have been avoided had Vidić been fit and marshalling the defence. Everything was being made too easy for Argentina, who were able to just control the ball, keeping possession with ease. The only blemish was the loss of Lucho González to injury after just 17 minutes, although with Cambiasso coming on to replace him *La Albiceleste* were about to score perhaps the greatest team goal in World Cup finals history.

Rodríguez-Heinze-Mascherano-Riquelme-Rodríguez-Sorin-Rodríguez-Sorin-Mascherano-Riquelme-Ayala-Cambiasso-Mascherano-Rodríguez-Sorin-Mascherano-Cambiasso-Riquelme-Mascherano-Sorin-Saviola-Riquelme-Saviola-Cambiasso-Crespo-Cambiasso: 54 seconds and 26 passes later Argentina had scored a truly incredible goal. Patient passing and cool heads meant that there were no mistakes as they moved their markers around before speeding up the play right on the edge of the area with the passes between Saviola, Riquelme, Cambiasso and Crespo all quick, instinctive flicks that caused confusion. Cambiasso was the one with the simple task of slotting the ball above the goalkeeper and doubling the lead. It is a goal that is hard to do justice by describing how it played out and is definitely worth searching for on YouTube.

That goal seemed to drain the last remaining bit of spirit that Serbia and Montenegro possessed and Argentina began turning the screw. Five minutes after going two goals up, Crespo had the ball in back of the net, only for the offside flag to deny him a second goal of the tournament. Replays suggested that the striker may have been hard done by in having the goal chalked off and, to add insult to injury, he was booked by the referee for playing on after the whistle had gone. A third goal was not too far away though, and it was another poor defensive showing. A long hopeful pass for Saviola was seemingly easy to deal with for Krstajić but he opted to try to shepherd the ball out of play and was robbed of possession by good harrying from Saviola. The Barcelona striker, one of just 33 players to play for both the Catalan outfit and their fierce rivals Real Madrid, drove into the area and poked a shot that was pushed away by Jevrić. The goalkeeper did the right thing by pushing the ball away wide of his goal but Maxi Rodríguez was the fastest to the loose ball and calmly slotted home from a tight angle. A three-goal lead at half-time and Argentina were showing the watching world why they were considered strong contenders to take home the title.

Although there were some signs of life from Serbia and Montenegro to begin the second half, with Milošević bringing about a good save by Abbondanzieri and narrowly missing getting on the end of a header back across goal by Kežman, the match fully went away from them when Kežman earned himself an early bath. With just over an hour gone, the striker had a little kick out at Riquelme after the playmaker had produced a clever back-heel to escape him, which earned him a talking to from the referee. Not content with the warning, two minutes later Kežman dived into a challenge near the halfway line on Mascherano and the Italian referee produced the red card. There was minimal contact on the Corinthians midfielder but the challenge was reckless and out of control, so the official had little choice but to expel him from the pitch.

With the game all but over, Pékerman decided now would be a good time to experiment and give the youngsters in his squad valuable game time. Prior to the sending-off, he had introduced a 22-year-old Carlos Tevez for Saviola and afterwards took off Maxi for Barcelona's 18-year-old Lionel Messi. It was the perfect opportunity for the two youngsters to show the watching Argentinian public that they were the future of their nation, but it was the established guard who added the next goal, with Crespo finally getting his name on the scoresheet. Riquelme, the best player on the pitch once again, played a quick free kick down the left for Messi to race on to and he just had to square a simple ball across the six-yard box for the Milan striker to tap home.

Goal number five came just six minutes later, with Riquelme again providing the assist, his second of the tournament, laying off a simple pass for Tevez, who beat two defenders and calmly put the ball into the far corner, sending the goalkeeper the wrong way. And there was still time for one more goal, and it was the one that was perhaps the most exciting for the Argentines in the crowd. Tevez collected the ball 30 yards from goal and played a nice one-two with Crespo before freeing Messi down the right-hand side. The now six-time Ballon d'Or winner took the ball in his stride, drove forwards and drilled a shot beyond Jevrić to wrap up the victory. It was just his second international goal and a sign of what was to come from the little maestro on both the domestic and international stage.

Six goals scored, qualification to the knockout stage secured and a statement of intent sent out to the other contenders for the title, this was a perfect performance from Argentina. Everything had gone their way and they had established themselves as the team to beat in the tournament. For Serbia and Montenegro, it was a devastating result that ended their chances of progressing and they looked a shadow of the team that had impressed so much in reaching the finals. The second goal seemed to drain all the self-belief from their players and Kežman's red card ended any hope of an improbable comeback. Unable to qualify, they would still have the opportunity to end their uneasy political union before becoming separate countries on a positive note with victory over

Ivory Coast. The importance of that match was yet to be decided, with it potentially being one to decide the qualification hopes of Ivory Coast or a dead rubber if they failed to get at least a point against the Netherlands.

The match-up at the Gottlieb-Daimler-Stadion in Stuttgart was critical for both nations as the Netherlands would qualify with a win, which would also end the hopes of the West Africans, while a victory for *The Elephants* would give them an excellent chance of qualifying, as the Netherlands would have the tougher match against Argentina to contend with. Perhaps the enormity of the occasion was on the minds of the players, as the opening exchanges of the contest were cagey and neither team was able to gain control. Ivory Coast thought they should have been awarded a penalty after Arsenal full-back Eboué went down in the box claiming that his shirt was being pulled, but the Colombian referee waved away the protests.

The first moment of real quality came from the Dutch after Van Persie had won a free kick just outside the Ivorian penalty area. The Arsenal forward dusted himself off, lined up the set piece and hit a venomous left-footed strike beyond the despairing dive of the keeper and into the top right corner of the goal. It was a beautifully struck free kick and there was little chance that Tizié would have been able to keep the shot out even if he had managed to get a hand to it. It was the first opening that either team had fashioned and it inspired the Dutch into life.

They doubled their lead just three minutes later. Robben picked up the ball on the left, cut inside, before playing an awkward one-two with Van Bommel. The winger played a clever reverse pass behind the defensive line for Ruud van Nistelrooy, who took a touch into the area before firing a clever finish over Tizié. The defenders immediately appealed for an offside as the Manchester United striker had been loitering on the last line of defence, as he had done throughout his career, but the replay showed that he had done brilliantly to keep himself just onside and he dispatched the chance in typical confident fashion.

It was a tough blow for the Ivorians to take, conceding twice in just three minutes, but they did not let that affect their game and were unlucky not to find a way back into the contest when midfielder Didier Zokora, who would join Tottenham from Saint-Étienne after the tournament, cut inside on to his right foot and unleashed a shot that flew beyond the dive of Van der Sar but crashed against the crossbar and bounced clear.

Buoyed by the Zokora effort, the Ivorians got their reward six minutes later when Bakari Koné picked up the ball just inside the Dutch half. He drove forwards, towards the right-hand side of the area, leaving two Dutch players in his wake, and fired an unstoppable shot across the goalkeeper and into the far top corner. It was a truly spectacular goal, continuing the trend from a tournament that was littered with goals of the highest order.

Outside of the goals, there was plenty of bark but little bite in the match. Drogba earned himself a yellow card for a late challenge on Van der Sar that saw the Dutch defenders crowd around the Ivorian captain. Van Bommel earned himself a caution as well for a poor stamp on the ankle of Arthur Boka, who himself was lucky that he had a covering defender when cynically tripping a Dutch player to prevent a counter-attack. There was plenty of shirt-pulling from set pieces, primarily against Drogba to limit the potential danger that he posed and, as such, the match was unable to ever settle into a pleasing rhythm. Half-chances came and went for Van Nistelrooy, who saw one effort saved and one well blocked by a defender when following in for a rebound from a Robben shot.

With their World Cup place at stake, Ivory Coast began to dictate the play, upping the tempo and trying to force the issue against their more illustrious opponents. Gilles Yapi Yapo, Aruna

Dindane and Kanga Akalé were all introduced to try to turn the tide and they did almost snatch an equaliser to keep them alive. A header back across goal by Drogba seemed destined to nestle in the net but Van Persie was in the right place at the right time to chest the ball off the line and the Dutch managed to escape unscathed. It was another critical moment from the striker, one at either end of the pitch. He was showing that he would be able to carry the hopes of an expectant nation, along with the other talented youngsters emerging.

Despite the best efforts of the West Africans, they were unable to fashion another chance and the game drifted to the final whistle, with a 2-1 victory meaning that the Dutch were safely through to the knockout stages with a match to spare. Ivory Coast, despite the expectations of being able to cause a few shocks, had been unable to cause an upset and were eliminated after just two matches. They had performed admirably in both against much more established opposition at this level, but that will have been little consolation for a team reaching the peak of its powers. It was a period of failed expectations for *The Elephants*, as they failed to progress from the group stages in three consecutive World Cups and reached the quarter-finals of the Africa Cup of Nations (AFCON) in all five editions between 2006 and 2013 but failed to win any, including losing finals on penalties in 2006 and 2012 to Egypt and Zambia respectively. They finally broke through on the continental stage in 2015, winning their second AFCON title, but there was definitely a feeling of a missed opportunity that this team featuring some of the best talents in world football had failed to make a bigger impact on the world stage.

* * *

With qualification secured, both Argentina and the Netherlands rotated their squads with Pékerman and Van Basten making five changes each to try to keep their fringe players match sharp and give them a chance to fight for their place in the starting line-up. Tevez and Messi both started after impressing in cameos from the bench for Argentina, while Van der Vaart and Kuyt were given a chance to fire the Dutch above their rivals and into top spot in the group. Usually, when these two nations met, there was a significant amount of pressure on the match. They had met at the World Cup on three previous occasions, including a resounding 4-0 victory for the Dutch in Germany during the 1974 edition and a 2-1 victory that saw them progress to the semi-finals in 1998. The biggest clash between the two came on Argentinian soil at the 1978 World Cup Final. Missing their talisman Johan Cruyff, the Netherlands had reached a second consecutive final through their brand of total football. There were rumours of Cruyff not going to the tournament for political reasons, allegations of corruption and bribery abounded and there was no shortage of controversy surrounding the tournament. Ultimately, the Dutch fell short once more, losing 3-1 after extra time as Argentina won their first title. It was rare for these two nations to meet with little on the line, but this match represented just that opportunity.

La Albiceleste started the brighter of the two, creating early chances through Cambiasso, who was well challenged by Khalid Boulahrouz, and Tevez, who curled an effort narrowly wide. There was a brief glimmer for the Netherlands when Kuyt won the ball back on the left in his typical hard-working style and drove into the box, only to see his effort pushed behind by Abbondanzieri, but the first half was comfortably dominated by the South Americans. Nicolás Burdisso had to be replaced by Newcastle United legend Fabricio Coloccini in the only blemish of the half, but Argentina would have been disappointed to not take a lead into the interval. Riquelme had a free kick on the left-hand side that he whipped low under the jumping Dutch wall, causing panic in the defence.

Boulahrouz was the first player to the ball but he turned it towards his own goal, fortunately seeing the ball cannon into the post and bounce clear. The respite was brief though, as less than a minute later Maxi fired a brilliant volley from the edge of the area that had Van der Sar scrambling, but it flew just wide of the post.

Although Argentina were playing like potential world champions, the second half was a drab affair with both teams seemingly content to just play out the remainder of the match trying to avoid injury and staying fit for their respective knockout ties. The best chances of the half fell to Argentina, with Riquelme shooting wide and Tevez having an effort saved, but the match came to an end with no real opportunities having been presented and the South Americans finishing their group stage as winners, setting up a match against the runners-up of Group D, while the Netherlands would be given the supposedly harder task of facing the winners of the same group.

All of 240 miles away in Munich, while the two qualified nations were playing out a drab 0-0 draw, Ivory Coast and Serbia and Montenegro were featuring in one of the best matches of the tournament. Freed from the pressures of the competition, having already been eliminated, both nations left Germany having put on a show in their final appearance despite a combined ten changes between them. The likes of Kolo Touré, Didier Drogba and Savo Milošević were all rested but those who took their place showed that there was little drop in quality between those who started the two defeats and those who missed out.

There was a dream start for the Eastern Europeans, who took the lead after just ten minutes. With Žigić starting, the Serbs and Montenegrins reverted to their longer ball tactic and stand-in captain Dejan Stanković played a simple ball over the top for the big striker to chase. Back-up Ivorian goalkeeper Boubacar Barry felt that he could reach the ball first but never got anywhere near it and Žigić controlled the ball well with his left foot, taking it around the stranded goalkeeper and tapping into the empty net. Things got even better ten minutes later when, after a poor touch by squad captain Cyril Domoraud in his own penalty area landed at the feet of Saša Ilić, the Galatasaray midfielder followed in his striker's footsteps and rounded the keeper before firing home.

In between the two goals, the Ivorians should have equalised when Dindane found himself free in the penalty area but could only direct his shot straight at the goalkeeper, who kept the ball out with his feet, before Akalé was rash with his effort. Everything seemed to be going the way of the Europeans and it looked like Ivory Coast would end their campaign with a whimper.

A steady rhythm developed after the second goal until a blatant handball from Milan Dudić gave the West Africans the perfect route back into the match. With Drogba on the bench, Dindane took the responsibility on his shoulders and calmly fired the ball to the goalkeeper's left but the Mexican referee was not happy with Jevrić moving off his line before the penalty was struck and ordered a retake. Unfazed by the added drama, Dindane stepped straight up and put the ball in the same spot to give the Ivorians a glimmer of hope to cling to for a comeback.

A back-and-forth match had broken out and the Serbian and Montenegrin's believed that they should have had a penalty of their own when Domoraud brought down Predrag Đordević on the edge of the area. The replay suggested contact was initiated by the Serb, but if the referee was giving a foul, then it happened inside the area so should have been a penalty. Dindane was booked a minute later for an alleged dive, although there was clear contact between himself and the goalkeeper. It was a tough first half to referee, with the pace of the match, but the Mexican officiating crew was having a difficult time getting the correct decisions between them. Hoping for a quiet end to the half may have been their wish, but Albert Nađ slid through the back of his opponent and gave the ref another key decision to make. He may have taken the ball, but he had got there by sliding through the striker, so there was little choice for the official but to show a second yellow card and a subsequent red.

Half-time. Three goals, a retaken penalty, potentially two more penalties, seven yellow cards and a red card. It was a match that had everything, being played at breakneck pace, and it would have been difficult for that to continue into the second period. Aside from another yellow being added to the tally and a speculative Arthur Boka effort, there was little action until the 68th minute when the Ivorians upped the pace through Abdul Kader Keïta, who was shining under the Munich spotlights. He floated an excellent cross into the area from the right on to the head of Dindane. The future Portsmouth forward generated the power and steered it beyond the dive of the goalkeeper to draw his nation level. The equaliser spurred both teams back into life and the tempo from the first half was matched for the final 20 minutes.

Both teams came close with a header a minute apart. Firstly, Milošević, on as a sub, worked himself into space in the penalty box and had a free header that he wastefully sent wide. It was a clear chance and definitely one that he would have backed himself to score the majority of the time. Then Yaya Touré found himself in similar space in the opposite area from a corner and he too could only steer his header comfortably wide.

With just six minutes remaining, Bonaventure Kalou sent a speculative shot towards goal that hit the arm of Dudić once again. This handball was a lot more contentious than the first, with an argument easy to make that his hand was being tucked into his body, but the referee pointed to the spot once again and the Ivorians were presented with the ultimate opportunity to get their first-ever World Cup victory. Kalou himself took the ball over Dindane, who was on a hat-trick and had already scored from the spot. Kalou followed his team-mate's previous effort, sending the ball to the keeper's left and giving his country the lead for the first time in the match.

There was still time for Domoraud to be given his marching orders as well, receiving a second booking for taking the legs out from under Milošević as he collected the ball with his back to goal on the halfway line. It was a needless challenge so late on, and a deserved booking. Fortunately for him, the referee soon blew the final whistle and brought this crazy contest to an end. Freed from the shackles of needing to pick up results to keep their tournament alive, both teams had given it everything and produced an incredible show for the watching crowd.

9pm, 10 June 2006
Volksparkstadion, Hamburg
Attendance: 49,480
Referee: Frank De Bleeckere (Belgium)

Argentina 2 (Crespo 24, Saviola 38)
Ivory Coast 1 (Drogba 82)

Argentina: Roberto Abbondanzieri, Nicolás Burdisso, Roberto Ayala, Gabriel Heinze, Juan Pablo Sorin (c), Maxi Rodríguez, Javier Mascherano, Esteban Cambiasso, Juan Román Riquelme (Pablo Aimar 90+3), Javier Saviola (Lucho González 75), Hernán Crespo (Rodrigo Palacio 64). **Manager:** José Pékerman.

Ivory Coast: Jean-Jacques Tizié, Emmanuel Eboué, Kolo Touré, Abdoulaye Méïté, Arthur Boka, Yaya Touré, Didier Zokora, Abdul Kader Keïta (Arouna Koné 77), Bonaventure Kalou (Aruna Dindane 55), Kanga Akalé (Bakari Koné 62), Didier Drogba (c). **Manager:** Henri Michel.

Booked: Saviola (41), Heinze (48), González (81); Eboué (62), Drogba (90+1)

3pm, 11 June 2006
Zentralstadion, Leipzig
Attendance: 43,000
Referee: Markus Merk (Germany)

Serbia and Montenegro 0
Netherlands 1 (Robben 18)

Serbia and Montenegro: Dragoslav Jevrić, Nenad Đorđević (Ognjen Koroman 43), Goran Gavrančić, Mladen Krstajić, Ivica Dragutinović, Dejan Stanković, Igor Duljaj, Albert Nađ, Predrag Đorđević, Savo Milošević (c) (Nikola Žigić 46), Mateja Kežman (Danijel Ljuboja 67). **Manager:** Ilija Petković.

Netherlands: Edwin van der Sar (c), John Heitinga, André Ooijer, Joris Mathijsen (Khalid Boulahrouz 86), Giovanni van Bronckhorst, Mark van Bommel (Denny Landzaat 60), Wesley Sneijder, Phillip Cocu, Robin van Persie, Ruud van Nistelrooy (Dirk Kuyt 69), Arjen Robben. **Manager:** Marco van Basten.

Booked: Stanković (34), Koroman (64), Dragutinović (81), Gavrančić (90); Van Bronckhorst (56), Heitinga (85)

3pm, 16 June 2006
Arena AufSchalke, Gelsenkirchen
Attendance: 52,000
Referee: Roberto Rosetti (Italy)

Argentina 6 (Rodríguez 6, 41, Cambiasso 31, Crespo 78, Tevez 84, Messi 88)
Serbia and Montenegro 0

Argentina: Roberto Abbondanzieri, Nicolás Burdisso, Roberto Ayala, Gabriel Heinze, Juan Pablo Sorin (c), Javier Mascherano, Lucho González (Esteban Cambiasso 17), Juan Román Riquelme, Maxi Rodríguez (Lionel Messi 75), Javier Saviola (Carlos Tevez 59), Hernán Crespo. **Manager:** José Pékerman.

Serbia and Montenegro: Dragoslav Jevrić, Igor Duljaj, Goran Gavrančić, Milan Dudić, Mladen Krstajić, Ognjen Koroman (Danijel Ljuboja 50), Albert Nađ (Ivan Ergić 46), Predrag Đorđević, Dejan Stanković, Savo Milošević (c) (Zvonimir Vukić 70), Mateja Kežman. **Manager:** Ilija Petković.

Booked: Crespo (36); Koroman (7), Nađ (27), Krstajić (42)
Sent off: Kežman (65)

6pm, 16 June 2006
Gottlieb-Daimler-Stadion, Stuttgart
Attendance: 52,000
Referee: Óscar Ruiz (Colombia)

Netherlands 2 (Van Persie 23, Van Nistelrooy 27)
Ivory Coast 1 (Koné 38)

Netherlands: Edwin van der Sar (c), John Heitinga (Khalid Boulahrouz 46), André Ooijer, Joris Mathijsen, Giovanni van Bronckhorst, Mark van Bommel, Wesley Sneijder (Rafael van der Vaart 50), Phillip Cocu, Arjen Robben, Ruud van Nistelrooy (Denny Landzaat 73), Robin van Persie. **Manager:** Marco van Basten.

Ivory Coast: Jean-Jacques Tizié, Emmanuel Eboué, Kolo Touré, Abdoulaye Méïté, Arthur Boka, Yaya Touré, Didier Zokora, Romaric (Gilles Yapi Yapo 62), Bakari Koné (Aruna Dindane 62), Didier Drogba (c), Arouna Koné (Kanga Akalé 73). **Manager:** Henri Michel.

Booked: Robben (34), Mathijsen (35), Van Bommel (58), Boulahrouz (90+4); Zokora (25), Drogba (41), Boka (66)

9pm, 21 June 2006
Waldstadion, Frankfurt
Attendance: 48,000
Referee: Luis Medina Cantalejo (Spain)

Netherlands 0
Argentina 0

Netherlands: Edwin van der Sar (c), Kew Jaliens, Khalid Boulahrouz, André Ooijer, Tim de Cler, Rafael van der Vaart, Wesley Sneijder (Hedwiges Maduro 86), Phillip Cocu, Robin van Persie (Denny Landzaat 67), Ruud van Nistelrooy (Ryan Babel 56), Dirk Kuyt. **Manager:** Marco van Basten.

Argentina: Roberto Abbondanzieri, Nicolás Burdisso (Fabricio Coloccini 24), Roberto Ayala (c), Gabriel Milito, Leandro Cufré, Maxi Rodríguez, Javier Mascherano, Esteban Cambiasso, Juan Román Riquelme (Pablo Aimar 80), Lionel Messi (Julio Cruz 70), Carlos Tevez. **Manager:** José Pékerman.

Booked: Kuyt (28), Ooijer (42), De Cler (48); Cambiasso (57), Mascherano (90)

9pm, 21 June 2006
FIFA World Cup Stadium, Munich
Attendance: 66,000
Referee: Marco Rodríguez (Mexico)

Ivory Coast 3 (Dindane 37 (p), 67, Kalou 86 (p))
Serbia and Montenegro 2 (Žigić 10, Ilić 20)

Ivory Coast: Boubacar Barry, Emmanuel Eboué, Blaise Kouassi, Cyril Domoraud (c), Arthur Boka, Abdul Kader Keïta (Bonaventure Kalou 73), Didier Zokora, Yaya Touré, Kanga Akalé (Bakari Koné 60), Aruna Dindane, Arouna Koné. **Manager:** Henri Michel.

Serbia and Montenegro: Dragoslav Jevrić, Nenad Đorđević, Goran Gavrančić, Milan Dudić, Mladen Krstajić (Albert Nađ 16), Dejan Stanković (c), Igor Duljaj, Saša Ilić, Predrag Đorđević, Ivan Ergić, Nikola Žigić (Savo Milošević 67). **Manager:** Ilija Petković.

Booked: Keïta (33), Domoraud (41), Dindane (43); Nađ (17), Dudić (35), Duljaj (37), Gavrančić (57)
Sent off: Domoraud (90+2); Nađ (45+1)

Group C	P	W	D	L	GF	GA	GD	PTS
ARGENTINA	3	2	1	0	8	1	+7	7
NETHERLANDS	3	2	1	0	3	1	+2	7
IVORY COAST	3	1	0	2	5	6	-1	3
SERBIA & MONTENEGRO	3	0	0	3	2	10	-8	0

Argentina and Netherlands qualified

Group D

WHEN IT comes to perennial World Cup contenders, one nation that might not jump immediately to mind is Mexico. Yet, apart from Brazil, Germany, Italy and Argentina, who had won 13 of the 17 tournaments held prior to 2006, no other nation had qualified for the tournament more times than *El Tri*. They had reached the finals on 13 occasions, including this tournament, a feat more impressive considering that they had never won the trophy so never received an automatic qualification spot that way, although they had qualified as hosts twice. Heading to Germany with their dark horse tag firmly applied once again, there was genuine hope that this could be the year that they progressed further than the quarter-finals. Ranked fourth in the world by FIFA and led by Barcelona central defender Rafael Márquez, whose international career spanned more than two decades and who had appeared in five consecutive World Cups from 2002 to 2018, there was real hope among the travelling Mexican squad.

Their first obstacle was an Iranian team that were also highly ranked by FIFA (23rd) and who would have had hopes of producing a shock result and reaching the knockout stages. Led by Bayern Munich striker Ali Karimi and captain, former Bayern striker and prolific international goalscorer Ali Daei, there was faint optimism that Iran would be able to improve on their World Cup best by simply qualifying from the group stage.

It was the underdogs who began the brightest, dictating the early proceedings under the baking sun in Nuremburg. The dangerous Karimi had a prime opportunity to run at the Mexican defence after just six minutes but was denied by an excellent recovery challenge from Márquez, before two good chances came and went within the space of a few seconds. First, a cross whipped in from the right-hand side narrowly evaded every Iranian in the penalty area before reaching the left-hand side, with the cross this time reaching the head of Vahid Hashemian, whose header was well saved by Oswaldo Sánchez. After the initial flurry of Iranian chances, Mexico began gaining control of possession but were struggling to carve out any meaningful opportunities, although they were looking threatening from set pieces, an avenue to goal that would prove fruitful just before the half-hour mark.

It was a free kick as simple as it was effective. Pável Pardo stood over the free kick on the right-hand side of the Iranian penalty area and floated a simple ball into the centre of the box, where Villarreal striker Guillermo Franco had drifted into an unmarked position to glance a header on. If leaving one player unmarked was poor defending, leaving two was asking for trouble, and that was exactly the problem for Iran, as Omar Bravo found himself free at the back post to tap the flick-on beyond the goalkeeper and give Mexico a lead very much against the run of play. The movement from the attackers was clever in finding the space that was available, but it was definitely a goal that Branko Ivanković would have been disappointed for his team to concede.

Despite the setback of conceding the first goal, Iran never wavered in their belief that they would be able to cause Mexico problems. Their deserved equaliser came with less than ten minutes remaining in the half and it was another set-piece goal that will be viewed in less than favourable light by the defending team. Rahman Rezaei managed to get his head to the corner but had his effort blocked by Sánchez, who was doing his best superman impression in reaching the ball. The ball bounced in the area and no Mexican defender could react quickly enough before Yahya Golmohammadi reached the loose ball and slammed it into the roof of the net. It was just reward for the positivity with which Iran had approached the first half and they will have perhaps been rueing the fact that they were only going into the half-time interval on level terms.

Clearly unhappy with his team's effort during the opening period, Mexico boss Ricardo La Volpe made two changes at the break. The introduction of Sinha and Luis Ernesto Pérez seemed to provide Mexico with a greater control over proceedings as they dominated the opening exchanges of the second half in a way that they never managed at any point during the first. Although they had begun to exert their dominance over the match, aside from a decent penalty shout after Márquez was bundled over by Golmohammadi, Mexico were unable to fashion any clear chances for themselves to grab a winner and the match appeared to be drifting harmlessly towards a draw until a quickfire double saw things swing in favour of *El Tri*. With just 15 minutes remaining, a poor clearance from the Iranian goalkeeper could only reach Rezaei, who was seemingly caught unawares and had the ball pinched off of his toe by Sinha. The half-time substitute played a simple ball in behind the off-balance Iran defence and left Bravo through one-on-one. He calmly slotted the ball home for his and Mexico's second.

If the match had been drifting into a lull, Bravo's goal sparked the Central Americans into life and they doubled their lead just three minutes later. It was Sinha again at the heart of the move, picking up the ball near halfway and driving at the Iranian defence before knocking a simple ball out to the right-hand side for Mario Méndez. The Monterrey defender knocked a clever cross to the centre of the penalty area where Sinha, continuing his run, arrived late to power a header beyond the keeper and all but secure Mexico the win. Sinha, who was actually born in Brazil, became the first foreign-born player to score a goal for Mexico at a World Cup. In the space of three minutes, he had assisted and scored the goals that drove Mexico to their opening win, having been a key reason why they had gained a stronger grip of the match after being introduced at half-time with his adopted nation struggling.

As the final whistle blew, confirming Mexico's win, the players all rushed to their goalkeeper Sánchez, who was overcome with the emotion of the occasion as he had only re-joined the squad the day before the match, having flown back home to attend the funeral of his father, who had passed away suddenly on the eve of the tournament. It was an understandable outpouring of emotion from the stopper who had helped his nation to their victory with some good saves in the first half.

Iran would have felt hard done by, having lost by two goals, as they contributed equally to an intriguing game of football, including being the better team during the first period. Although they had started the group with a defeat, they had certainly shown that they were not a team that could be taken lightly.

Politics and sports should never mix. Or at least that is the popular retort when sports or their stars try to use their platform to tackle issues that make those at the top of the game take an introspective look into their own actions. At some point, that sentiment becomes hard to take seriously as political influences and topics interject themselves into sporting occasions in a way that cannot be ignored. This was particularly true of the first-ever match for Angola at a World Cup finals.

Angola had done brilliantly to reach this stage, edging out a Nigeria squad containing Obafemi Martins, Yakubu and Jay-Jay

Okocha on head-to-head record. Their reward was a tough group draw, one that contained their former colonisers as an opening match. Portugal had been rulers over Angolan land for nearly 500 years before the Angolan War of Independence set about trying to end that. The conflict lasted 13 years, ultimately ending when an overthrow of the Portuguese government saw a new regime end all Portuguese military actions in Africa. Angola was finally an independent nation. As can often happen when a nation is left without the rule of its coloniser, civil war broke out. This war raged on for decades, only ending properly in 2002, but the country was left in crisis. Those crises can be dated back to the Portuguese departure as they offered no help and left the country to be engulfed by conflict. Those players selected to represent their nation are likely to have each had a personal story from the conflict and there would be extra incentive to make their mark on their former colonisers.

For Portugal, in a footballing sense there were high expectations heading to Germany. Rated as the seventh-best team in the world, there was hope that they would be able to go one step further than two years earlier when they finished runners-up to surprise champions Greece on home soil at Euro 2004. Wanting to lay down an early marker for the competition, *A Seleção* almost opened the scoring inside the first ten seconds when Pauleta was slipped in behind the Angolan defence but could only drag his shot wide of the post. The disappointment of the early miss was short-lived, however, as the PSG striker opened the scoring after just four minutes. Captain Luís Figo, operating behind the striker in a central role, collected the ball inside the Angolan half and drove at the defence, easily knocking it beyond Jamba and beating him for pace before squaring the ball into the centre of the box to give Pauleta the easy task of tapping the ball into the back of the net.

Unsurprisingly, the early proceedings were being dominated by the European nation. Clear-cut chances were certainly hard to come by but Pauleta almost added a second after reaching a hopeful long ball by Ricardo Carvalho but he could only chip wide after goalkeeper João Ricardo had needlessly rushed out to the edge of his area. Simão also went close when sending a shot from the edge of the area over the bar, before Mateus repeated the feat at the other end for Angola. The Mateus effort seemed to spark some intent into the West African nation, with a cross from the right-hand side finding all-time top goalscorer Akwá in the penalty area but he could only send his acrobatic effort over the crossbar.

Despite the increased positivity, it was still Portugal's match for the taking. With Figo, Simão and Cristiano Ronaldo playing as the three behind the striker, the Angolan defence was struggling to keep them quiet and it was the Manchester United winger who should have increased Portugal's lead. A cross from Simão found him free at the back post but the ball could only bounce off him and roll behind for a goal kick. He may have been surprised that the ball reached him at all but he still should have done a lot better once it did arrive. Perhaps frustrated by that miss, he began to stamp his mark on proceedings, firing a header against the crossbar, nearly getting a free header before the intervention of Jamba and seeing a shot from the edge of the area well saved by the goalkeeper.

Although Portugal were turning the screw on their opposition, Angola were still creating the odd opportunity and nearly drew level just before half-time when André Macanga drilled a low shot from distance towards goal that was heading straight into the bottom corner before an excellent save from Ricardo in the Portuguese goal.

The second half began in similar fashion but Portugal still found themselves unable to add to their early goal. Tiago had an effort easily stopped, as did Pauleta, but the match was struggling to truly click into a high gear. It was a Portuguese performance that was very much in the mould of England's opener against Paraguay in that they had seemed as if they were going to blow their opponents away after taking the lead incredibly early and creating chances but they struggled to find any fluency. Like their English counterparts, as the match drew on, they retreated deeper and allowed the other team to come on to them. Fortunately for Scolari's men, Angola were also struggling to create any chances, but with just ten minutes remaining, they were presented with the opportunity to create something of note with a free kick in a promising position just outside the Portuguese penalty area. Yet, instead of sending the ball into the box and hoping to win either the header or the second ball, they opted to go short and Portugal easily regained possession.

As they entered the final ten minutes, Angola did manage to fashion out potential opportunities, with a Mantorras cross being well cleared by Carvalho, and Ricardo saving comfortably from Mateus's shot, but it was Portugal who came closest to adding another goal. Simão headed over just before the two Angolan chances and Maniche produced the best moment of the second half when firing a shot on goal from distance that required a smart save from João Ricardo.

With the final whistle, Portugal would have been pleased with the result if not the overall performance. Winning the opening fixture of an international tournament is always a key moment, with no team having won the World Cup after losing their opening match previously, but Portugal would certainly need to sharpen their game if they had their sights set on winning the competition. With Luis Felipe Scolari, the manager who had led Brazil to the title four years earlier, they had a seasoned campaigner who knew that it was how much better a team got as the tournament progressed, rather than how they started, that would determine whether true success was possible.

* * *

Having won their opening match with a scoreline that appears more comfortable than the reality, Mexico knew that they had a perfect opportunity to all but seal their place in the knockout stages with victory over Angola. Recognising the change that helped turn the match against Iran, Sinha earned his place in the starting line-up to replace Bolton Wanderers striker Jared Borgetti. For Angola, they knew that a defeat would leave their hopes hanging on life support. However, a victory would see them in prime position to upset one of the more established international football nations, although there was little from their opening match to suggest that this was a realistic possibility.

Under the floodlights in Hanover, Mexico started the brighter. Their first real chance came after ten minutes when Pável Pardo saw his free kick easily caught by the Angolan goalkeeper and then just two minutes later Rafa Márquez watched in hope as his free kick took a deflection off the wall that steered it out of the reach of the desperate dive of the keeper, only to see the ball strike the base of the post and go out for a corner. Despite the early flurry of free kicks, the West Africans would have felt that they had the better of the first half. Perhaps taking confidence from the way they battled against Portugal, Angola started with positivity and held their own against the more storied opposition. Unfortunately, the efforts that they had were mostly speculative ones. Both Paulo Figueiredo and Mendonça wasted chances that they sent harmlessly over the bar, and Mendonça tried an audacious free kick after spotting Sánchez standing off his line, but his attempt to catch the goalkeeper unawares sailed over the bar once again. Striker Mateus nearly had the best opening of the half just before half-time, but the ever-impressive Márquez narrowly beat him to a header to clear the danger for Mexico.

As the half-time whistle blew, the match was delicately balanced. Neither team had created a true clear-cut chance, with the majority of the shots on goal being speculative efforts from distance, but both had been playing good football and the match was progressing with a nice flow to it. No result could seal the fate for either team before the Portugal-Iran match, but both knew a victory was crucial, especially Angola, who knew that anything other than a win would make qualification extremely unlikely.

Wanting to keep matters firmly in their own hands, Mexico began the second half stronger than they had appeared at any point in the first, moving the ball nicely and attempting to break the well-organised shape of the Angolan defence. Eleven minutes into the half the best chance so far came and went for the Central Americans. Guillermo Franco was played through one-on-one and the Villarreal striker tried to chip the ball over the onrushing goalkeeper, but João Ricardo managed to deflect the ball down before it could properly loop over him. The rebound fell kindly for substitute Jesús Arellano, whose goalbound effort was brilliantly cleared off the line by Angolan defender Jamba.

Although possession remained with Mexico, they were becoming increasingly frustrated by the stubbornness of their opponents, a theme that was an undercurrent throughout the entire tournament. Aside from a Bravo effort that was straight at the goalkeeper, Mexico were unable to break the Angolan resistance. The introduction of substitutes to try to change things simply served to disrupt the rhythm that had existed in the first half and the match seemed to be drifting towards a 0-0 draw that would leave the group precariously balanced. Yet, with just ten minutes left, the complexion of the match changed as Mexico sought to break down the right-hand side before André Macanga stuck out his arm and stopped the ball from going beyond him. Having already been booked in the first half, the flash of second yellow card from the Singaporean referee meant that, for the final exchanges, Angola would have to cope with one player less.

Having that man advantage, Mexico upped the intensity further to try to snatch their victory. Francisco Fonseca volleyed wide and Márquez unleashed a brilliant 40-yard strike that was superbly tipped wide by João Ricardo. From the resulting corner, Ricardo flapped at the cross and the ball reached Bravo but simply bounced off the striker before striking the post and being cleared. Despite the extra player and keeping the ball well, *El Tri* were unable to find a way to break down the Angolan defence. The final whistle blew and Angola had earned their first-ever point at the World Cup finals. Mexico had perhaps edged the match but they certainly could not complain too much about the result as they played without any cutting edge. It had certainly been a performance that would have left La Volpe worried about their prospects as they lacked the ability to finish their chances, which would be crucial when they faced opposition of a higher quality.

The result was not perfect for Angola either, but it kept them alive heading into the final group fixtures. If Portugal could beat Iran, then the West Africans could qualify with a win and a Mexico defeat in the final round, depending on the goal difference, as it was three goals in favour of the Central Americans. Entering the last match against Iran with a prospect of qualifying was perhaps the best that Angola could have hoped for prior to the tournament and they had given themselves a chance of conducting one of the more shocking upsets in World Cup history.

In Frankfurt, the equation for Portugal was simple. Win against Iran and they would qualify for the knockouts with a match to spare. Having started rapidly against Angola and then fading as the match drew on, this was an opportunity for Scolari's men to start finding their best form so that they could match the expectations that had been placed upon them. The task at hand was just as simple for Iran, but in the opposite direction. A defeat would end their competitive aspect of the tournament a match early, with a draw making it highly unlikely that they would progress either. Although he was their all-time record appearance-maker and goalscorer, the fact that captain Ali Daei was now 37 years of age meant that playing two matches in quick succession was perhaps a step too far, so he was left on the bench with the possibility of featuring as a super sub.

In a similar manner to their opening match, Portugal nearly took the lead inside the opening minute. Figo was the orchestrator, cutting the ball back for Deco, who had been recalled to the starting line-up, but the Barcelona creator was unable to dig the ball out from under his feet to get a strike at goal. The early breakthrough did not arrive this time, but Portugal were definitely creating enough openings to put the game to bed. Deco saw his strike pushed over by the Iranian keeper, Maniche's volley was deflected behind for a corner and Ronaldo had a free header that hit his shoulder rather than making any clean contact and was easily chested off the line.

There was a contentious issue just before half-time when Hossein Kaebi raised his foot to win the ball and caught Figo in the face. Although the incident was accidental, it was a reckless challenge that could have easily brought a card of either colour, one that would certainly be checked by VAR in the modern age of football.

As half-time came, little had changed, with Portugal controlling the play but lacking any cutting edge. Despite having Deco back on the pitch, the creator was struggling to affect the match in a positive way. The Brazilian-born Portuguese star was coming into the tournament fresh from having won the Champions

League with Barcelona, his second triumph in the competition after winning in 2004 with Porto, and being named UEFA's best midfielder for the preceding season as well. This tournament was seemingly coming at the peak of his abilities and he was viewed by many as the missing piece of the Portuguese puzzle as they attempted to finally win a major international tournament.

Yet his inclusion in the Portugal squad was not welcomed by all. Born in Brazil, Deco was a nationalised Portuguese citizen, having resided in the country for over six years. Having never been capped by Brazil and having Portuguese citizenship, when he was first being discussed as a potential option for the national team, the debate seemed tribal in nature as Porto fans felt he should be called up and those of their rivals did not, broadly speaking. Yet, when he was named in the squad for their home European Championship in 2004, his captain fanned the flames further. Figo was not diplomatic when asked about the decision, saying, 'I don't think people would be happy in Spain if I became a Spanish national and played for the Spanish side. It's something that distorts team spirit and I don't agree with it.' Hardly a welcoming message from his national team captain but something that raised plenty of debate.

France had won the World Cup in 1998 with a squad containing many immigrants or sons of immigrants, much to the annoyance of National Front leader Jean-Marie Le Pen, who said France could not recognise itself in its national team. Yet every nation at the tournament was made up of a multicultural background and was better for it. Ideas permeated. Perspectives changed. As Guus Hiddink, manager of Australia at this tournament and managing a third different international team suggested, the world was increasingly global and nationalism and patriotism were not as strong as they had been previously. Would those who objected to Deco's inclusion not celebrate if he scored the winning goal in the final? Would Figo not? Like everything, if Deco proved useful then those critics would soon disappear.

Back under the German sun and Portugal continued to toil away in search of the goal that would secure their progress and also some fluency to take with them into their next matches. Ronaldo saw his low shot pushed away by the Iranian keeper but it was ultimately the naturalised Portuguese midfielder that would provide the breakthrough. Deco started the move, picking the ball up in midfield and switching play out wide left for his captain Figo. The experienced winger drove inside before laying the ball off for Deco, who had continued his run to the edge of the area. He fired a right-footed rocket into the corner of the net, leaving Mirzapour rooted to the spot. It was the first true moment of quality that Deco had brought to the match and it saw Portugal finally break down the stubborn Iranian defence.

With the result as it stood ending their competitive participation early, Iran had little choice but to come out and attack. Rasoul Khatibi was played in behind the Portuguese defence but could only drag his shot wide of the post, before Hashemian steered his header into the waiting arms of goalkeeper Ricardo. Rather than holding the ball to waste some time, the Sporting goalkeeper sent a quick kick forwards that eventually landed with Deco. Once again, the Barça playmaker freed Figo down the left and this time he took on his man, driving into the penalty area and drawing the foul from a desperate lunch by Golmohammadi. Having struggled to make a notable impact on the opening two matches to this point, Ronaldo took the responsibility of making Portugal's lead a comfortable one and duly obliged by sticking the spot kick into the top left corner, striking it so well that even if the keeper had dived the correct way, there was no chance he would have been able to save it.

Aside from Golmohammadi being forced off with what appeared to be a dislocated shoulder, little else happened as both teams just saw the final ten minutes of the match out, Iran seemingly resigned to their fate. Victory meant that a point in the final group match against Mexico would see Portugal top the group but they were assured of a place in the knockout stages no matter what. This result meant that it was either Mexico or Iran that would progress, with the Central Americans the clear favourites as a draw or better against Portugal would secure their progress. If they lost, however, Angola could surprise everyone and reach the knockout stages at their first-ever World Cup finals appearance, although they would be reliant on a three-goal swing in goal difference, as Mexico held the advantage there as well.

* * *

Already assured of their place in the knockout stages, Scolari opted to ring the changes ahead of the final group match, bringing in five new names and giving rests to the likes of Deco, Ronaldo and Pauleta. While giving the replacements a chance to earn their place in the starting line-up, it may have also offered hope to Mexico that they could get the point they needed to qualify, as a Portugal without those key players was an easier proposition.

If there was to be any disjointed play from the Portuguese it was not evident in the opening exchanges as they once again got off to a fast start and seemed intent on putting the game to bed as early as possible. In fact, it only took six minutes for them to make the breakthrough. Simão, starting in place of Ronaldo, gathered the ball on the left-hand side and was afforded the time and space to drift towards the penalty box unchallenged and roll a simple ball across the area. It was behind Hélder Postiga but it was perfectly placed for the arrival of Maniche late into the area and the experienced Dynamo Moscow midfielder, who had spent the second half of the previous domestic season helping Chelsea retain their Premier League title, lashed the ball into the roof of the net.

There was no sense of Portugal taking their foot off the gas as they continued moving the ball well, not allowing Mexico to settle into any sort of rhythm. The perfect opportunity to double their advantage was handed to them on a silver platter when Rafa Márquez raised his hand while trying to head clear a corner and the ball bounced off of it, leaving the Slovakian referee with little option but to point to the spot. Having provided the opener, Simão was the one who stepped up to take the penalty and opted to go for power, driving it to the keeper's right. Sánchez guessed correctly and the penalty was not right in the corner, but the sheer power that was on the strike saw it fly into the back of the net.

With just 25 minutes played Mexico found themselves two goals down and at risk of exiting the tournament at the first round if Angola beat Iran by any scoreline. Trying to regain control over their own fate, Mexico began to grow into the match and nearly pulled one back when Omar Bravo found himself free at the back post from a free kick. He caught his strike well enough but Ricardo scrambled across his goal quickly, managed to deflect the ball up and was fortunate enough to watch as it landed on the roof of his goal. From the resulting corner, Francisco Fonseca evaded his marker and found himself with a free header from the edge of the six-yard box. His flicked header nestled perfectly just inside the far post.

The first half had been played at breakneck speed, with both teams contributing to an open, end-to-end match, and the second period followed in the same manner. Sinha had once again been brought on at half-time to try to swing the momentum in Mexico's favour, and they certainly were in the ascendancy through the opening exchanges of the half. It took just 12 minutes for that superiority to come to fruition when Luis Pérez turned well in the penalty area and Miguel dived into a challenge, which the referee decided was worthy of a penalty. Whether the foul was awarded for the contact on Pérez, which was minimal, or for the ball hitting the arm of the stricken defender while he lay on the floor, the Slovakian official saw enough to warrant providing Mexico with the perfect opportunity to equalise. Bravo, who had already scored twice at the tournament so far, took the ball and calmly placed it on the spot. Standing in his way was Ricardo, who had an excellent record at saving penalties. He was the hero two years earlier against England at Euro 2004 when he took off his gloves before saving Darius Vassell's effort and then stepping up to score the winning spot kick himself immediately after. Perhaps fearing Ricardo's record, Bravo opted to go for power and aimed for the top corner. Unfortunately for Mexico, the accuracy was lacking and the effort was blazed high over the crossbar.

Undeterred by the missed penalty, Mexico continued to push forward in search of the all-important equaliser and just three minutes later had another shout for a penalty for another foul on Pérez, again by Miguel. The Portuguese defender appeared to bundle the striker over but whether there was enough contact for a foul was debatable. The referee, however, decided that the Monterrey forward had dived in an attempt to win a second penalty. Having been shown a yellow card for a high foot in the first half, the second booking meant that his afternoon was over after just an hour and *El Tri* would need to find their second goal with just ten players. Miguel, who himself had already been booked, was clearly walking a tightrope at this stage and Scolari reacted quickly, replacing him with Chelsea right-back Paulo Ferreira.

Rather than wilting, Mexico kept attacking and, a mere three minutes after going down to ten players, Bravo found himself in behind the Portuguese defence and one-on-one with the goalkeeper. Perhaps still thinking about the missed penalty, the striker lacked the composure he had shown against Iran and could only send his effort harmlessly over the bar. In the space of seven minutes, Mexico had missed a penalty, had a half-decent appeal for another turned down and seen another guilt-edged chance wasted. The watching public could have been forgiven for thinking that everything was transpiring against them in their bid for qualification.

After the breathless opening hour, the match began to settle down a little, with Portugal dropping deeper in an attempt to stem the Mexican onslaught. Nuno Gomes did have an excellent chance to restore Portugal's two-goal advantage in a rare venture forwards in the second half but could only send the ball over the bar with a snapshot effort from eight yards out. Less than a minute later and Mexico were appealing for another penalty after Ferreira clumsily slid through the back of Bravo as he tried to make sure the ball went behind rather than allowing the striker to run towards goal. It was clumsy at best and had the referee pointed to the spot for the third time in the match, the full-back could certainly have had zero complaints.

Despite the player disadvantage, Mexico were the stronger as the match drifted towards its conclusion, not wanting to give any edge to Angola in the battle for qualification. There were few more actual chances created though, as creativity seemed to wane as the Mexicans tired. Portugal almost increased their advantage when Maniche's effort was well saved by Sánchez but neither team could add to the scoreboard and Portugal had ground out a hard-fought victory that saw them join Germany as the only nation to win all three matches so far. It had been a spirited performance by La Volpe's team but their fate had been taken out of their hands. If Angola had managed to win by three goals, then they would surprise everyone by qualifying at the Mexicans' expense.

Having not scored in their opening two matches, the chances of Angola scoring at least three goals were incredibly slim but stranger things have happened in football. Playing an Iran that were already eliminated could be a blessing, as they had nothing to play for, or a curse as that freedom could unleash the shackles, allowing them to play without fear.

Knowing that anything less than a win would end their hopes, Angola started with intent, Mateus firing a snapshot over the bar after just ten minutes. But the early promise from the African nation was stunted as two early injuries unsettled the flow of the match, with both nations losing a player inside the opening 25 minutes. The disruption actually favoured Iran, as they began to create some chances of their own after the injuries. They had two quickfire headed chances, with the returning Ali Daei wasting his by sending a free header wide and Hashemian saw his goalbound effort stopped at the post by Mendonça.

The match had been slow to burst into life but those Iranian chances and the news that Portugal had taken a 2-1 lead over Mexico early in the first half seemed to inject energy into Angola's play towards the end of the first period. Despite the new-found energy that they were playing with, it was still Iran who were creating the more clear-cut chances, with Andranik Teymourian seeing his low shot well saved by João Ricardo, with the rebound narrowly evading Daei for a tap-in.

Half-time arrived and, as it stood, Angola were heading out. Backed by a raucous travelling support that had not stopped singing throughout the entirety of the tournament, Angola started the second half with a greater degree of intent than they had showed all tournament so far, with Mendonça narrowly sending a low shot beyond the post within two minutes of the restart. As the match ticked into the hour mark, while Mexico were missing a penalty that would have taken Angola's chances out of their own hands, the African nation made their breakthrough. Zé Kalanga received the ball on the right-hand side and floated a cross over to the back post, finding substitute Flávio, whose header looped back over the goalkeeper and nestled into the back of the net. It was a textbook example of sending the header back the way it had come from and it gave Angola a lifeline. With Mexico losing by one goal and down to ten men, Angola only needed a two-goal swing now and were hoping for a favour from Portugal that would reduce their own task to a single goal.

Somehow, the volume from the Angolan crowd increased once more, trying to inspire their team towards one of the more remarkable World Cup storylines. It was Mendonça again who came closest to increasing the advantage when he watched hopefully as two efforts came agonisingly close but ultimately snuck the wrong side of the post. Time was still on their side with 20 minutes remaining, but the key would be the next goal, as an Iranian equaliser would completely end any real chance that Angola had of qualification.

Despite their best endeavours, Angola were unable to carve out any openings that truly threatened the Iranian defence and the worst-case scenario came true with just 15 minutes left. A corner from the vastly experienced Hamburger SV midfielder Mahdavikia perfectly picked out Bakhtiarizadeh, whose header was so perfectly placed into the far corner that the goalkeeper had no chance of reaching it. It was the goal that the wonderful Angolan support had been dreading and it seemed to take away all the remaining optimism of the players on the pitch. Back to needing three goals to qualify, barring a miracle that would not arrive in the other match, the Angolan players were seemingly content with just ending the match.

The last real chance fell to Iran and Khatibi, whose shot was well tipped over, before the full-time whistle went to confirm the reality that Angola had been coming to terms with for the last 15 minutes. Their first World Cup journey was coming to an end. Although it had ended after the minimum three fixtures, the fact that they had managed to get to the final 15 minutes with a genuine chance of reaching the knockout stages should be remembered as a fantastic achievement. In a group containing the fancied Portugal, a perennial World Cup finalist Mexico and an experienced Iran, to not be outclassed and bringing back two points was an achievement that should be fondly remembered. Iran had also never appeared outclassed and could perhaps have felt a tad unlucky to have only won a solitary point. They had outplayed Mexico before mistakes took away their momentum and they had kept Portugal close until late in the second half.

Ultimately, it was the two fancied nations that had progressed to the knockout stages and with Portugal topping the group ahead of Mexico, they had created two very intriguing clashes for the Round of 16. Mexico as runners-up would face Group C winners Argentina, while Portugal would entertain the Netherlands. Both matches would become remembered in World Cup history, although for vastly different reasons.

6pm, 11 June 2006
Frankenstadion, Nuremburg
Attendance: 41,000
Referee: Roberto Rosetti (Italy)

Mexico 3 (Bravo 28, 76, Sinha 79)
Iran 1 (Golmohammadi 36)

Mexico: Oswaldo Sánchez, Rafael Márquez (c), Ricardo Osorio, Carlos Salcido, Mario Méndez, Pável Pardo, Gerardo Torrado (Sinha 46), Gonzalo Pineda, Omar Bravo, Jared Borgetti (Francisco Fonseca 52), Guillermo Franco (Luis Ernesto Pérez 46). **Manager:** Ricardo La Volpe.

Iran: Ebrahim Mirzapour, Hossein Kaebi, Yahya Golmohammadi, Rahman Rezaei, Mohammad Nosrati (Arash Borhani 81), Mehdi Mahdavikia, Javad Nekounam, Andranik Teymourian, Ali Karimi (Mehrzad Madanchi 62), Ali Daei (c), Vahid Hashemian. **Manager:** Branko Ivanković.

Booked: Torrado (18), Salcido (90+1); Nekounam (55)

9pm, 11 June 2006
RheinEnergieStadion, Cologne
Attendance: 45,000
Referee: Jorge Larrionda (Uruguay)

Angola 0
Portugal 1 (Pauleta 4)

Angola: João Ricardo, Locó, Jamba, Kali, Delgado, Zé Kalanga (Edson Nobre 70), André Macanga, Mateus, Paulo Figueiredo (Miloy 80), Mendonça, Akwá (c) (Mantorras 60). **Manager:** Luís Oliveira Gonçalves.

Portugal: Ricardo, Miguel, Fernando Meira, Ricardo Carvalho, Nuno Valente, Tiago (Hugo Viana 83), Petit (Maniche 72), Cristiano Ronaldo (Costinha 60), Luís Figo (c), Simão, Pauleta. **Manager:** Luiz Felipe Scolari.

Booked: Jamba (38), Locó (45+3), Macanga (52); Ronaldo (26), Valente (79)

9pm, 16 June 2006
Niedersachsenstadion, Hanover
Attendance: 43,000
Referee: Shamsul Maidin (Singapore)

Mexico 0
Angola 0

Mexico: Oswaldo Sánchez, Rafael Márquez (c), Ricardo Osorio, Carlos Salcido, Mario Méndez, Gerardo Torrado, Sinha (Jesús Arellano 52) Pável Pardo, Gonzalo Pineda (Ramón Morales 78), Omar Bravo, Guillermo Franco (Francisco Fonseca 74). **Manager:** Ricardo La Volpe.

Angola: João Ricardo, Locó, Jamba, Kali, Delgado, André Macanga, Zé Kalanga (Miloy 83), Paulo Figueiredo (Rui Marques 73), Mateus (Mantorras 68), Mendonça, Akwá (c). **Manager:** Luís Oliveira Gonçalves.

Booked: Pineda (59); Delgado (13), Macanga (44), Kalanga (50), Ricardo (86)
Sent off: Macanga (79)

3pm, 17 June 2006
Waldstadion, Frankfurt
Attendance: 48,000
Referee: Éric Poulat (France)

Portugal 2 (Deco 63, Ronaldo 80 (p))
Iran 0

Portugal: Ricardo, Miguel, Fernando Meira, Ricardo Carvalho, Nuno Valente, Costinha, Maniche (Petit 66), Luís Figo (c) (Simão 88), Deco (Tiago 80), Cristiano Ronaldo, Pauleta. **Manager:** Luiz Felipe Scolari.

Iran: Ebrahim Mirzapour, Hossein Kaebi, Yahya Golmohammadi (c) (Sohrab Bakhtiarizadeh 88), Rahman Rezaei, Mohammad Nosrati, Andranik Teymourian, Javad Nekounam, Mehrzad Madanchi (Rasoul Khatibi 66), Ali Karimi (Ferydoon Zandi 65), Vahid Hashemian. **Manager:** Branko Ivanković.

Booked: Pauleta (45+1), Deco (48), Costinha (61); Nekounam (20), Madanchi (32), Kaebi (73), Golmohammadi (88)

4pm, 21 June 2006
Arena AufSchalke, Gelsenkirchen
Attendance: 52,000
Referee: L'uboš Micheľ (Slovakia)

Portugal 2 (Maniche 6, Simão 24 (p))
Mexico 1 (Fonseca 29)

Portugal: Ricardo, Miguel (Paulo Ferreira 61), Fernando Meira, Ricardo Carvalho, Marco Caneira, Tiago, Petit, Maniche, Luís Figo (c) (Luís Boa Morte 80), Simão, Hélder Postiga (Nuno Gomes 69). **Manager:** Luiz Felipe Scolari.

Mexico: Oswaldo Sánchez, Francisco Javier Rodríguez (Sinha 46), Ricardo Osorio, Carlos Salcido, Mario Méndez (Guillermo Franco 80), Pável Pardo, Rafael Márquez (c), Luis Ernesto Pérez, Gonzalo Pineda (José Antonio Castro 69), Francisco Fonseca, Omar Bravo. **Manager:** Ricardo La Volpe.

Booked: Miguel (26), Maniche (69), Boa Morte (88), Gomes (90+1); Javier Rodríguez (22), Ernesto Pérez (27), Márquez (65), Sinha (87)
Sent off: Ernesto Pérez (61)

4pm, 21 June 2006
Zentralstadion, Leipzig
Attendance: 38,000
Referee: Mark Shield (Australia)

Iran 1 (Bakhtiarizadeh 75)
Angola 1 (Flávio 60)

Iran: Ebrahim Mirzapour, Hossein Kaebi (Arash Borhani 67), Rahman Rezaei, Sohrab Bakhtiarizadeh, Mohammad Nosrati (Masoud Shojaei 13), Mehdi Mahdavikia, Andranik Teymourian, Ferydoon Zandi, Mehrzad Madanchi, Vahid Hashemian (Rasoul Khatibi 39), Ali Daei (c). **Manager:** Branko Ivanković.

Angola: João Ricardo, Locó, Jamba, Kali, Delgado, Zé Kalanga, Miloy, Paulo Figueiredo (Rui Marques 73), Mateus (Love 23), Mendonça, Akwá (c) (Flávio 51). **Manager:** Luís Oliveira Gonçalves.

Booked: Madanchi (37), Teymourian (55), Zandi (90+1); Locó (22), Mendonça (45+1), Kalanga (67)

Group D	P	W	D	L	GF	GA	GD	PTS
PORTUGAL	3	3	0	0	5	1	+4	9
MEXICO	3	1	1	1	4	3	+1	4
ANGOLA	3	0	2	1	1	2	-1	2
IRAN	3	0	1	2	2	6	-4	1

Portugal and Mexico qualified

Group E

WHILE GROUP C was considered by many to be the so-called 'Group of Death' at this World Cup, Group E was one that was almost impossible to predict the outcome of. It contained Italy, three-time World Cup winners and one of the favourites to win despite the cloud of the Calciopoli scandal, Czech Republic, semi-finalists at Euro 2004, ranked second in the world and many pundits' dark horse prediction, USA, ranked fifth in the world with a squad that had a nice blend of experience and youth that was aiming to better the quarter-final appearance four years earlier, and Ghana, the debutants with a squad that could match any in the tournament and would be no easy game for anyone. One poor result in this group could be the difference between success and failure, so every nation needed to be on the top of their game from the first whistle.

The two highest-ranked teams in the group, USA and Czech Republic, got the action underway in the early evening in Gelsenkirchen, knowing that a fast start was crucial. It was the Czechs that delivered it. They had been dictating the play and a simple ball out to the right found Zdeněk Grygera in space. He delivered a pinpoint cross on to the head of the 6ft 8in Borussia Dortmund striker Jan Koller, who powered his header beyond Kasey Keller after just five minutes. The early going was being dominated by the European team, with Juventus midfielder Pavel

Nedvěd pulling the strings in what appeared to be a free role in the space behind Koller. It was the experienced playmaker who created the next opening when his cross from the left narrowly evaded Koller but found Grygera at the back post, whose header went just wide. It was a clearly defined tactic from the Czechs to utilise Koller's physical prowess as their long balls into the striker were sticking, with Nedvěd and Koller's Dortmund team-mate Tomáš Rosický playing off of him and taking control of the second ball.

Although the Czechs were clearly in the ascendancy, the Americans were ranked highly by FIFA for a reason and still looked dangerous when they were able to break forwards. Much like Nedvěd, the Americans' good play was largely coming through their talisman, Manchester City midfielder Claudio Reyna, whose son Giovanni is a star in the current USA national team. Before Grygera's missed header, Reyna found himself in a good crossing position but lost his footing at the key moment. Then his strike from 25 yards out beat Petr Čech but unfortunately bounced off the post and rebounded clear. The Americans were increasingly gaining and keeping possession, moving the ball but without any creative edge to break down their opponents; however, the Czechs still appeared to be the stronger team and doubled their lead just ten minutes before the half-time interval.

Nedvěd once again found himself in space on the left-hand side and his cross was headed clear by Oguchi Onyewu, landing at the feet of Rosický. The playmaker took a touch on to his right foot and from 30 yards out unleashed a swerving rocket that flew perfectly into the net beyond the dive of Keller. It was an unstoppable effort that no goalkeeper would have been able to stop and was another goal-of-the-tournament contender just three days in, to go alongside Lahm and Frings from Germany's opening match.

It was the perfect opening half of the tournament for the Czechs, two goals to the good against a strong USA team and dictating the tempo, the ideal start for a team that many fancied for a run to the latter stages of the competition. However, their first blemish came with a couple of minutes left in the half when Koller, having tormented the USA defenders for the entire first half, was battling for a ball near the penalty area and went down holding his hamstring. The big striker was stretchered off the pitch, replaced by Vratislav Lokvenc, but how damaging losing their focal point would be was yet to be seen.

Unhappy with the way the first half had played out, Bruce Arena made two changes at the break, bringing on John O'Brien and Eddie Johnson, but the substitutes could do little to change the momentum of the match. The Czechs created a flurry of chances, with Ujfaluši heading over a Poborský free kick, Lokvenc wasting a one-on-one with Keller after a clever through ball from Poborský, before the winger himself fired over from a tight angle after a good cross from Nedvěd. Lokvenc had done a good job standing for the Koller, holding the ball up well and allowing the Eastern Europeans to continue with their tactic that had worked so well in the first half. The chances continued to flow, with Milan left-back Jankulovski breaking in behind before a heavy touch allowed DaMarcus Beasley to get back and clear the danger. Rosický, Nedvěd and Poborský were still dictating the tempo, with the former trying to add another goal-of-the-tournament contender to his earlier effort when shooting from 30 yards again, only to watch his effort bounce back off the crossbar.

Rosický did manage to add his second with 15 minutes left, playing a neat one-two with Nedvěd on the halfway line that allowed him the space to run through the entire American half unchallenged before firing his effort over the advancing Keller. A three-goal lead and a dominating performance. It was the dream start for the Czechs and one that laid the perfect foundation for a second successful tournament in a row. As for the USA, the opening match could hardly have gone worse and they would need a rapid turnaround in fortunes to have any chance of qualifying from the group. Unfortunately, their second match was against the Italian team that many saw as the favourite to go on to win the tournament.

For Italy at this World Cup, opening with a win was paramount. Coming into the tournament under the dark cloud of the Calciopoli scandal, they needed to put in a good performance early on to switch the focus of the commentary from the state of their domestic game to the quality of their football. Needing that opening win to belay the critics, being matched up against debutants Ghana was not the kindest of draws. Although appearing at their first World Cup, Ghana had international pedigree, having won the AFCON on four occasions, and this was easily the most-talented squad that the West African nation had produced since their 1982 AFCON triumph, with a 17-year-old talent Abedi Pele and George Alhassan, nicknamed Jair due to his similar play to Brazilian World Cup winner Jairzinho. This iteration of the *Black Stars* contained quality throughout, with goalkeeper Richard Kingson, midfield duo of captain Stephen Appiah and Chelsea favourite Michael Essien, and two exciting attacking prospects in 21-year-old Sulley Muntari and 20-year-old Asamoah Gyan, both of Udinese. Ghana entered the tournament with the youngest squad, with an average age of just over 24 and a half, and the least experienced, with an average of just under 17 caps, but they were certainly no pushovers.

The match started predictably under the night sky in Hanover with Italy controlling the early exchanges. Palermo full-back Fabio Grosso was proving to be a hard to handle outlet on the left-hand side, winning an early corner that captain Fabio Cannavaro could only head over. Grosso was one of four Palermo players that made up the Italian squad, the third most behind Juventus and Milan, perhaps a surprising number given that they only managed the eighth-highest points total in the league, although they would ultimately finish fifth and be awarded a UEFA Cup spot after the punishments for the Calciopoli scandal were finalised. The Italians were pressing for the early goal led by Andrea Pirlo's sublime playmaking ability but the real star of the early goings for the *Azzurri* was Fiorentina's Luca Toni.

This tournament came at the perfect moment for Toni, the late bloomer who was at the height of his ability. He had spent the early stages of his career languishing in the Italian lower leagues without setting the world alight until a move to Palermo in 2003 kickstarted his development. He helped them to promotion back to Serie A, finishing with a record of 51 goals in 83 matches and earning a move to Fiorentina. His one season in Florence before this tournament was the best of his career as he scored at nearly a goal-a-game in all competitions, 33 in 42, and becoming the first Italian to win the European Golden Shoe.

The key players were coming to the fore early for the Italians, with Toni narrowly missing a cross from Simone Perrotta before firing an overhead kick straight as Kingson. Pirlo and Totti were masterfully moving the ball, not allowing Ghana a moment to settle, and the big Fiorentina striker was in total control of his contest with the central defenders. The in-form forward nearly produced one of the best goals of the tournament just before the half-hour mark. A ball from Daniele De Rossi into the feet of Toni's strike partner Alberto Gilardino was cleverly flicked up, Toni won the ball with his head and sent the defender the opposite way with his movement, giving himself an extra yard of space. He caught the ball with a near-perfect volley, smashing it over the head of Kingson only to see it rattle the underside of the crossbar and bounce down and away. It was a moment of quality that deserved a goal but perhaps summed up the Italian first half: lovely build-up play but lacking a decisive finish.

With Italy not taking advantage of their early momentum, Ghana began to grow into the match. Borussia Dortmund's Matthew Amoah narrowly shot wide from just outside the box, Essien drove into the Italian penalty area but could only send his effort wide of the goal and Emmanuel Pappoe was free in the area but rushed his shot and fired comfortably over the crossbar. While the West Africans were improving, the threat from Italy was still ever-present. Totti stung the palms of Kingson, who did well to turn his 40-yard effort from a free kick over the bar, Cannavaro saw another header go over the bar before the Roma captain Totti once again tested the goalkeeper from a free kick. The match was becoming increasingly end to end and it was perhaps as Ghana were beginning to feel confident of snatching a result that Italy made their breakthrough.

Totti played a simple short pass from a corner to Pirlo, who had inexcusably been left unmarked. The Milan playmaker drove towards the centre of the pitch before unleashing a curling effort beyond the dive of Kingson and into the far corner of the goal. It was a lovely goal but one that Ghana would look back on with a degree of disappointment as Pirlo was afforded far too much time on the edge of the area to measure up the effort. There was still time for Italy to go close to a second before half-time when Grosso, again getting down the left, found himself free in the box and opted for a shot that was saved when squaring the ball for Toni in the middle may have been the better option. It was a first half played at a near-breathless pace, one that both teams contributed equally to.

The second period continued in the same vein with Gilardino and Perrotta both having efforts well saved by Kingson either side of Essien testing Buffon with a shot from distance. There was a worry for Italy when John Paintsil trod on the knee of Totti, given that the No. 10 had only just returned from a three-month absence with a broken leg. Lippi wasted no time in bringing the Roma man off. It was not Totti at his influential best but it was certainly an encouraging hour-long appearance and the hope was that he would keep getting sharper and play a crucial role in the latter stages of the tournament should Italy get there.

With Ghana continuing to push for their equaliser, Italy knew that a second goal was crucial and they nearly had a wonderful opportunity to find it when a counter-attack saw them with two attackers free in the Ghanaian half, only for a questionable offside flag to bring it to a halt. Had the incident occurred in modern-day football, the flag would have remained down and VAR would have made the final decision had Italy scored. Alas, the chance was blown dead and just a couple of minutes later Italy may have been ruing that decision when De Rossi leaned into Asamoah Gyan in the penalty area a little forcibly, but the referee decided there was no infringement.

An offside denying Italy and a penalty appeal waved away for Ghana just a few minutes apart repeated itself five minutes later when substitute Vincenzo Iaquinta was bursting through and brought down by Samuel Kuffour. Had the offside, which replays suggested was the wrong decision, not been given, then Ghana may have been down to ten men. Not worrying about the favourable decision in their favour, Gyan continued causing problems for the Italian defence, driving between De Rossi and Zaccardo and being brought down, but again saw his appeal waved away. The replays were inconclusive but had the penalty been awarded, it would have been hard to argue against it.

As Ghana pushed, spaces began to appear in their defensive set-up and Pirlo was the perfect player to take advantage. With just over five minutes remaining, he collected the ball and played it long, over the top of the defence. Kuffour failed to deal with it and under-hit his back-pass, allowing Iaquinta to race clear, round the keeper and tap into the empty net. It was the nail in the coffin of Ghana's chances in the match and the last few minutes petered out with little action. It was an impressive performance from both nations, with Italy beginning with a strong win and Ghana showing that they were not afraid of anyone they came up against.

* * *

With the Czech Republic winning their opener and Ghana losing theirs, a victory for the Europeans would leave them on the verge on qualification and eliminate the West Africans. A Ghana victory, however, would leave the group precariously balanced and leave every team in with a chance of qualifying. The concern for the Eastern Europeans was how they would cope without the presence of Jan Koller leading the line. Vratislav Lokvenc had stepped in well during the second half against the USA but the Red Bull Salzburg striker did not represent as threatening a target as Koller, and Milan Baroš, who had won the golden boot at Euro 2004, was not fully fit after a foot injury.

As well as not having either of their main two strikers available, the Czechs got off to the worst possible start, conceding after just two minutes. An early corner for the Ghanaians was cleared but Stephen Appiah cleverly brought the ball under control and clipped a pass into the path of Gyan. The Udinese striker controlled well on his chest before hitting a low, hard shot with his left foot, giving Petr Čech no chance. It was a well-worked goal for Ghana, but the Czechs should have done better, as Ujfaluši attempted to intercept the ball before it reached Gyan but completely missed it, giving the striker the time to control and finish.

However, the Czechs did not wilt after the early goal and responded brightly. Nedvěd could only direct his shot straight at the keeper, Rosický created space with a brilliant run but could not find the striker and Poborský dragged his effort across the box but wide of the goal. Meanwhile, much like the Italy match, Ghana were always threatening when they moved forwards and the play was increasingly becoming end to end. Muntari, Amoah and Gyan all had good opportunities and should have done better, with only Gyan finding the target, and that was a weak effort straight at Čech.

The midfield battle between the two teams was an intriguing match-up, with Rosický and Nedvěd squaring off against Essien and Appiah. Four outstanding midfielders all attempting to stamp their authority over the match and both teams would have been feeling like they could click into a higher gear. The absence of Koller seemed to prevent the Czechs from being able to find that next level though. With the way that Toni's physicality had caused problems for the Ghanaian defenders in the opening match, Koller would have surely proven too much to handle. Lokvenc as his replacement could not occupy the central defenders in the same manner and it completely blunted the Czech attacking options.

The second half continued in a similar way to the first with both teams creating openings, Nedvěd having a fine header disallowed for offside and Gyan seeing his shot well saved by Čech after a clever run through the defence. The Czechs, trailing by the early Gyan goal, knew that they had to come out for the second half with a renewed vigour and they nearly scored a lovely goal when Rosický cleverly dummied a Jiří Štajner cross, allowing the ball to reach Monaco's Jaroslav Plašil. His effort was destined for the back of the net until a strong hand from Kingson tipped it over the bar.

It was a missed chance that the Czechs would come to rue just a few minutes later when Muntari's run down the left-hand side freed up space for Amoah, who was tripped by Tomáš Ujfaluši as he drove into the penalty area. It was a clear penalty and a second yellow card was produced for the Fiorentina defender. While the Argentine referee was seeing to the sending-off, Gyan stepped up and took the penalty anyway. It was a decision that saw the forward receive a yellow card, his second of the tournament, and one that would rule him out of his nation's final group fixture, a potentially costly absence. Undeterred by the thought of missing the next match, the Udinese striker stepped up again and sent Čech the wrong way, only to see his penalty rattle the post and bounce clear.

Despite the missed penalty, Ghana continued to press forward to take advantage of the extra player they had. A second goal could be crucial and would surely see off any remaining challenge from the Czechs. Unfortunately, they were facing one of the best goalkeepers in world football in Petr Čech. The Chelsea shot-stopper had been truly remarkable in the two seasons that he had been with the West London club. Since joining in the summer of 2004, he had appeared in 90 matches across all competitions, keeping a remarkable 49 clean sheets, only conceding 54 goals and going 1,024 minutes without allowing the opposition to score in the Premier League, a competition record at the time. His rewards were two league titles, a League Cup success, a Professional Footballers' Association team of the year appearance and a golden glove. He was a goalkeeper at the peak of his powers and the Czechs were reliant on him in keeping Ghana at bay.

The Chelsea keeper was in fine form, producing smart saves from Amoah and Muntari in quick succession. Both Muntari and Essien had chances to get a shot away but could not quite get the ball out from under their feet before the Chelsea midfielder forced another good save from his club team-mate. It was a procession of chances for the *Black Stars* and their second goal seemed inevitable. It finally came with eight minutes remaining as Appiah and Gyan combined well to free Muntari into space in the penalty area. He smashed his effort beyond Čech and into the roof of the net. It was a deserved second for Ghana, even if it had been harder to attain than they would have liked, and it all but secured their victory.

Although one player down, the Czechs nearly grabbed themselves a goal at the end, but both Libor Sionko and Jan Polák saw their headers well saved by Kingson. It was a brief flurry but it was too late. They had failed to truly get going in the match, clearly missing the presence of Koller, and had made it too easy for Ghana to take control. That, however, should not take away from the quality of the West Africans' performance. Every player had been outstanding, especially their key men Essien, Appiah, Gyan and Muntari. They had proven that they could compete with the teams highly ranked by FIFA and had blown Group E wide open, with every single nation in the group in with a chance of qualification in the final round of fixtures, regardless of the outcome between Italy and USA.

Although there was no result that could secure qualification, the Italians knew that a victory over the Americans would see them in a perfect position before their final match. If both teams' performances in their openers was anything to go by, then Marcelo Lippi's team would be fine, as the USA had failed to make any real impact and it seemed like a disappointing tournament was unfolding for one of the dark horses. Bruce Arena had responded to that performance with two changes, bringing in Fulham defender Carlos Bocanegra and a 23-year-old Clint Dempsey, who would later become a Fulham player himself, but there still seemed little hope for the Americans.

As the old cliché goes, football is not played on paper, and despite the match-up seeming like an easy Italian victory, it was the USA that actually started on the front foot. Led by Dempsey and Reading's Bobby Convey, they were pressing high and not giving the Italian defenders a moment to rest. Both had good chances in the opening 20 minutes, with Dempsey just unable to get a shot away inside the area and then shooting narrowly wide, either side of Convey firing a free kick into the Italian wall that deflected behind. It was a promising start, one that seemed unlikely before the match, but they were made to rue those missed chances. An Italian free kick from the right-hand side was taken by Pirlo, whose usual excellent delivery reached Alberto Gilardino. The Milan forward's stooping header across Keller was the ultimate sucker-punch.

The floodgates could easily have opened at this point, with American heads possibly dropping at going behind despite being on top in the opening exchanges. This was, however, one of the best USA men's national teams ever produced and they were not going to go quietly. Just five minutes after going behind they had their own free kick from the right. Convey, who had been at the heart of everything good in their play, whipped a dangerous free kick across the Italian box and Zaccardo attempted to clear with his left foot but only succeeded in slicing the ball into his own goal. It was the perfect response and no less than Arena's team deserved.

If the American equaliser was bad for Italy, worse was about to come just seconds later. A loose ball deflected into the air and was contested by Brian McBride and Daniele De Rossi. Inexplicably, the Roma midfielder opted to swing his elbow wildly, catching the striker in the face, drawing plenty of blood. It was a moment of madness from the Italian and earned him an instant red card. The incident earned him a four-match ban, ruling him out until the final, should Italy reach that stage, and the annoyance of his team-mates, with Pirlo saying in his autobiography *I Think Therefore I Play* that the Italy squad 'weren't exactly the most tactful to begin with' as they knew that they were losing a key player. The sending-off provided the perfect opportunity for the USA, giving them the ideal opportunity to leave the group precariously balanced with all teams level on three points, should they push and get a winner.

They did continue to push, causing more problems for the talented Italian back line. Bocanegra headed wastefully over, Mastroeni curled an effort off the top of the netting and captain Reyna saw his shot well blocked by Alessandro Nesta. With half-time fast approaching, the USA knew that getting into the interval with the scores level was not a bad outcome and they could regroup and push for the winner with the man advantage during the second period. What they could not account for was the late, reckless lunge from Pablo Mastroeni that caught the ankle of Pirlo. It was a poor challenge and left the Uruguayan official with little choice but to send the Colorado Rapids midfielder off.

With the match level in terms of scoreline and players on the pitch, the second half was intriguingly poised. Having been the better team for the first period, the Americans knew more of the same would give them a great opportunity of producing a massive upset. However, any hopes that they may have had were wiped away just two minutes after half-time. After already being booked for a foul that could have been a red card for being the last man, when Eddie Pope clipped the heels of Gilardino as he attempted to turn and break, there was little choice but to show a second yellow card and leave the USA with just nine players on the pitch. In a mad three-minute spell either side of the interval, they had seen their one-player advantage turn into a one-man deficit and their hopes of a victory all but disappear.

With Totti having been substituted for Gattuso to shore up the middle of the pitch when the USA had the numerical advantage, Lippi introduced Del Piero for Zaccardo and set about pushing for a win that would see them to the verge of the knockout stages. But even with their extra player, Italy were unable to find their rhythm and allowed the Americans to create the better chances, with McBride shooting wide when he really should have hit the target and a DaMarcus Beasley strike finding the back of the net but being ruled out for offside as McBride was standing in Buffon's line of sight.

With just 20 minutes remaining, Italy finally began exerting some pressure on the depleted USA team. Del Piero was finding space around the penalty area and a delightful dink over the back line from Pirlo found the Juventus striker free but his clever stabbed effort was superbly clawed away by Kasey Keller, before the follow-up was deflected behind for a corner. It was the best opening Italy had created and Keller had been its match. Keller again found himself the American hero when stretching well to push away a curling, goalbound effort from Del Piero from 25 yards out. It was increasingly a case of nearly moments for the *Azzurri*, with their forwards just unable to find any way to create a clear-cut chance. Iaquinta nearly found himself free in the box with just a few minutes remaining, but the American defenders were again up to the challenge and cleared for a corner.

Even with just nine players left on the field, the USA had caused problems for Italy and no one watching could have begrudged them victory. With Italy down to ten men, the opportunity had been there but two rash decisions either side of half-time had cost them a chance of going in search of a historic victory. The draw left the group wide open, with all four teams having the possibility of reaching the knockout stages. Italy, the Czech Republic and Ghana all knew that a win for them in their final match would secure qualification, with the USA needing a favourable outcome in the Italy-Czech Republic match, but no matter what happened, the final fixtures would be exciting.

* * *

With all four teams still alive, the calculations for the final outcome were surprisingly straightforward. Italy knew a draw would be enough to see them qualify, the USA needed to win and hope the Czechs failed to win, Ghana and the Czechs knew a win would see them through, and a draw in both matches would see Italy and the Czechs qualify. Relatively simple, right?

The all-European tie was taking place in Hamburg and, with the return of Milan Baroš to the starting line-up, the Czechs set about trying to cause problems for Italy as quickly as possible. The Aston Villa forward had the first opening of the match, seeing his effort well smothered by Buffon. After the disappointment of the Ghana match, it was important that they started well and rediscovered the quality of their play from their first match and there were definite signs of improvement in the opening exchanges. Nedvěd, against the country that had become his adopted home, was running the show. He was dictating the tempo of the play and also providing the best goal threat for his country. It was becoming a running battle between the Juventus team-mates of Nedvěd and Buffon, with the keeper coming out on top on both occasions, following up the second effort with a good save from a rebound from Marek Jankulovski.

As usual with the Italians, their strength lay in their defensive quality. With Alessandro Nesta and Fabio Cannavaro as their central partnership, they boasted perhaps the best defensive pair in the entire tournament. When the Milan defender signalled to the bench after just 17 minutes with nobody around him and no obvious challenge having been made on him, it was a major concern for Lippi's team. It was a cruel blow for Nesta who had seen his experiences at the previous two World Cups cut short due to injury, and the hope was that this was just a slight tweak and the change was precautionary, although that seemed unlikely. The replacement for Nesta was his cross-town rival Marco Materazzi, who would feature in a prominent role coming off the bench.

Having only been on the field for ten minutes, the Internazionale defender rose highest in the penalty area to power home a header from a Totti corner to give Italy the lead. Much like against the USA, it was a goal that came against the run of the play, not that the Italians would particularly care. Unlike the previous match, however, there was no immediate response from their opposition. For all their early positivity, the Italian goal seemed to take all the wind out of the sails of the Czechs. They continued to keep possession of the ball but lacked any spark of creativity to unlock the Italian defence. Half-time was fast approaching and if Czech coach Karel Brückner could get his team back in at the break just the one goal down at worst, then they could regroup. The last thing they needed was for things to slip further from their grasp.

That worst-case scenario was realised in the second minute of added time at the end of the first half when Totti collected the ball near the halfway line and Jan Polák tried to win it back but only succeeded in swiping the legs from the Roma legend instead. It was a clear booking, even if the reaction from Totti was exaggerated, and having already been booked, it meant that the Czechs were down to ten men for the second consecutive match. A man down and a goal down at the break and it certainly felt like all hope was lost for the Eastern Europeans.

It was almost footballing miracle territory but the Czechs were not ranked second-best in the world for no reason and they were refusing to go down without a fight. There was spirit and quality right through the spine of the team. Čech produced a good save from Totti's 20-yard strike before Nedvěd once again burst beyond the Italian defence but found Buffon standing tall to deny him. Baroš and Camoranesi traded headers that went wide of the target before substitute Filippo Inzaghi was played in via a deflection from a Czech defender but dragged his shot beyond the far post. It was a chance that the veteran poacher would have expected to finish, and it would likely have ended the contest.

The Czechs were still alive though, and to their credit never stopped pushing for their equaliser. Predictably, it was Nedvěd running the show with his clever movement and vision, although he still could not find a way past Buffon, no matter what he tried. Everything good was flowing through the blonde-haired playmaker but space was being left as the Czechs pushed forwards and Italy were the perfect team to capitalise on any gaps left. The match was stretched but chances were hard to come by and time was rapidly ticking away. With just three minutes left, Perrotta won the ball in his own half and played it through for Inzaghi to chase. Left free with the entire Czech half to run into, he bore down on Čech, with Simone Barone for company. As expected, *Superpippo* was selfish and used his team-mate's run as a decoy, rounded the goalkeeper and tapped home into the empty net.

It was the goal that clinched the result and sealed both teams' fate. Italy were heading into the knockout phase, while the Czechs were heading home despite their empathetic opening victory. It was a disappointing end to a disappointing tournament for the Eastern Europeans, competing for the first time as a sovereign nation. The loss of Koller was a crucial blow that altered their outlook, but they knew that they had come up short and missed out on the opportunity to shock the watching footballing world and go deep in an international tournament for a second successive showing. The result also meant that the equation in the other match being played at the same time was simple. If the USA could beat Ghana, then, improbably, they would qualify. Any other outcome and the *Black Stars* would reach the knockout stages in their first World Cup.

Ghana and the USA were 400 miles to the south, both attempting to take advantage of the Czechs losing to Italy. Both teams were forced into changes due to suspensions, with Pope and Mastroeni missing for the Americans and, perhaps more crucially, Muntari and Gyan out for Ghana, having been booked in both matches so far. It would have offered a little more optimism for Arena's team, knowing that the two livewires for Ghana would be missing for the biggest match.

Both teams would have been looking for a fast start and it was the Americans who created the first opening of the match, with Dempsey sending a header into the arms of Kingson in the Ghanaian goal. It was a scrappy opening 20 minutes, neither team really able to gain a foothold in midfield and settle into a rhythm. Ghana's first opportunity came from a good press by Haminu Draman, starting in place of Muntari, as he harried Reyna on the ball and stole possession. He took the ball and drove into the USA penalty area before firing a low shot across Keller and into the far corner of the goal. It was a well-taken finish and a goal entirely created by his own tenacity. After losing the ball, Reyna had stayed down, clutching his right knee. In his press, Haminu had clattered into the American captain, with knee-to-knee contact causing pain for the Manchester City midfielder. He tried to battle on, attempting to help drag his team towards the finish line, but could only last 15 minutes longer before being stretchered off and replaced. It was a huge dent in the American chances, as Reyna was their talisman and driving force.

Perhaps inspired by losing their star, the Americans pressed on in search of an all-important equaliser before half-time. When they tried to play more direct, they caused problems for the West Africans, with a long ball flicked on by McBride reaching Landon Donovan, who could only slice his effort wide. Their direct play did eventually pay off just a couple of minutes before half-time when DaMarcus Beasley intercepted a sloppy pass from Derek Boateng and drove towards the left edge of the penalty area. He whipped a brilliant cross in behind the Ghanaian defence to find Dempsey rushing in to lash the ball perfectly into the corner of the goal. It was a counter-attack executed to perfection and gave the USA the perfect platform to build the second half from. Or so they thought.

Just three minutes after getting themselves level, a cross into their penalty area was met by the head of Standard Liège defender Oguchi Onyewu. It was a seemingly good defensive header by the American but the German referee disagreed. Believing that Onyewu had been too forceful on Razak Pimpong in reaching the ball first, the official pointed to the penalty spot and gave Ghana the perfect opportunity to retake the lead before half-time. The replays were pretty conclusive in showing that Markus Merk had made the wrong call, with Pimpong being on the floor seemingly convincing the official that a foul had been committed even though the American defender had won the ball fairly.

The legitimacy of the penalty decision was the least of the concerns of the Ghanaian players and the responsibility was entrusted to their captain, Appiah. The Fenerbahçe midfielder, who had been playing for his country for the previous 11 years and was the crossing point of generations, having replaced Ghanaian legend Abedi Pele on his international debut, was perhaps the most logical choice given that usual penalty taker Gyan was suspended. Any nerves that he may have had were not evident as he stepped up, sent the goalkeeper the wrong way and fired his spot kick into the top left-hand corner of the goal. It was a near-perfect penalty and gave Ghana the all-important lead at the interval.

With the sense of injustice over the penalty decision in their minds, the USA began the second half with a determination about their play. They were causing problems for their opponents with their movement and direct play but were unable to fashion themselves a clear goalscoring opportunity. Donovan came closest to creating a chance for his nation, but his dangerous free kick evaded everyone in the area. It was a theme throughout the tournament for Donovan, who, after winning the best young player award four years earlier in Japan and South Korea, struggled to make any significant impact in this edition and was subject to heavy criticism in the press back home.

As time ticked away, the desperation in the American play became more evident. Decisions were rushed, passes were misplaced and the rhythm that had begun to settle into their play towards the end of the first half had all but disappeared. They never gave up, though, and did nearly find their equaliser when Eddie Lewis worked a little space on the left and played a cross to the near post. McBride, reading the ball better than anybody, got in front of his marker and directed a header towards goal that beat Kingson. Unfortunately for the forward, it bounced off the outside of the post and went wide. It was the best chance that they had created all half and it would have given them enough time to push for the winner they needed.

Time kept ticking away and the Americans kept pushing but they never seemed likely to grab even one goal, let alone the two they needed to qualify. Ghana had produced the performance they needed, although they were helped enormously by a contentious refereeing decision. Despite this clearly going against the Americans, Ghana had been the surprise package of the tournament and fully deserved their place in the knockout stages. They had come through arguably the toughest group in the tournament and had played outstanding football at times. They had a difficult match-up next, with Brazil probably waiting for them in the Round of 16, but they must have fancied their chances against anyone.

6pm, 12 June 2006
Arena AufSchalke, Gelsenkirchen
Attendance: 52,000
Referee: Carlos Amarilla (Paraguay)

USA 0
Czech Republic 3 (Koller 5, Rosický 36, 76)

USA: Kasey Keller, Steve Cherundolo (John O'Brien 46), Eddie Pope, Oguchi Onyewu, Eddie Lewis, DaMarcus Beasley, Claudio Reyna (c), Pablo Mastroeni (Eddie Johnson 46), Bobby Convey, Landon Donovan, Brian McBride (Josh Wolff 77). **Manager:** Bruce Arena.

Czech Republic: Petr Čech, Zdeněk Grygera, David Rozehnal, Tomáš Ujfaluši, Marek Jankulovski, Tomáš Galásek (c), Karel Poborský (Jan Polák 82), Tomáš Rosický (Jiří Štajner 86), Pavel Nedvěd, Jaroslav Plašil, Jan Koller (Vratislav Lokvenc 45). **Manager:** Karel Brückner.

Booked: Onyewu (5), Reyna (60); Rozehnal (16), Lokvenc (59), Rosický (81), Grygera (88)

9pm, 12 June 2006
Niedersachsenstadion, Hanover
Attendance: 43,000
Referee: Carlos Simon (Brazil)

Italy 2 (Pirlo 40, Iaquinta 83)
Ghana 0

Italy: Gianluigi Buffon, Cristian Zaccardo, Alessandro Nesta, Fabio Cannavaro (c), Fabio Grosso, Simone Perrotta, Andrea Pirlo, Daniele De Rossi, Francesco Totti (Mauro Camoranesi 56), Alberto Gilardino (Vincenzo Iaquinta 64), Luca Toni (Alessandro Del Piero 82). **Manager:** Marcello Lippi.

Ghana: Richard Kingson, John Paintsil, John Mensah, Samuel Kuffour, Emmanuel Pappoe (Illiasu Shilla 46), Stephen Appiah (c), Eric Addo, Michael Essien, Sulley Muntari, Asamoah Gyan (Alex Tachie-Mensah 89), Matthew Amoah (Razak Pimpong 68). **Manager:** Ratomir Dujković.

Booked: De Rossi (10), Camoranesi (62), Iaquinta (88); Muntari (41), Gyan (65)

6pm, 17 June 2006
RheinEnergieStadion, Cologne
Attendance: 45,000
Referee: Horacio Elizondo (Argentina)

Czech Republic 0
Ghana 2 (Gyan 2, Muntari 82)

Czech Republic: Petr Čech, Zdeněk Grygera, David Rozehnal, Tomáš Ujfaluši, Marek Jankulovski, Tomáš Galásek (c) (Jan Polák 46), Karel Poborský (Jiří Štajner 56), Tomáš Rosický, Pavel Nedvěd, Jaroslav Plašil (Libor Sionko 68), Vratislav Lokvenc. **Manager:** Karel Brückner.

Ghana: Richard Kingson, John Paintsil, John Mensah, Illiasu Shilla, Habib Mohamed, Otto Addo (Derek Boateng 46), Michael Essien, Stephen Appiah (c), Sulley Muntari, Matthew Amoah (Eric Addo 80), Asamoah Gyan (Razak Pimpong 85). **Manager:** Ratomir Dujković.

Booked: Lokvenc (49); Addo (18), Essien (37), Gyan (66), Boateng (75), Muntari (84), Mohamed (90+3)
Sent off: Ujfaluši (65)

9pm, 17 June 2006
Fritz-Walter-Stadion, Kaiserslautern
Attendance: 46,000
Referee: Jorge Larrionda (Uruguay)

Italy 1 (Gilardino 22)
USA 1 (Zaccardo 27 (o.g.))

Italy: Gianluigi Buffon, Cristian Zaccardo (Alessandro Del Piero 54), Alessandro Nesta, Fabio Cannavaro (c), Gianluca Zambrotta, Simone Perrotta, Andrea Pirlo, Daniele De Rossi, Francesco Totti (Gennaro Gattuso 35), Luca Toni (Vincenzo Iaquinta 61), Alberto Gilardino. **Manager:** Marcello Lippi.

USA: Kasey Keller, Steve Cherundolo, Eddie Pope, Oguchi Onyewu, Carlos Bocanegra, Clint Dempsey (DaMarcus Beasley 62), Claudio Reyna (c), Pablo Mastroeni, Bobby Convey (Jimmy Conrad 52), Landon Donovan, Brian McBride. **Manager:** Bruce Arena.

Booked: Totti (5), Zambrotta (70); Pope (21)
Sent off: De Rossi (28); Mastroeni (45), Pope (47)

4pm, 22 June 2006
Volksparkstadion, Hamburg
Attendance: 50,000
Referee: Benito Archundia (Mexico)

Czech Republic 0
Italy 2 (Materazzi 26, Inzaghi 87)

Czech Republic: Petr Čech, Zdeněk Grygera, Radoslav Kováč (Marek Heinz 78), David Rozehnal, Marek Jankulovski, Jan Polák, Karel Poborský (Jiří Štajner 46), Tomáš Rosický, Pavel Nedvěd (c), Jaroslav Plašil, Milan Baroš (David Jarolím 64). **Manager:** Karel Brückner.

Italy: Gianluigi Buffon, Gianluca Zambrotta, Alessandro Nesta (Marco Materazzi 17), Fabio Cannavaro (c), Fabio Grosso, Gennaro Gattuso, Andrea Pirlo, Simone Perrotta, Mauro Camoranesi (Simone Barone 74), Francesco Totti, Alberto Gilardino (Filippo Inzaghi 60). **Manager:** Marcello Lippi.

Booked: Polák (35); Gattuso (31)
Sent off: Polák (45+2)

4pm, 22 June 2006
Frankenstadion, Nuremberg
Attendance: 41,000
Referee: Markus Merk (Germany)

Ghana 2 (Draman 22, Appiah 45+2 (p))
USA 1 (Dempsey 43)

Ghana: Richard Kingson, John Paintsil, John Mensah, Illiasu Shilla, Habib Mohamed, Derek Boateng (Otto Addo 46), Stephen Appiah (c), Michael Essien, Haminu Draman (Alex Tachie-Mensah 80), Matthew Amoah (Eric Addo 59), Razak Pimpong. **Manager:** Ratomir Dujković.

USA: Kasey Keller, Steve Cherundolo (Eddie Johnson 61), Oguchi Onyewu, Jimmy Conrad, Carlos Bocanegra, Clint Dempsey, Landon Donovan, Claudio Reyna (c) (Ben Olsen 40), DaMarcus Beasley, Eddie Lewis (Bobby Convey 74), Brian McBride. **Manager:** Bruce Arena.

Booked: Essien (5), Shilla (32), Mensah (81), Appiah (90+1); Lewis (7)

Group C	P	W	D	L	GF	GA	GD	PTS
ITALY	3	2	1	0	5	1	+4	7
GHANA	3	2	0	1	4	3	+1	6
CZECH REPUBLIC	3	1	0	2	3	4	-1	3
USA	3	0	1	2	2	6	-4	1

Italy and Ghana qualified

Group F

WHEREAS GROUP E seemed like an even group with no clear favourite, Group F appeared on paper a simple battle for the second qualification spot behind holders Brazil. Previously, being defending champions secured your place in the following edition of the competition, but the rules had been changed prior to 2006, so Brazil had to complete the arduous task that is South American World Cup qualifying. They made light work of the challenge, topping the group and finishing nine points clear of the inter-confederation play-off place that Uruguay failed to take advantage of. *La Celeste* did not manage to qualify as they lost on penalties after a 1-1 aggregate draw against Australia, who would, coincidentally, face Brazil in this group.

Australia had qualified for their first appearance at the finals since 1974 and, led by Guus Hiddink, would be a tricky opposition for any nation that they faced. The *Socceroos* were one of three teams that seemed destined to be fighting to take the second qualification spot along with Croatia and Japan. Croatia had finished third in 1998 on debut but were seeing the end of that generation fade away and the beginnings of the one that would take them to the World Cup Final in 2018 emerge, so it seemed that reaching the knockout stages would be their best scenario. Japan were arriving after their best showing as hosts four years earlier and, with Brazilian legend Zico at the helm, optimism that they would at least match that performance was high.

While Australia would be unable to be drawn into a World Cup group with Japan now, back in 2006 they were still competing in qualifying from the Oceania federation rather than Asia, so they were the opening match-up of Group F. It took only two minutes for the first opening to present itself and it was a self-inflicted one that Australia will have been warning themselves about before the match began. The watching footballing world knew that a major aspect of Japan's play would come from set pieces, as they possessed one of the best dead-ball specialists in world football at the time in Shunsuke Nakamura. The Celtic playmaker, who had just finished his first season in Glasgow, was entering the tournament having provided six goals and ten assists as Celtic won the Scottish Premier League and Scottish League Cup, and was arguably in the best form of his career. He was renowned for his ability to score from free kicks, seemingly able to bend the ball to his will whenever he struck it from a dead-ball situation. Fortunately for Australia, on this occasion the wall did its job and the ball was cleared.

Ultimately, despite Australia controlling the opening exchanges of the match, it was Nakamura who would break the deadlock, albeit in controversial circumstances. He picked the ball up on the right-hand side and floated a hopeful cross into the Australian penalty area. As goalkeeper Mark Schwarzer came to claim the ball, it evaded everyone and ended up in the back of the net. Australia, and particularly Schwarzer, were outraged that the goal was awarded, believing that there had been a foul on the keeper as he came to gather the cross. The replay showed that there was definitely contact between Schwarzer and Atsushi Yanagisawa, which hindered Schwarzer, and had the referee decided to give a free kick to Australia, no one would have batted an eyelid. Yet the Egyptian official saw nothing untoward with the challenge and allowed the goal to stand.

Although it was Japan who had the lead, the *Socceroos* were still making the majority of the running. Mark Viduka was proving too much to handle for the Japanese defenders and he did well to free Bresciano, who should have finished the chance presented to him. Harry Kewell, perhaps Australia's most-talented footballer, was showing all his quality in this match and almost responded immediately after Nakamura's fluked opener but he could only fire his effort over the crossbar.

As the match ticked into the second half, the pattern continued with Australia controlling the tempo and Japan keeping them at a relative distance. Viduka was Australia's biggest outlet and had their best chance of the second period, firing a low free kick under the wall that forced a smart save from the Japanese goalkeeper.

Early in the second half, Hiddink rolled the dice and sent Everton's Tim Cahill on in the hope of forcing an equaliser. He struggled to get into the match but, with just six minutes remaining, he repaid his manager's faith. A long throw from Lucas Neill was missed by the keeper as he came to claim and the ball bobbled free in the area, where Cahill was waiting to tap the ball home and draw his nation level. It was a completely deserved equaliser and sparked something of a chaotic final few minutes. A couple of minutes after the goal, Komano drove into the Australian penalty area and was clearly fouled by Cahill. The referee could not have seen it as it was a stonewall penalty and would have presented the perfect opportunity for a Japanese winner.

The failure to award Japan a clear penalty would come back to haunt them a few minutes later when Aloisi played a simple pass into Cahill's feet on the edge of the area and he whipped a shot across the keeper, against the far post, then watched in relief as the ball rolled across the goal line and into the net. Two goals in five minutes and Cahill had single-handedly turned the match around, although he had nearly cost his team in between.

With Japan pushing forward to grab a leveller of their own, space began opening up and Aloisi had the freedom of the half to drive towards goal before adding the finishing touch and securing the victory for Australia. They had struggled to break Japan down but then scored three goals in the final ten minutes to turn the match on its head. It was the perfect start for Hiddink's team as they had played well and got the result that their performance deserved. Japan had held out for the majority of the match and seemed to be heading towards an undeserved victory but the manner of the defeat will have been deflating for Zico's team. With Croatia and Brazil still to come for both, Australia's incredible turnaround may well have been the spark for their tournament to become memorable.

Between Australia, Japan and Croatia, there were a total of five appearances across all the previous 17 World Cups. Brazil, the other team in the group, had won the tournament on five occasions, while appearing in all 17 editions. To say Brazil had pedigree in the competition would be an understatement and it was obvious why this iteration of the national team was seen as favourites to win the competition once again. They entered the tournament with four players who had reached the 1998 and 2002 finals, as well as a further seven who had been a part of the winning squad four years earlier. There was star quality throughout and the depth to match. Interestingly, only eight players have ever won the Ballon d'Or, European Cup/Champions League and World Cup in their careers, and two of those were featuring in this Brazil squad in Ronaldinho and Kaká.

Although Brazil were strong favourites, Croatia were not a team that could be taken lightly. They had reached the semi-finals on World Cup debut in 1998, narrowly losing to eventual winners France, and always proved to be tricky opposition for the royalty of world football. Although this team was perhaps the mixing point of two great generations, with Zlatko Kranjčar at the helm and talented players still in the squad, Croatia fancied their chances of reaching the knockout stages and causing some upsets on the way.

Predictably, Brazil started the match with the more attacking intent. Playing with a 4-2-2-2 formation to accommodate their so-called magic quartet, Kaka, Ronaldinho, Ronaldo and Adriano, the link-up play was slick but chances were hard to come by. Kaká, the Milan playmaker, was at the heart of most of it, sending his own effort wide, before Stipe Pletikosa produced two quality saves from Roberto Carlos and Ronaldinho. Despite controlling the ball, the *Seleção* were being frustrated by their Croatian counterparts. Even with the loss of future Bayern Munich and Monaco manager Niko Kovač to injury, they were well organised, forcing Brazil into shooting from distance. They even nearly took the lead when Igor Tudor narrowly missed reaching a free kick that would have presented him with a free header on goal.

With half-time fast approaching, the Croatian defensive line was finally breached and it came from the exact type of chance they had been happy to limit their illustrious opponents to. Cafu, at 36 years old and winning his 139th international cap, showed his continued quality with a driving run down the right before laying a simple pass inside to his club colleague Kaká, who turned on to his left foot beyond his two markers before bending a delightful effort beyond Pletikosa's despairing dive. If either team deserved to be leading, it was definitely Brazil, but Croatia could reasonably be disappointed to be going into the interval trailing as they had done a very good job at defending their own penalty box. Yet one moment of true quality from one of the best players on the planet had changed the match.

No longer having the option to defend to pinch a point from the reigning champions, Croatia began to push forward themselves and showed that they were certainly no pushovers. Rangers striker Dado Pršo had been their best outlet in the first half with his running and he had the first opening of the second, running in behind once again, only to see his low effort saved by Dida before being cleared for a corner. As the Europeans pushed forwards, space opened up and Brazil saw chances for Ronaldinho and the unusually quiet Ronaldo come and go, but the match was simmering rather than boiling as neither team was really able to take charge under the Berlin floodlights. The fabled Brazilian attack was unable to get going, with only Kaká able to stamp any authority over proceedings. However, it was only Brazil's opening match of the tournament so the quartet could easily click into gear as it progressed but there was certainly worrying signs throughout this performance.

With Brazil misfiring, Croatia knew that they had an opportunity to produce a moment of magic to snatch a point that could start their tournament well. Marko Babić saw his header saved by Dida before Niko Kranjčar, son of coach Zlatko, could only head over from a clever Pršo cross. Play had to be halted briefly because of a pitch invader and flares being set off in the Croatian section of the crowd, as the travelling support continued to enjoy themselves and make sure that they were heard by all. Sadly, the pyrotechnics in the crowd were the biggest highlights of the final exchanges of the match. Neither team got into a free-flowing rhythm and the outcome was a poor spectacle. With the quality of players in the Brazil squad, it seemed to be a question of whether they could get all their stars singing from the same hymn sheet, a task that manager Carlos Alberto Parreira needed to quickly figure out. For Croatia, a 1-0 defeat to the best international team on the planet was nothing to be ashamed of and, if they could find that spark going forwards, they would be a problem for both Japan and Australia.

* * *

As both teams had lost their opening fixtures, the clash between Japan and Croatia took on extra importance as both knew that a defeat now would see them on the verge of elimination from the tournament. With so much riding on the outcome, it was understandable that the opening exchanges were extremely cagey as nobody wanted to make a mistake that would give their opponent the advantage. The first 20 minutes saw little action, with both teams seemingly content trying to retain possession, although even that was proving tricky in the pressurised atmosphere. Eventually that dreaded mistake did come, though, with Gamba Osaka defender and Japanese captain Tsuneyasu Miyamoto misjudging the flight of the ball and allowing Pršo to sneak in behind. In the panic to try to rectify his mistake, Miyamoto clipped the heels of the Rangers striker and the Belgian referee pointed to the spot to give Croatia the perfect opportunity to take the lead.

The responsibility was handed to Shakhtar Donetsk legend Darijo Srna and it felt like it was in good hands. The full-back, at this stage just 24 years old, was well on his way to a great career that would see him become the most-capped Croatian at one point, as well as Shakhtar's all-time record appearance holder, turning down moves to elite European clubs such as Chelsea and Bayern Munich to stay in Ukraine. His goalscoring record was not a bad one either, finishing his career with 57 goals in 648 club matches and 22 in 134 for his nation, a brilliant return for a player who spent the majority of his career playing as a defender. Back in the sunshine in Nuremburg and Srna stepped up to face Yoshikatsu Kawaguchi with the weight of the nation on his back. He sent his penalty to the goalkeeper's left with pace and accuracy but, unfortunately for him, Júbilo Iwata guessed correctly and brilliantly tipped the ball behind for a corner.

The resulting corner saw a header for Kranjčar, starting after an impressive cameo against Brazil, ripple the side-netting before the match became a series of long-range efforts. The future Portsmouth and Tottenham midfielder, who would earn his move to England after this tournament, was central to Croatia's attacking efforts, rattling the crossbar from 25 yards out, and was the one player on the pitch who seemed capable of producing a moment of quality. Hidetoshi Nakata responded with a long-range effort of his own from 35 yards that was well pushed behind by Pletikosa, before two quickfire Croatian opportunities came and went with Klasnić's effort tipped behind and Pršo heading over when free in the box, a chance he should have done better with.

Where the first half struggled to get going, the second began in a lively fashion with both teams having a good chance in the opening ten minutes. First, Atsushi Yanagisawa pulled a shot wide in front of an open goal, although replays suggested he may have been offside in any case, before Kranjčar found himself with another opening, stabbing an effort wide while on the stretch. It was a difficult chance but one that he would have fancied to at least hit the target with. This brief flurry of activity could have been the spark for an entertaining game of football to break out, but rather than trying to force a winner that could have altered their fortunes dramatically, both teams remained cagey and opted for a risk-free approach that limited the odds of their opponents getting a goal. As Jonathan Wilson noted about Croatia in *Inverting the Pyramid*, 'they played stodgy, tedious football' and 'however aggressive Srna and Marko Babić were as wing-backs, it couldn't disguise the fact that … they were effectively playing with seven defenders'. His sentiments were entirely correct, as although they needed to take charge of the match and attempt to force the issue, their play was predictable and relied on moments of individual brilliance from Kranjčar or a fresh-faced Luka Modrić, who was earning just his sixth international cap and making his World Cup debut.

Despite both teams being passive in possession, the draw kept them both alive in the group. Croatia would have perhaps been the most optimistic, having already played Brazil, while Japan would have to beat the pre-tournament favourites to stand any chance of progression. For Croatia, however, the worry would have been that they had played 180 minutes of World Cup football and had failed to score, only managing nine shots on target. They were playing like a team lacking any belief in themselves and would need a drastic turnaround in fortunes as, no matter the outcome in the other match in the second round of matches, they needed to beat Australia to make it out of the group, as they would have expected prior to the tournament.

Whereas Japan and Croatia were playing to keep their tournament hopes alive, Brazil and Australia knew that victory would confirm their place in the knockout stages of the tournament, a prerequisite for Brazil and a remarkable achievement for Australia. The *Socceroos* knew that they would be up against it but, with Guus Hiddink at the helm, there was every possibility that they could produce a shock result. The veteran Dutch coach, who is the most successful manager his storied nation has ever produced in terms of trophy count, was seasoned at helping his teams punch above their traditional weight, as evidenced by taking PSV to the Champions League semi-finals in 2005 before losing on away goals to Milan, and he would have been hoping to add Brazil to his list of scalps.

With the air of inevitability, Brazil started on the front foot, with Kaká volleying narrowly wide after just three minutes. There was a confidence in their play in the opening exchanges before a strong challenge from Vince Grella on Ronaldo after ten minutes, one he was lucky to escape a card for, changed the feeling. It was a moment that seemed to energise Australia and rattle Brazil, as for the remainder of the first half the South Americans could hardly keep possession with any comfort and their opponents were stifling all their creativity.

The next opening fell to the underdogs, with Jason Culina firing a long-range effort straight into the arms of Dida. Australia had succeeded in turning the match into a battle, with strong challenges, allowing their illustrious opponents no time on the ball and not giving up another clear-cut chance in the opening period. It was exactly as Hiddink would have schemed, and the second half was set for the Australians to go out and produce one of the World Cup's greatest-ever shocks.

Australia, however, were not the only nation with an experienced coach. Carlos Alberto Parreira knew exactly how to guide his nation through the tournament to a successful ending, having been in charge when Brazil won at USA 1994. That experience may have been influential at the interval as Brazil started the second period with a renewed vigour and it only took four minutes for them to find a breakthrough. It was a goal that involved three members of Brazil's fabled magic quartet. Barcelona midfielder Ronaldinho dropped into a deeper, more central role and collected the ball before turning into space, playing a pass into the path of Ronaldo. The striker, who had done brilliantly to arc his run to remain onside, held up the ball while surrounded by two defenders. He in turn played the ball across the edge of the penalty area for his strike partner, who took a touch on to his left foot and unleashed a low, powerful, trademark finish beyond the despairing dive of Schwarzer.

This was the peak of Adriano's powers. In the previous two years, the Internazionale forward had scored 19 goals in 23 international appearances, and 47 in 89 for the *Nerazzurri*. His arrival on the global stage was heralded across Brazil as he was seen as the perfect player to take on Ronaldo's mantle after he retired. Ronaldo's career was clearly drawing to a close, with a lot of media attention being drawn to his form and weight, and the hope and perhaps even expectation was that Brazil could retain their title with both strikers in place and then Adriano would help the *Seleção* remain at the sharp end of future World Cups. Unfortunately for both player and nation, Adriano's stock fell sharply after 2006 was over and he never managed to reach the heights expected of him. Personal issues off the field and struggles on it combined to see a highly promising player fade into the footballing abyss, condemned to be remembered more for his legendary status on video game Pro Evolution Soccer 6 than any achievements in the real world.

Adriano's goal, rather than breaking the Australians' spirit, simply served to motivate them to another level. They almost immediately had a great chance, with Bresciano bursting free down the left-hand side, but as he tried to cut back on to his right foot, Zé Roberto managed to get back to make the crucial challenge. Then came the moment that Australia had been waiting for. A looped ball into the box was fumbled by Dida who simply dropped it directly at the feet of Harry Kewell with an open goal to aim for. The Liverpool winger had to take his shot quickly, acting largely on reflex, but could only send his effort over the crossbar, although the diving presence of the Brazil goalkeeper may have put him off.

The tricky winger continued to be an outlet for his nation, bursting forwards on the counter-attack a few minutes later only to be denied by another excellent Zé Roberto tackle. The third opening for Kewell since being introduced as a substitute arrived shortly after, when he broke free on the left and saw Dida off his line and backpedalling. Kewell attempted to lob the ball over him, watching as it narrowly went over, flicking the top of the net on its way.

As the match entered the final ten minutes, it became increasingly stretched as Australia pushed for an equaliser and left space on the counter for Brazil. Robinho narrowly volleyed over after cleverly setting himself up, before Bresciano saw his acrobatic effort clawed away by a scrambling Dida. Kaká then saw his header from Ronaldinho's corner hit the crossbar, before Mark Viduka chipped over Dida as he rushed out, seeing his effort land on top of the goal. As added time approached, Robinho found space on the right and fired a low shot beyond Schwarzer that rebounded back off the post. It fell straight to the feet of Fred, who had only been on the pitch for a minute, and he could not miss the open goal, tapping in for confirmation of the victory for Brazil.

It had been a battling performance for the world champions against a well-organised and talented Australian outfit, and they would have been relieved to come away with the three points, despite their coach saying the result was never in doubt. The win had secured their qualification into the knockout stages with a match to spare and, as they had yet to find their best form, the hope was that they could improve before peaking at the business end of the tournament. For Australia, three points from the first two matches was an expected outcome and the final match against Croatia was always likely to have been key to their chances of progression. They entered that match knowing that a draw would be enough to see them reach the next round and, after pushing Brazil to the limit, they would have certainly fancied their chances.

* * *

Having only picked up a single point against Australia and Croatia, Japan knew that their chances of reaching the knockout stages for a second consecutive tournament were incredibly slim. The *Samurai Blue* needed to beat Brazil by three goals and would then have to rely on Croatia and Australia drawing. Brazil, knowing that a point would be enough to secure top spot and a meeting with Ghana in the second round, rotated their team, making five changes, giving starts to Juninho and Robinho and resting Cafu, Roberto Carlos and Zé Roberto for the knockout phase.

Even with the changes, Brazil seemed more fluent than they had at any point in the tournament, perhaps freed by the pressure being lifted from their shoulders. Inside the opening 25 minutes, Japanese goalkeeper Kawaguchi produced five top-quality saves to keep the scores level. Ronaldo and Robinho both saw two efforts turned behind for corners, while Juninho's 25-yarder was brilliantly tipped over by the best save of the lot. There was even time for Kaká to shoot over from the edge of the area as well. Under the floodlights in Dortmund, Brazil were showing why they had entered the tournament as favourites to lift the trophy. They were moving the ball with confidence, creating space for each other and could have been out of sight if not for the sharp reflexes of the Japanese goalkeeper. Then, in true unpredictable football style, the opening goal came for Japan.

Although it was against the run of play, the opening goal was brilliantly executed. Japan's Alessandro Santos, the left-back more commonly known as Alex, carried the ball on into the opposing half, taking advantage of the space left in behind Brazil's right-back Cicinho, who had pushed forwards. Cutting inside, Alex's options seemed limited but he managed to play a fine disguised pass with the outside of his left foot that freed Keiji Tamada in behind the Brazil defence. The Nagoya Grampus Eight striker did not even need to take a touch, simply letting the ball run beyond him before rifling a fierce shot beyond Dida at his near post, the sheer power on the strike making it impossible to save.

Having taken the shock lead, if they could hold out until half-time, Zico and Japan would have been feeling confident. And they seemed to be heading to the interval with their lead intact. Brazil had gone back to keeping the ball and moving it but were wasting half-chances with wayward finishing. Undeterred, the champions built slowly and forced the Japanese defenders into chasing the ball, allowing space for Ronaldinho to float a cross to the back post for Cicinho. The Real Madrid full-back, in the most advanced position of any of his team-mates, reacted with a forward's instinct and headed the ball back across the penalty area for his more accomplished club and international team-mate Ronaldo, who had the simple task of powering a header beyond the keeper, in doing so becoming the 20th player in history to score at three World Cup finals. Brazil had been playing some outstanding football during the half, the best they had managed all tournament to this point, and their goal seemed to take all the wind out of Japanese sails.

It only took eight minutes of the second half for Brazil to claim the lead. After his heroics of the first half, the second Brazilian goal can only be described as a glaring error by Kawaguchi. Olympique Lyonnais midfielder Juninho received the ball in acres of space and 30 yards from goal. He hit a speculative shot but it was fired directly at the goalkeeper. However, he was unable to lay a glove on the ball, watching helplessly as it flew past his hands and into the back of the net. It was a well-hit shot but one the keeper would have been disappointed had gone beyond his grasp.

Once Brazil had taken the lead there was only one outcome, the only question being how impressive the final result would ultimately look. Just six minutes later Ronaldinho, who was producing his best performance of the tournament, turned into space on the halfway line before playing Hertha Berlin defender Gilberto in down the left-hand side. Having reached the penalty area and realising that there was no sensible passing option for him, he decided to strike a shot on goal, sending it low and out of reach of the keeper, who could only watch as the ball nestled almost perfectly in the bottom corner. It was a goal befitting a striker rather than the only international goal of Gilberto's career.

With the result all but secure and both teams' fates settled, the match drifted towards its conclusion, although there was time for another goal, and it was an important one at that. Central defender Juan, most well-known for his spells in Germany and Italy with Bayer Leverkusen and Roma, channelled his inner adventurer and brought the ball forwards from the back, linking nicely with Ronaldo before the striker swivelled on to his right foot and fired a brilliant effort into the bottom corner. More than just the icing on the cake, this goal was the 14th that the striker had recorded at the World Cup, equalling the all-time record of legendary German striker Gerd Müller. With Brazil looking their sharpest and showing signs of clicking into top gear, it appeared likely that that record would soon be broken.

Japan's tournament ended with little more than a whimper, although there was a brief ten-minute spell towards the end of the first half when qualification seemed possible. Had they held on against Australia and won their opening match, the atmosphere in the camp may have been different and they may have proven more difficult opposition. Alas, it was an early exit for the island nation, unable to match their achievement from four years prior as hosts and a disappointing World Cup as a whole.

With Japan losing to Brazil in Dortmund, the situation nearly 300 miles away in Stuttgart was clear. Australia knew a single point was enough to see them qualify for the knockout stages for the first-ever time, while Croatia needed a victory that would see them pip their opponents to the finish line. Knowing the onus was on them to attack, Croatia could hardly have wished for a better start, taking the lead after just three minutes. Winning a free kick slightly left of centre about 25-yards from goal, Darijo Srna, who had missed the vital penalty against Japan, stepped up and perfectly whipped the ball over the top of the wall and into the top corner. It was the dream start for Croatia and the perfect way for Srna to make amends.

With so much resting on the outcome, it would have been easy to understand had the match settled into a tense affair. However, both teams seemed determined to get the result on their own terms and the contest was played at an electric pace more akin to a basketball game. Australia had a penalty shout denied when Mark Viduka claimed he was being held by Stjepan Tomas, before Kewell's long-range strike was well saved. Neither team were creating many good openings, despite the high-octane nature of the play, and it took a defensive mistake to allow Australia back into the contest. While attempting to clear the ball from a simple cross, Tomas got it all wrong and the ball struck his outstretched left arm. Referee Graham Poll had little option but to award a penalty. Craig Moore, the Newcastle United defender, was perhaps a surprising choice to take the pressurised spot kick but he stepped up confidently and sent the ball into the roof of the net, waiting for the keeper to move before striking the ball to maximise the chances of scoring. It was a calm penalty under the circumstances and a goal that saw Australia through if the scores remained the same.

Viduka and Pršo both had chances before half-time, with the Australian heading straight at Pletikosa, before the Croat dragged his effort wide when he really should have at least hit the target. Thanks to the profligacy of both teams, the score remained level at 1-1 at the interval and Australia knew that if they could wrestle control over the match, they would be able to progress with this scoreline.

However, Croatia were showing a resilience and attacking intent that had been missing during their previous two matches and retook the lead just 12 minutes into the second half, with their captain Nico Kovač shooting from range and watching as his shot bobbled over the gloves of Zeljko Kalac in the Australian goal. It had been a surprise decision from Hiddink to drop Mark Schwarzer in favour of the Milan goalkeeper Kalac, and as Kovač's shot settled in the back of the net, it may well have been a decision that the Dutch coach was regretting. The pressure was now back on Australia to force the issue and to their credit they did push forward in search of that vital goal.

Harry Kewell watched as his shot was tipped over by Pletikosa, before the Shakhtar Donetsk keeper produced a world-class double save, diving at the feet of multiple Australians and managing to grab hold of the loose ball to stop it rolling over the line. It was a remarkable double save and one that would have had the Australians doubting whether it was going to be their day. Those doubts would have only increased when they had another shout for a penalty waved away by Poll, even though the replays showed that it was a very similar incident to the one that he had given a penalty for in the first half.

With just 11 minutes remaining, Mark Bresciano sent in a hopeful cross that was flicked on by John Aloisi. The ball reached Kewell, who controlled calmly on his chest before smashing the ball into the back of net. It was a moment of quality from Kewell who had too often failed to produce when the stakes were at their highest, but he had just scored possibly the most important goal in Australian footballing history.

The match sparked into madness within the last five minutes and it all revolved around the officials. With just five minutes remaining, and with Croatia pushing for an equaliser, the Australians tried to waste time whenever possible, and with

Kewell doing that job well, Dario Šimić decided to speed play along and swiped away his legs. It was a clear booking and the second one the defender had received, so he was given his marching orders. The extra player advantage should have given Australia the momentum they needed to see the match out but the numerical disparity only lasted two minutes as Brett Emerton, already on a booking, clearly handled a ball that was heading down the side line and was correctly shown a red card. Two red cards in two minutes and the match was quickly descending into chaos.

If two red cards and four goals were not enough, one of the most infamous incidents in World Cup history was about to unfold. With cards being distributed freely, Josip Šimunić earned himself a yellow card as the match headed into injury time. Graham Poll took his name and number and walked away to set up the Australian free kick. The peculiarity came from the fact that Šimunić had already been shown a yellow card earlier in the half, so the yellow card just received should have been followed by a red. In subsequent interviews, Poll has admitted to taking down the wrong player details for the first yellow card, mistaking the Croat for an Australian, presumably due to Šimunić's Australian accent as he had been born in Canberra. Despite the mitigating circumstances, it was a nightmare for the English official and it was the last match that he would officiate at the tournament.

With so little time left, more drama seemed unlikely. Yet Australia found time to score a winning goal to cement their passage to the next round, but the whistle had mysteriously been blown and, with no foul being signalled, the only conclusion was that the whistle was the final one. Confusion seemed to be everywhere in the ground except for Šimunić, who, seemingly determined to help Poll correct his mistake, finally received his marching orders after confronting the ref. Four goals, three red cards, and a player not being sent off after two yellow cards. It was a chaotic fixture helped by suspect officiating and it created a memorable spectacle for the watching world. The final result, a 2-2 draw, meant that Australia had qualified for the knockout stages on their return to the tournament, a remarkable achievement by Hiddink and his squad.

Croatia would have been disappointed to see their tournament end in this manner but this was the meeting point of two outstanding generations of footballers in their nation. Failure to make it out of the group at this edition was unfortunate, but the rise of Luka Modrić had been a success and would become the catalyst for Croatia reaching the 2018 World Cup Final in Moscow, sadly losing 4-2 to France, and then the semi-finals at the 2022 edition.

3pm, 12 June 2006
Fritz-Walter-Stadion, Kaiserslautern
Attendance: 46,000
Referee: Essam Abd El Fatah (Egypt)

Australia 3 (Cahill 84, 89, Aloisi 90+2)
Japan 1 (Nakamura 26)

Australia: Mark Schwarzer, Craig Moore (Joshua Kennedy 61), Lucas Neill, Scott Chipperfield, Luke Wilkshire (John Aloisi 75), Brett Emerton, Vince Grella, Mark Bresciano (Tim Cahill 53), Jason Culina, Harry Kewell, Mark Viduka (c). **Manager:** Guus Hiddink.

Japan: Yoshikatsu Kawaguchi, Keisuke Tsuboi (Teruyuki Moniwa (Masashi Oguro 90+1)), Tsuneyasu Miyamoto (c), Yuji Nakazawa, Yūichi Komano, Hidetoshi Nakata, Takashi Fukunishi, Alessandro Santos, Shunsuke Nakamura, Naohiro Takahara, Atsushi Yanagisawa (Shinji Ono 79). **Manager:** Zico.

Booked: Grella (33), Moore (58), Cahill (69), Aloisi (78); Miyamoto (31), Takahara (40), Moniwa (68)

9pm, 13 June 2006
Olympiastadion, Berlin
Attendance: 72,000
Referee: Benito Archundia (Mexico)

Brazil 1 (Kaká 44)
Croatia 0

Brazil: Dida, Cafu (c), Lúcio, Juan, Roberto Carlos, Emerson, Zé Roberto, Kaká, Ronaldinho, Adriano, Ronaldo (Robinho 70). **Manager:** Carlos Alberto Parreira.

Croatia: Stipe Pletikosa, Dario Šimić, Robert Kovač, Josip Šimunić, Darijo Srna, Igor Tudor, Niko Kovač (c) (Jerko Leko 41), Marko Babić, Niko Kranjčar, Ivan Klasnić (Ivica Olić 56), Dado Pršo. **Manager:** Zlatko Kranjčar.

Booked: Emerson (42); N. Kovač (32), R. Kovač (67), Tudor (90)

3pm, 18 June 2006
Frankenstadion, Nuremberg
Attendance: 41,000
Referee: Frank De Bleeckere (Belgium)

Japan 0
Croatia 0

Japan: Yoshikatsu Kawaguchi, Akira Kaji, Tsuneyasu Miyamoto (c), Yuji Nakazawa, Alessandro Santos, Hidetoshi Nakata, Takashi Fukunishi (Junichi Inamoto 46), Mitsuo Ogasawara, Shunsuke Nakamura, Naohiro Takahara (Masashi Oguro 85), Atsushi Yanagisawa (Keiji Tamada 61). **Manager:** Zico.

Croatia: Stipe Pletikosa. Dario Šimić, Robert Kovač, Josip Šimunić, Darijo Srna (Ivan Bošnjak 87), Igor Tudor (Ivica Olić 70), Niko Kovač (c), Marko Babić, Niko Kranjčar (Luka Modrić 78), Ivan Klasnić, Dado Pršo. **Manager:** Zlatko Kranjčar.

Booked: Miyamoto (21), Kawaguchi (42), Santos (72); R. Kovač (32), Srna (69)

6pm, 18 June 2006
FIFA World Cup Stadium,, Munich
Attendance: 66,000
Referee: Markus Merk (Germany)

Brazil 2 (Adriano 49, Fred 90)
Australia 0

Brazil: Dida, Cafu (c), Lúcio, Juan, Roberto Carlos, Emerson (Gilberto Silva 72), Zé Roberto, Kaká, Ronaldinho, Adriano (Fred 88), Ronaldo (Robinho 72) **Manager:** Carlos Alberto Parreira

Australia: Mark Schwarzer, Craig Moore (John Aloisi 69), Lucas Neill, Tony Popovic, Mark Bresciano, Vince Grella, Scott Chipperfield, Jason Culina, Tim Cahill (Harry Kewell 56), Mile Sterjovski, Mark Viduka (c). **Manager:** Guus Hiddink.

Booked: Cafu (29), Ronaldo (31), Robinho (83); Emerton (13), Culina (39)

9pm, 22 June 2006
Westfalenstadion, Dortmund
Attendance: 65,000
Referee: Éric Poulat (France)

Japan 1 (Tamada 34)
Brazil 4 (Ronaldo 45+1, 81, Juninho 53, Gilberto 59)

Japan: Yoshikatsu Kawaguchi, Akira Kaji, Keisuke Tsuboi, Yuji Nakazawa (c), Alessandro Santos, Shunsuke Nakamura, Hidetoshi Nakata, Junichi Inamoto, Mitsuo Ogasawara (Kōji Nakata 56), Seiichiro Maki (Naohiro Takahara 56 (Masashi Oguro 66)), Keiji Tamada **Manager:** Zico.

Brazil: Dida (c) (Rogério Ceni 82), Cicinho, Lúcio, Juan, Gilberto, Juninho, Gilberto Silva, Kaká (Zé Roberto 71), Ronaldinho (Ricardinho 71), Robinho, Ronaldo **Manager:** Carlos Alberto Parreira.

Booked: Kaji (40); Gilberto (44)

9pm, 22 June 2006
Gottlieb-Daimler-Stadion, Stuttgart
Attendance: 52,000
Referee: Graham Poll (England)

Croatia 2 (Srna 2, N. Kovač 56)
Australia 2 (Moore 38 (p), Kewell 79)

Croatia: Stipe Pletikosa, Dario Šimić, Stjepan Tomas (Ivan Klasnić 83), Josip Šimunić, Darijo Srna, Igor Tudor, Niko Kovač (c), Marko Babić, Niko Kranjčar (Jerko Leko 65), Ivica Olić (Luka Modrić 74), Dado Pršo. **Manager:** Zlatko Kranjčar.

Australia: Zeljko Kalac, Craig Moore, Lucas Neill, Scott Chipperfield (Joshua Kennedy 75), Mile Sterjovski (Mark Bresciano 71), Vince Grella (John Aloisi 63), Brett Emerton, Jason Culina, Tim Cahill, Harry Kewell, Mark Viduka (c). **Manager:** Guus Hiddink.

Booked: Šimić (32), Tudor (38), Šimunić (61), Pletikosa (70), Šimunić (90); Emerton (81)
Sent off: Šimić (85), Šimunić (90+3); Emerton (87)

Group C	P	W	D	L	GF	GA	GD	PTS
BRAZIL	3	3	0	0	7	1	+6	9
AUSTRALIA	3	1	1	1	5	5	0	4
CROATIA	3	0	2	1	2	3	-1	2
JAPAN	3	0	1	2	2	7	-5	1

Brazil and Australia qualified

The decision to award Germany the right to host the 2006 World Cup was not without its controversy

Germany's Philipp Lahm scores a brilliant opening goal of the tournament, setting the tone for the rest of the competition

The Czech Republic were predicted by many to be a surprise package but flattered to deceive, exiting at the group stage

Esteban Cambiasso celebrates scoring the greatest team goal in World Cup history during Argentina's demolition of Serbia and Montenegro

18-year-old Lionel Messi wheels away after scoring his first World Cup goal.

Peter Crouch gives England the lead against a resolute Trinidad and Tobago with a helping handful of Brent Sancho's dreadlocks

This tournament came just too soon for the blossoming Spanish generation but this was the point when the momentum began to shift

Not every match can be a classic, with Switzerland and Ukraine playing out the dullest one in World Cup history

Russian referee Valentin Ivanov handed out a record four red cards during Portugal's infamous last-16 tie with the Netherlands

The tournament's motto may have been 'A Time to Make Friends' but no love was lost between Germany and Argentina after their quarter-final meeting

As always, the Brazilian line-up was littered with incredible talent, but they failed to make it count

The England line-up before their quarter-final defeat on penalties to Portugal

Wayne Rooney sees red after a stamp on Ricardo Carvalho. England would go on to lose on penalties once again

Unlikely hero Fabio Grosso runs away in disbelief after scoring Italy's match-winning goal in the 119th minute of the World Cup semi-final win over Germany

German fans showing their pride for their nation at the Fan Fest at the Brandenburg Gate during the third-place play-off

The world holds its breath as Zidane attempts the audacious, breathing a sigh of relief as his Panenka penalty bounces off the crossbar and behind Gianluigi Buffon's goal line

Marco Materazzi powers over Patrick Vieira to cancel out Zidane's opener. It would not be the last connection between the two

The last act of Zidane's remarkable footballing career

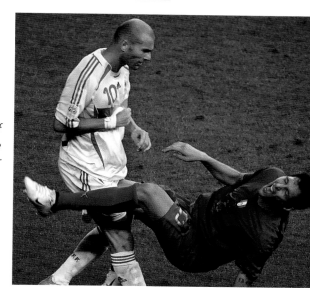

Zidane exits the football stage past the trophy he had almost single-handedly dragged his nation to for a second time

Fabio Grosso celebrates scoring the winning penalty in the final as Italy beat France 5-3 in the shoot-out after a tense 1-1 draw

Fabio Cannavaro raises the World Cup trophy aloft after captaining his nation to their fourth World Cup title

Group G

IF, AS HAS become a key tradition in the build-up to a World Cup, you were filling in a pre-tournament bracket to predict the final outcome, then Group G would have seemed like one of the more easily predictable groups. There was France, the clear favourites to top the group, debutants Togo, the weakest team, and Switzerland and South Korea left to battle for the second qualification spot. If form and history held, with France winning all their matches and Togo losing all theirs, then the match between the Swiss and South Koreans would be the key one. Yet football is not a game played on paper and France were not exactly the dominant power that they had been in recent years. After winning the 1998 edition on home soil as well as the European Championship two years later, they had entered the World Cup in 2002 with expectations of retaining their title, as a large majority of their squad remained intact. Instead, they had been eliminated after the group stages, having earned a solitary point and failing to score a single goal.

Qualification for 2006 had also been a struggle. Drawn into a relatively simple group containing Switzerland, Israel, Republic of Ireland, Cyprus and the Faroe Islands, France toiled, drawing with both Israel and Switzerland and needing to coax Zidane, Thuram and Vieira out of international retirement to secure qualification. The qualifying group had been extremely tight, with France topping it with 20 points, followed by Switzerland and Israel on 18 and Ireland with 17. The Swiss went into the play-offs, courtesy of their better goal difference, and progressed via the away goals rule in a fiery clash with Turkey.

While the two European nations were preparing to meet for a third competitive fixture in 18 months, the group was being opened in Frankfurt by South Korea and Togo. South Korea were coming into the tournament after their best-ever showing at a World Cup, finishing fourth as hosts in 2002, although that was certainly not without its controversy. On their run to the semi-finals they had been the beneficiaries of numerous favourable decisions, notably in their quarter-final clash with Italy, and there had been suggestions of a conspiracy designed to help one of the two hosts reach the latter stages of the tournament, although these largely came from the Italian media, who were disgruntled at their country's exit from the competition.

If South Korea were unlikely to repeat their exploits from the previous tournament, the odds were stacked even further against Togo. At 61st in the FIFA rankings, they were the lowest-ranked team in the tournament. Togo, the West African nation situated alongside Benin between Ghana and Nigeria and with a population of approximately eight million, were entering their first World Cup and had just a handful of appearances in the AFCON, finishing without a single point during the edition held earlier in 2006. Much like Angola being drawn in the same group as their former colonisers Portugal, Togo had been afforded the same opportunity against France, although the meeting would be the final group game rather than the opener. The fact that Togo had even reached this stage at all was a remarkable achievement in itself.

The smallest African nation in terms of population to ever reach the finals of the World Cup, *Les Éperviers*, the Sparrowhawks, had navigated a tricky qualifying group containing Senegal, who had reached the World Cup quarter-finals four years earlier. Heading into the final qualification fixtures, Togo had a surprising two-point lead over Senegal and held their fate in their own hands, being propelled by the goals of Arsenal striker Emmanuel Adebayor, who finished as top scorer with 11. With Senegal three goals ahead and cruising in Dakar against Mali, Togo were faltering, 2-1 behind away to Congo. With the pressure now firmly on, it was time for a national hero to emerge and it came in the form of Mohammed Kader. The striker, playing for mid-table Guingamp in the French second division, had only scored once all qualifying campaign but stepped up when it really counted and scored twice in ten minutes to turn the match completely on its head. Togo held on to the lead and earned themselves their first-ever appearance at the World Cup finals.

The drama for Togo, however, was not just limited to the pitch. With World Cup qualifying doubling as qualifying for the AFCON being held at the start of the same year, Togo's impressive performance had also earned them a place in the tournament being held in Egypt. A poor performance during the competition, losing all three matches they participated in, saw Nigerian coach Stephen Keshi replaced by experienced German manager Otto Pfister. The German was expected to make Togo competitive and hopefully produce a shock on the biggest stage. Instead, he became the story. Pfister quit his position in charge on the eve of the tournament, citing his inability to work under the conditions imposed by the Togolese football federation. The players apparently stepped in and persuaded their new coach to return, but the roots of discontent had been fully exposed at this point.

The Togolese players, instrumental in bringing their coach back, were also gaining their own headlines when they went on strike prior to the tournament. Their strike was in protest over unpaid bonuses in relation to them reaching the finals in Germany. Or at least that was their side of the story. The other side was that the originally agreed money had been paid to the players but now they were demanding more, or increased bonuses for their matches in the tournament itself. The players were allegedly asking for $200,000 for their successful qualifying campaign and $40,000 per win at the finals. With the players and the coach back, attention could finally turn back to the pitch and their opening fixture against South Korea.

As would be the case throughout a majority of the tournament, the weather played a factor in the opening exchanges. The players were feeling the effects of the heatwave that was being experienced across Europe, hitting Germany particularly hard, and this led to the matches sometimes failing to kick into the highest gear. This was in the days before FIFA introduced cooling breaks for matches played above certain temperatures, and the players would certainly feel the effects of the searing heat. In Frankfurt for Group G's opening fixture the heat created a cagey opening half an hour. Adebayor and Kader nearly combined, but the Arsenal striker's cross narrowly evaded his strike partner, who claimed he had been fouled as the ball came over, but it would have been a harsh penalty.

The first true moment of quality came just after the half-hour mark and it fell to the debutants. A hopeful ball forward was misjudged by the South Korean defender and Kader took a composed touch before firing a low shot across the goalkeeper and into the back of the net. The opening chance of the game had led to the opening goal. Kader's strike put the tails up for Togo and they nearly doubled their lead before half-time when Yao Junior Sènaya struck a free kick on target, producing a fine stop from South Korean captain and keeper Lee Woon-jae. The interval arrived and Togo had the lead in their first-ever World Cup match and had looked solid in achieving it. Getting through the first ten minutes of the second half unscathed would have been the message from Pfister.

That plan lasted all of eight minutes. Manchester United midfielder Park Ji-sung won possession and was bursting through the middle of the pitch when he was clearly impeded by Jean-Paul Abalo. The referee had little choice but to show the APOEL Nicosia defender and Togolese captain a second yellow card and send him for an early bath. As if the sending-off was not punishment enough, when Lee Chun-soo whipped the resulting free kick over the wall and across the goal into the back of the net to bring South Korea level, the punishment doubled. Things could have become even worse just two minutes later when Lee Young-pyo was bundled to the floor in the penalty area for what looked like a clear penalty, but English ref Graham Poll was unconvinced and waved play on.

Seemingly undeterred by the red card, Togo still retained belief that they could get something from the match. They nearly retook the lead when a cross into the area found Adebayor but the star man could not bring the ball under control, then Salifou wasted a chance when shooting over from outside the area.

Despite their endeavour, Togo were always fighting an uphill battle and South Korea began slowly turning the screw. The pressure eventually told when Ahn Jung-hwan received the ball on the edge of the area, turned smartly to his right before hitting a shot into the top corner, albeit via a deflection from Daré Nibombé. The Duisburg striker nearly doubled the advantage just three minutes later but found his effort well saved, before Adebayor managed to fashion a shooting opportunity for himself, although he had fouled his marker in finding the space and was penalised before he could get his shot away.

With a player advantage and fatigue setting in due to the extreme heat the match was being played under, the last ten minutes passed by without any incident, South Korea controlling the closing moments professionally. It was a vital victory that looked unlikely at the interval and one that started their campaign in the perfect way. Togo could perhaps feel unfortunate with the outcome of the match, given that they were the only team to create anything in a cagey first half. Ill-discipline and a lack of clinical finishing had cost them their first-ever point, and facing Switzerland and France next hardly offered much hope of having anything positive to show from their first World Cup.

Reaching the finals had been no easy feat for either of the two European nations in Group G, with both progressing from the same qualifying group. The matches between the two had both ended in draws, with France also failing to win against Israel home and away and being held in Paris by Ireland. The Swiss had similar woes, ultimately drawing six of their ten matches. France were struggling to find traction in the rebuild that new French coach Raymond Domenech had been tasked with, so he turned to the French hero from the 1998 World Cup, trying to coax Zinedine Zidane out of international retirement. The Real Madrid playmaker answered his nation's call and even went one step further, convincing Juventus's Lilian Thuram and Chelsea's Claude Makélélé to join him in returning to the international set-up. What followed were two wins and a draw before a 4-0 thumping of Cyprus in their final group match, which saw France top the group ahead of Switzerland, who had been held in Dublin by the Irish in a result that was not ideal for either team.

Despite that draw, Switzerland remained in second place in the qualifying group and earned a spot in the play-offs, being unseeded due to the fact they were the fifth-lowest-ranked nation. Perhaps fortunately they avoided Spain and the Czech Republic, being matched with Turkey, World Cup semi-finalists from four years earlier but not as effective a team anymore. The first leg in

Berne was fairly comfortable for Switzerland, with goals from Philippe Senderos and Valon Behrami earning an impressive 2-0 victory to take to Istanbul four days later. When Alexander Frei converted a penalty just two minutes into the return leg, everything seemed to be in the Swiss' favour as the away goals rule meant Turkey now needed four goals without reply. Tuncay Şanlı, most notable for his hat-trick for Fenerbahçe against Manchester United in the Champions League, scored twice before half-time, then Necati Ateş calmly converted a penalty soon afterwards to give Turkey a 3-1 lead on the night and level the scores on aggregate, although the Swiss still had the away goal advantage.

With the Turks pushing to grab their winner, they were hit with a sucker-punch as Marco Streller took the score to 4-3 overall. This was just the start of the drama though. Tuncay completed his hat-trick with a minute remaining in normal time and Turkey had hope once more. They threw everything they had at the Swiss, backed by a raucous Istanbul crowd, but could not find that extra gear to convert a chance that would have given them the overall lead. As the final whistle blew, players and officials from both teams sprinted towards the tunnel as chaos erupted. Tensions had been high after the first leg in which Turkish players claimed that they had been treated unfairly and the Swiss had been disrespectful by disrupting the Turkish national anthem. The Turkish assistant manager appeared to aim a kick at Valon Behrami, sparking scenes of players from both teams kicking out and a brawl erupting in the depths of the stadium, leading to Swiss defender Stéphane Grichting being hospitalised.

The fallout was exacerbated by FIFA President Sepp Blatter, a Swiss national, seemingly laying the entire blame for the confrontation at the feet of the Turks and threatening to ban them from the 2010 World Cup. Turkish officials felt the sanctions were ultimately political and based on Blatter's nationality rather than the actual events. It was an unsavoury ending to a two-legged contest marked by tension and unease, but the Swiss had confirmed their place in Germany and a third competitive meeting with neighbours France in just over a year.

France were in the midst of rebuilding their national set-up after the retirement of several stars of the previous generation. This was evident in their line-up for the opening match, with just five starters in the line-up that also started the World Cup against Senegal four years earlier. Despite this, the average age of the XI selected by Domenech was just shy of 30, with just one player aged under 26. It was the old guard that created the opening chances as well, with Sylvain Wiltord crossing for his one-time Arsenal team-mate Henry, who could not quite get over the ball and headed over. Then another player with a French-Arsenal connection, Patrick Vieira, got free at the back post from a corner but could only bobble his shot into the ground and it bounced harmlessly over the bar.

If the experienced French players had been the ones to start well, it was the youngest player in the squad who was capturing the headlines by the end of the first half. Fresh from a first season with Marseille and helping the famous club to a French Cup final, there were high hopes resting on the shoulders of Franck Ribéry. The tricky winger was used to the attention of the media being firmly fixated on him, especially after his move from Galatasaray to Marseille. Having helped win the Turkish Cup with a goal and an assist against bitter rivals Fenerbahçe, his stock was rising among the Istanbul faithful. Yet, at the end of the 2004/05 season he announced that he would be joining Marseille, with his current employers unaware of the development and Ribéry still having three years left on his contract.

The Frenchman claimed that he had only been paid once since arriving in the Turkish city and asked FIFA to invalidate his contract to allow him to join Marseille. His request was agreed by the governing body, leading to Galatasaray launching an appeal with the Court of Arbitration for Sport. The verdict was finally reached in April 2007, with Ribéry nearly at the end of his second season back in France and a couple of months away from joining Bayern Munich, and was decided against the Turkish club, saying that Ribéry ended his contract on valid grounds and the club was not entitled to the €10 million that they had been claiming from Marseille.

On the pitch, in arguably the biggest match of his young career so far, Ribéry was the shining star. Playing on the left of the attacking trio behind Henry, he was finding space to cut on to his favoured right foot and was causing problems for the Swiss defence. He was direct with his running and created two good openings for himself, wriggling free on the edge of the area before shooting over and, perhaps not showing a selfishness that would arrive later in his career, having an opportunity to get a shot away but instead squaring the ball to Henry, whose shot was blocked by the arm of Patrick Müller, although the referee did not think it was worthy of a penalty.

Although Ribéry was showing the watching football world the talent that would see him remain at the elite level of football for nearly 15 years, the match itself was a drab affair. With the temperature reaching nearly unprecedented heights, the match was slow, lacking in any urgency as both teams struggled to combat the heat.

The Swiss did grow into the contest in the second period, with Tranquillo Barnetta doing well to burst into the French penalty area, only to see his shot cleared by Abidal, before Lille forward Daniel Gygax found himself free at the back post but could only steer his effort straight at Barthez, who reacted well to keep the ball out.

With substitutions disrupting the flow even further, the second half drifted towards an inevitable conclusion. France did have enough in the legs to create one last chance for themselves, with substitutes Louis Saha and Vikash Dhorasoo combining well before the PSG striker drilled his shot wide. It was a rare moment of quality, created by star man Zidane, but was a fleeting glimpse of the capability of the talented French. The full-time whistle was a blessing when it came, for the players and the fans. Not every match can be a classic and the hope was the best for both teams was yet to come.

* * *

Since 1950, when the World Cup had a group stage as the opening round, France had appeared at eight finals. They had either reached the semi-finals or been knocked out at the group stages across all those appearances. They won their opening match on three occasions, drew once and lost four, with all the wins leading to semi-final appearances and any failure to win leading to a group-stage exit except for one tournament. Back in 1982, France lost their opening match 3-1 to England before sneaking through the group in second place, controlling the second group stage by winning both matches, before facing West Germany in the semi-finals in what would become a World Cup classic.

With the neutrals openly supporting the French over the West Germans after the 'disgrace of Gijón', Jupp Derwall's squad further turned public sympathy against them during their match against France. With the scores level at 1-1 after an hour, French captain Michel Platini picked up the ball in midfield and played a beautiful pass through the German defence, freeing Patrick Battiston on goal. The Saint-Étienne defender chipped the ball over the charging German goalkeeper, Harald Schumacher, but wide of the post; however, as the ball drifted wide, the keeper jumped and turned his hip into Battiston, clattering him square in the face. The defender was knocked unconscious and his team-mates and German captain Manfred Kaltz immediately called for a stretcher to aid the stricken player.

The incident was about as blatant as they come and is worth searching for on YouTube if you have not seen it before, for the sheer temerity of it. The only people who seemingly missed the assault were the officiating team, as all that was given was a goal kick. Television replays clearly showed that it was a deliberate act, and there is the image of Schumacher, stood, hands on hips, apparently irritated at the delay in allowing him to take the goal kick while Battiston lay prone on the pitch with three broken teeth, cracked ribs and damaged vertebrae. The clash overshadowed what was one of the best World Cup matches of all time. It finished 3-3, with four goals coming in extra time, before the West Germans fully cemented their status as villains of the 1982 tournament by winning the resulting penalty shoot-out. Ultimately their luck would run out in the final, with Italy emerging victorious with a strong 3-1 victory.

With the weight of their own history behind them, France knew it was important to put an improved performance in against South Korea and to pick up three points to give them a strong chance of qualification. They got off to the ideal start. Claude Makélélé won possession and released Sylvain Wiltord. The forward could only scuff his shot but fortunately the ball fell kindly to his former Arsenal team-mate, Henry, who made no mistake, giving his team the lead after just nine minutes. They continued to make the majority of the running, with Florent Malouda and Zidane both narrowly missing chances that they should have done better with.

With half an hour gone, and France on top, they thought they had doubled their lead when Vieira rose highest from a corner and powered his header towards goal. The South Korean goalkeeper scrambled the ball off the goal line and it eventually fell harmlessly wide. Vieira and the French players were convinced that the ball had crossed the line before the keeper had saved it and the replays certainly supported that claim. It was another favourable decision that had fallen the Asian nation's way after their controversial run to the semi-finals four years earlier and it seemed to take any momentum away from the French.

While the first half had shown some signs of improvement from the Switzerland match, the second saw the return of the tepid France that had shown up during that opener. Passes were misplaced, runners were not spotted and there appeared to be a complete lack of confidence and harmony within the squad. This disunity was a feature of French squads at other international tournaments, most notably in 2010 when there was mutiny among the squad that saw them exit the tournament at the first hurdle.

Fortunately, it appeared that South Korea were also unable to muster enough energy to cause problems for their European counterparts, as they struggled to create any chances during the opening 80 minutes. The only notable moment came when Lee Ho took a knee from Vieira to the face and had to be taken off the pitch. But, with the score still stuck at 1-0, it would only take one chance to turn the match on its head. That chance came with just nine minutes remaining.

Seol Ki-hyeon, the first South Korean player to score in the Champions League, played a simple lofted ball over the top for Manchester United's Park Ji-sung to chase on to, and he knocked the ball over the head of the outrushing Barthez. The goalkeeper was unable to claw the ball away despite getting fingertips to it, and William Gallas also could not quite reach the ball as it landed in the back of the net, drawing South Korea level. It was a sucker-punch that had seemed unlikely to arrive, but it was the price that Domenech's team deserved to pay for their lacklustre second half performance.

With the threat of not winning either of their two opening matches for a second consecutive tournament looming large over their heads, France suddenly rediscovered their attacking form. Vieira found himself free on the edge of the box but could only send his effort high over the crossbar, before Henry had two separate efforts in the space of two minutes, one being saved and one headed over. It showed that the quality was still there, but it was just failing to be properly unlocked until their backs were against the wall. The match ended 1-1, and the bad news for France continued as, in between the two Henry chances, Zidane received a yellow card, his second of the tournament, so he would now miss the crucial clash against Togo.

The fact that the final group match was against arguably the weakest team in the group would have been a blessing to Domenech, but he would have known that he needed to inspire his team into better performances and quickly. France were almost sleepwalking their way through another World Cup, continuing their recent disappointing form in international tournaments. South Korea, on the other hand, now had four points from their opening two matches and were in a strong position to qualify. A win over Switzerland would see them qualify and a draw would probably be enough, although goal difference would be needed to separate potentially three teams. The group that had looked fairly straightforward on paper was proving to be quite different once played on the pitch.

With South Korea's late equaliser against France, the Swiss knew victory over Togo in their second match would keep their fate in their own hands. Togo needed to avoid defeat to keep any slim qualification hopes alive, with any positive result for the West Africans also helping South Korea edge closer to the knockout stages. However, the build-up to this match was once again dominated by off-field issues affecting the Togolese.

With coach Otto Pfister having been the centre of the commotion prior to the opening match, it was the turn of his players to disrupt the preparations and continue turning their first World Cup experience into a complete circus. Pfister had threatened to quit due to the disunity that was running through the squad in the build-up to the tournament and now the players decided that they were going on strike and refused to participate or even travel to Dortmund for their match against the Swiss. Having reached their first-ever finals, the Togolese players were expecting to be awarded bonuses between $150,000 and $200,000 per appearance but they were informed before the tournament that those bonuses would not be paid out. Citing economic concerns, with the average annual income just $316, the conflict became about more than just bonuses. For many it was seen as the greed of modern football taking over as people believed that simply playing for your nation at the most prestigious tournament should be reward enough, while the players were arguing that they were just getting what they had been promised before qualifying.

As often happens, arbitrary black-and-white lines were drawn and the court of public opinion ruled in favour of one or the other, seemingly falling against the Togolese players. In reality the truth was more delicately balanced. The financial aspect of football has run amok, with players' wages and transfer fees rising, nation states adding their wealth to the pot and fans increasingly priced out of following their teams and countries, with ticket prices and TV subscription costs increasing year on year. Yet this generation of Togolese footballers had achieved what no previous or subsequent one ever managed and reached the finals of the World Cup. If their footballing federation had offered unaffordable bonuses for their players in expectation that they were unlikely to qualify, then those bonuses deserved to be paid if the target was met, especially as each nation was awarded $5.7million for qualification and a share of sponsorship money would also reach the bank accounts of the Togolese federation. In any other industry or profession, it would be expected, and football should be no different.

Ultimately, it was up to FIFA to step in to prevent one of the matches at their flagship event from not going ahead. Threatening potential disqualification from future tournaments and economic penalties including fines and forfeiting of revenues from the World Cup campaign, the governing body forced the hand of the Togo players. Having been strong-armed by the organisers, Togo eventually made their way to Dortmund to take on the Swiss, and if their off-pitch preparations had been less than ideal, they got off to an equally bad start on it.

The contest was only 16 minutes old when a deep Swiss cross from the left found Barnetta at the back post. He played a clever ball back across the penalty area first time for Alexander Frei. The Rennes striker, who would sign for Borussia Dortmund during the tournament, did not make the cleanest contact of his career, the ball ultimately going in off his knee, but he made contact nevertheless, and they all count the same. This tournament represented a chance for Frei to perhaps redeem himself in the eyes of the watching public. Two years earlier when playing for his country against England at Euro 2004, television cameras captured footage that appeared to show the striker spit towards Steven Gerrard. Nothing was spotted during the match but Frei was withdrawn from the squad before the next match against France, and UEFA suspended him for 15 days. Frei denied the charges in front of the disciplinary panel but allegedly admitted to his federation that he had aimed a spit at the Liverpool captain. Frei had top-scored for his nation during qualification for the tournament with seven goals and, if he could lead Switzerland on a deeper than expected run through the knockout stages, then perhaps all would be forgiven. After all, football often has a short memory.

Frei's early goal had come against the run of play as Togo had started brightly. Mohamed Kader was once again at the heart of everything positive from the West Africans and saw two clever efforts saved in the opening exchanges. His partnership with Adebayor was causing the usually resolute Swiss defence problems, and the Arsenal man felt he should have been awarded a penalty after being tripped, but the contact was minimal. The half-time interval came at perhaps the best time for Switzerland and allowed their coach Köbi Kuhn to make changes and inspire his team into a better performance.

Whatever words were said, Switzerland were much improved in the second period. There was not a flurry of chances to reflect the change in momentum but they were in greater control of the tempo of the play. Passes were connecting easier. Possession was being retained. They used the opening 15 minutes of the second half to almost squeeze the last remaining fighting breaths from their opponents. Barnetta and Frei both had chances, with one saved and one deflected over. Raphaël Wicky attempted an audacious chip from the halfway line that would have been the goal of the tournament had it dropped just under rather than just over the crossbar. Togo had little in response to the greater intensity of the Swiss. Knowing that they had to score to retain any slim chance of reaching the knockout stages, they could not get anything going. Adebayor and Kader were unable to exert similar levels of influence over the match as they had during the first half and it looked as if the off-field events in the build-up had finally caught up with the players. They seemed tired and devoid of energy, resigned to their fate.

As time ticked away, Switzerland continued to dictate the tempo, eventually doubling their lead when Barnetta, arguably the best player on the pitch, found himself free on the right edge of the area. Having seen numerous chances saved or blocked, the Bayer Leverkusen midfielder steadied himself and drilled a low shot beyond the dive of Agassa. If Togo had any faint flicker of hope beforehand, it was extinguished as the ball settled in the corner of the goal. The final whistle confirmed what had been on the cards for the entirety of the second period, Togo's World Cup campaign was over after their opening two matches. Their on-field performances had been spirited and they had not been outclassed at any point. They may have even won the South Korea match had they not been reduced to ten players just after half-time. Although the outcome of the match would not change the fortunes of Togo, there was no doubt that their final game was one of huge significance. Against France, their former colonisers, they had the opportunity to stop the French from reaching the knockout stages of a second consecutive World Cup. Surely that was more motivation than any potential win bonuses that may or may not have been promised.

* * *

Switzerland vs South Korea. Saturday night. Hanover. Winner takes all. It was that simple. The winner would qualify as group winners and the loser would be left sweating on France's result. Should France fail to win then both nations would qualify regardless of the outcome. Neither would have emerged on to the pitch under the floodlights with any other goal than to win to take any doubt out of the equation. It is always better to be in charge of your destiny, after all.

The match started brightly with Ji-sung Park and Tranquillo Barnetta exchanging long-range efforts that were stopped by the respective goalkeepers. Throughout the opening match against France and the first 45 minutes against Togo, Switzerland had appeared laboured, struggling to find any intensity in the baking heat. Something must have been said during half-time in that victory over Togo, as from that moment they began playing with a bit more confidence and control. Limiting their opponents was always going to be their best chance of progressing, but it had come at the cost of attacking impetus at the start of the tournament. Now they appeared to be willing to take the game to their opposition.

Switzerland's early endeavour was rewarded midway through the first half. It was a simple goal. Hakan Yakin sent a simple free kick into the penalty area and Arsenal defender Philippe Senderos powered a brilliant header into the back of the net. The 21-year-old central defender had thrown himself at the ball and ran away celebrating with blood pouring from his nose, having clashed heads with the South Korean he had bullied out of the way to win the duel.

There was hope that this tournament would mark the starting point of a long and distinguished career for Senderos, particularly in North London where Arsenal had won the race with Real Madrid to sign the promising young defender from Servette. He had come to the attention of the elite European clubs during the 2002 Under-17 European Championships. Having been redesignated as an under-17 rather than under-16 tournament, Switzerland surprised most pundits by remaining unbeaten, conceding only twice in six matches and winning the competition. Senderos was the standout in the Swiss team, with Tranquillo Barnetta also impressing enough to merit inclusion in the 2006 World Cup squad. Their most impressive performance came in the semi-finals against the highly fancied England squad containing Wayne Rooney. The Everton striker was kept quiet and unable to influence the game in the way he would just two years later at the senior edition of the tournament, and it was this match that encouraged Arsenal, Real Madrid and other elite European clubs to battle for his signature. Unfortunately for all parties, his career was blighted by recurring injuries that meant he was never able to fulfil the potential that was so evident. It was a shame to see his career fizzle out in the manner that it did, as aside from his footballing ability, this was a young man that was well-read, well-liked and would have been a key cog in any dressing room due to his ability to speak seven languages, a trait that would be perfect in the multinational dressing rooms that Premier League clubs often have now.

While Senderos was marshalling the defence, Yakin and Frei were in complete control of the match. Yakin was the star of the first half, creating the goal and seeing two shots on goal diverted wide, one by the gloves of the keeper and one by a defensive block. The South Koreans did not seem able to get close to the playmaker to slow down the momentum that Switzerland seemed to be gathering.

The second half saw Frei begin to receive the goalscoring chances that had evaded him in the first. He dragged a shot wide just before the hour mark and rattled the woodwork a few minutes later when making a clever run in behind the defence. The second goal came eventually and, when it did, it was in controversial circumstances.

With South Korea pushing forwards in search of a crucial equaliser, the Swiss countered and tried to play the ball around the edge of the Korean penalty area. The ball eventually ran through to Frei, who rounded the goalkeeper and slotted the ball into the empty net. It clearly reached him in an offside position and the assistant referee raised his flag to rule the goal out. Horacio Elizondo, the Argentine referee, had a different view. In his eyes the ball had been played through to Frei by a South Korean defender, meaning that Frei was onside. After discussing with his assistant, with inevitable input from players from both teams, the referee awarded the goal, doubling the Switzerland lead and all but securing their place in the knockout stages. It has been described as a controversial goal in many reports since, but the video evidence clearly shows the ball being played by a South Korean defender to reach Frei and, considering the controversy surrounding South Korea's run to the final four in 2002, it was clearly the correct decision and only deemed controversial to provide a talking point after the match for pundits and reporters.

The final whistle confirmed what appeared a foregone conclusion for the final 15 minutes. On their return to the World Cup finals after a 12-year and two-tournament absence, Switzerland had reached the knockout stages and had hopes of matching their best-ever finish of a quarter-final place. They had proven hard to beat and had yet to concede a goal. South Korea, on the other hand, were now waiting on the outcome of the concurrent match being played in Cologne, as a France victory would see their competition end. They had failed to get going in this match and paid the price dearly, so their fate was now out of their hands. Having impressed in the opening two matches, and wanting to show the footballing world that reaching the semi-finals on home soil was not just down to controversial refereeing performances, a group stage exit would have been a harsh return for the Asian nation.

Despite labouring through their opening two matches, France knew that they were still in a position of strength. Public opinion in France was not exactly at its highest, with many believing that their nation would be exiting another World Cup prematurely and wasting another tournament for their greatest-ever generation. In purely footballing terms, France were clear favourites over Togo even without the suspended Zidane. Their players were lighting up the biggest stages, featuring regularly in the latter stages of the Champions League and had a remarkable trophy count, while many of the Togolese were plying their trade in the lower leagues in those same countries that their counterparts were dominating. Yet there was a heavy political undercurrent to the match that meant it would not be as simple as it seemed.

Much like Angola when they played Portugal, Togo's history cannot be told without a heavy French presence. During the First World War, British and French troops invaded what was then known as Togoland, which was under German control, and divided it among themselves. Togo as it appears on a map today was split in two, one half controlled by Britain and the other France. Unlike Portugal and Angola, after Togo gained independence, they could still rely on French aid as they signed a mutual defence agreement that ensured protection in the event of aggression from another nation. There are strong trade links between the two and those ties seemingly continue to strengthen. It was no perfect relationship as it never is between coloniser and colonised, but it was a stronger relationship than other similar ones.

The World Cup had been a sporting disaster for Togo. Two defeats, two strike threats and a fine from FIFA, but this match represented the opportunity to gain a truly memorable result for themselves and eliminate France. The key for *Les Bleus* was going to be a fast and controlled start, something that they had not managed in either of their opening matches. They nearly got the perfect start as well, and it came from two of the players who had been brought in for this match.

It was as simple as it gets as Franck Ribéry and David Trezeguet both broke beyond the Togolese defensive line and the young winger laid the ball perfectly into the path of the more experienced striker, who tapped the ball home. The assistant referee immediately raised his flag and, unlike in the Switzerland vs South Korea match, the referee concurred and ruled the goal out. The television replays showed that Ribéry was clearly offside when receiving the first pass, but it was a much tighter call when he played Trezeguet in. The ball travelled forwards but the question was whether or not the Juventus striker was in front or level with the Marseille winger as the pass was made. The replay was inconclusive, although it perhaps leaned more towards offside than onside, but there was still anger among the French camp at the officiating decisions when combined with the goal they were not awarded against South Korea that could have made their progress much smoother.

Once the goal had been disallowed, France seemed to lose all sense of composure that their experience should have brought to the occasion. The entire forward line was guilty of squandering good chances, with Henry's tame shot being easily gathered, Ribéry blazing over the bar when through one-on-one and Trezeguet having a good header tipped over brilliantly by Agassa. The Togo goalkeeper was having the match of his life during the first half, stopping everything that came his way, and he was due the stroke of good fortune he received five minutes before half-time. He handled a long-range Malouda strike poorly and the ball landed at the feet of Trezeguet, whose effort bounced off the stricken keeper, who was able to bravely dive on the loose ball before it crept over the line.

Half-time arrived and, as it stood, France were heading out. It represented perhaps the most important team talk of Raymond Domenech's career. Without the game-changing presence of his nation's best player, did he stick with the XI that started or gamble on a substitute being able to make the difference? He opted to stick and the decision was vindicated just ten minutes into the second half. After Ribéry had wasted another good chance, it felt like it was going to be one of those days where nothing came off for France, but their stand-in captain Patrick Vieira grabbed the match by the scruff of the neck and dragged his nation forwards. In a manner that Arsenal fans had become accustomed to seeing, he drove on with the ball, laid it off to Ribéry out left, who gave it straight back to him. The midfielder needed just one touch to get the ball out from under his feet and another to curl it beyond Agassa and into the far corner. It was a vital goal at a vital time.

The moment seemed to settle the nerves and allowed France to show their true quality. The Arsenal connection again paid dividends, with Vieira winning a header on the edge of the area and flicking the ball on to Henry, who took a touch and drilled a shot beyond the goalkeeper. Two goals in six minutes and France were in firm control over the match. It had been a spirited effort again from Togo, but the lack of elite quality showed through ultimately. Once France had broken the deadlock, there was no other likely outcome to the match. Togo's performance throughout the tournament was confusing, as usually underdog nations that put up valiant efforts against more established nations become fan favourites, yet they never received that status. Their off-field issues had spoiled what should have been a momentous occasion for their nation and, to date, they have never managed to reach the same heights again.

France, however, had managed to drag themselves out of the group stages despite never managing a truly convincing performance. With Zidane back for the first knockout round, there would need to be rapid improvements if they were going to have any hopes of adding to their solitary World Cup trophy. There was hope from this match, with both Vieira and Henry showing glimpses of their true ability, having stepped up in the absence of their captain, and the emergence of Ribéry as an international-quality star, but there was a lack of fluidity among the squad that would be exposed by the top-tier nations left in the competition. At least that is how it seemed.

3pm, 13 June 2006
Waldstadion, Frankfurt
Attendance: 48,000
Referee: Graham Poll (England)

South Korea 2 (Lee Chun-soo 54, Ahn Jung-hwan 72)
Togo 1 (Kader 31)

South Korea: Lee Woon-jae (c), Choi Jin-cheul, Kim Young-chul, Kim Jin-kyu (Ahn Jung-hwan 46), Song Chong-gug, Lee Ho, Lee Eul-yong (Kim Nam-il 68), Lee Young-pyo, Park Ji-sung, Cho Jae-jin (Kim Sang-sik 83), Lee Chun-soo. **Manager:** Dick Advocaat.

Togo: Kossi Agassa, Massamasso Tchangai, Jean-Paul Abalo (c), Daré Nibombé, Ludovic Assemoassa (Richmond Forson 62), Junior Sènaya (Assimiou Touré 55), Alaixys Romao, Chérif Touré Mamam, Moustapha Salifou (Yao Aziawonou 86), Mohamed Kader, Emmanuel Adebayor. **Manager:** Otto Pfister.

Booked: Young-chul (41), Chun-soo (51); Abalo (23), Romao (24), Tchangai (53)
Sent off: Abalo (53)

6pm, 13 June 2006
Gottlieb-Daimler-Stadion, Stuttgart
Attendance: 52,000
Referee: Valentin Ivanov (Russia)

France 0
Switzerland 0

France: Fabien Barthez, Willy Sagnol, Lilian Thuram, William Gallas, Eric Abidal, Patrick Vieira, Claude Makélélé, Sylvain Wiltord

(Vikash Dhorasoo 84), Zinedine Zidane (c), Franck Ribéry (Louis Saha 70), Thierry Henry. **Manager:** Raymond Domenech.

Switzerland: Pascal Zuberbühler, Philipp Degen, Patrick Müller (Johan Djourou 75), Philippe Senderos, Ludovic Magnin, Tranquillo Barnetta, Ricardo Cabanas, Johann Vogel (c), Raphaël Wicky (Xavier Margairaz 82), Alexander Frei, Marco Streller (Daniel Gygax 57). **Manager:** Köbi Kuhn.

Booked: Abidal (64), Zidane (72), Sagnol (90+3); Magnin (42), Streller (45), Degen (56), Cabanas (72), Frei (90+3)

9pm, 18 June 2006
Zentralstadion, Leipzig
Attendance: 43,000
Referee: Benito Archundia (Mexico)

France 1 (Henry 9)
South Korea 1 (Park Ji-sung 81)

France: Fabien Barthez, Willy Sagnol, Lilian Thuram, William Gallas, Eric Abidal, Patrick Vieira, Claude Makélélé, Sylvain Wiltord (Franck Ribéry 60), Zinedine Zidane (c) (David Trezeguet 90+1), Florent Malouda (Vikash Dhorasoo 88), Thierry Henry. **Manager:** Raymond Domenech.

South Korea: Lee Woon-jae (c), Lee Young-pyo, Choi Jin-cheul, Kim Young-chul, Kim Dong-jin, Lee Ho (Kim Sang-sik 69), Kim Nam-il, Lee Eul-yong (Seol Ki-hyeon 46), Lee Chun-soo (Ahn Jung-hwan 72), Cho Jae-jin, Park Ji-sung. **Manager:** Dick Advocaat.

Booked: Abidal (79), Zidane (90+1); Lee Ho (11), Dong-jin (29)

3pm, 19 June 2006
Westfalenstadion,, Dortmund
Attendance: 65,000
Referee: Carlos Amarilla (Paraguay)

Togo 0
Switzerland 2 (Frei 16, Barnetta 88)

Togo: Kossi Agassa, Assimiou Touré, Massamasso Tchangai (c), Daré Nibombé, Richmond Forson, Thomas Dossevi (Junior Sènaya 69), Alaixys Romao, Kuami Agboh (Moustapha Salifou 25), Chérif Touré Mamam (Robert Malm 87), Mohamed Kader, Emmanuel Adebayor. **Manager:** Otto Pfister.

Switzerland: Pascal Zuberbühler, Philipp Degen, Patrick Müller, Philippe Senderos, Ludovic Magnin, Tranquillo Barnetta, Johann Vogel (c), Ricardo Cabanas (Marco Streller 77), Raphaël Wicky, Alexander Frei (Mauro Lustrinelli 87), Daniel Gygax (Hakan Yakin 46). **Manager:** Köbi Kuhn.

Booked: Salifou (45), Adebayor (47), Romao (53); Vogel (90+2)

9pm, 23 June 2006
RheinEnergieStadion, Cologne
Attendance: 45,000
Referee: Jorge Larrionda (Uruguay)

Togo 0
France 2 (Vieira 55, Henry 61)

Togo: Kossi Agassa, Massamasso Tchangai, Jean-Paul Abalo (c), Daré Nibombé, Richmond Forson, Junior Sènaya, Yao Aziawonou, Moustapha Salifou, Chérif Touré Mamam (Adékambi Olufadé 59), Mohamed Kader, Emmanuel Adebayor (Thomas Dossevi 75). **Manager:** Otto Pfister.

France: Fabien Barthez, Willy Sagnol, Lilian Thuram, William Gallas, Mikaël Silvestre, Franck Ribéry (Sidney Govou 77), Patrick Vieira (c) (Alou Diarra 81), Claude Makélélé, Florent Malouda (Sylvain Wiltord 74), David Trezeguet, Thierry Henry. **Manager:** Raymond Domenech.

Booked: Aziawonou (38), Mamam (44), Salifou (88); Makélélé (30)

9pm, 23 June 2006
Niedersachsenstadion, Hanover
Attendance: 43,000
Referee: Horacio Elizondo (Argentina)

Switzerland 2 (Senderos 23, Frei 77)
South Korea 0

Switzerland: Pascal Zuberbühler, Philipp Degen, Patrick Müller, Philippe Senderos (Johan Djourou 53), Christoph Spycher, Johann Vogel (c), Tranquillo Barnetta, Hakan Yakin (Xavier Margairaz 71), Ricardo Cabanas, Raphaël Wicky (Valon Behrami 88), Alexander Frei. **Manager:** Köbi Kuhn.

South Korea: Lee Woon-jae (c), Lee Young-pyo (Ahn Jung-hwan 63), Choi Jin-cheul, Kim Jin-kyu, Kim Dong-jin, Kim Nam-il, Lee Ho, Park Ji-sung, Lee Chun-soo, Park Chu-young (Seol Ki-hyeon 66), Cho Jae-jin. **Manager:** Dick Advocaat.

Booked: Senderos (43), Yakin (55), Wicky (69), Spycher (82), Djourou (90); Chu-young (23), Jin-kyu (37), Jung-hwan (78), Jin-cheul (78), Chun-soo (80)

Group G	P	W	D	L	GF	GA	GD	PTS
SWITZERLAND	3	2	1	0	4	0	+4	7
FRANCE	3	1	2	0	3	1	+2	5
SOUTH KOREA	3	1	1	1	3	4	-1	4
TOGO	3	0	0	3	1	6	-5	0

Switzerland and France qualified

Group H

RECENT INTERNATIONAL football cannot be talked about without Spain taking centre stage. Between 2008 and 2012, Spain entered four competitions and won three, two European Championships and a World Cup, with their only failure coming in the Confederations Cup in 2009 where they were surprisingly beaten in the semi-finals by the USA. The old style of *La Furia Roja* (The Red Fury) as was decreed by an Italian journalist after the 1920 Olympics in Antwerp due to the physical style of Spain's play, had been replaced by head coach Luis Aragonés. The veteran coach had introduced a variation of the tiki-taka style that was beginning to take shape at Barcelona, who had just won the Champions League and would soar to new heights when Pep Guardiola took over. Based on their final position at the last World Cup, Spain would hardly seem to be in need of a major cultural rebuild.

Being eliminated in the quarter-finals by co-hosts South Korea may not have been the result expected of the Iberian nation, but there were certainly mitigating circumstances that can be pointed to. Having knocked out Italy in the Round of 16 in controversial fashion that caused ire in the Italian press, the Spanish were seen as a step too far for the South-East Asian nation. The match was hardly a classic, with Spain continuing their theme from the tournament and not playing in an overly positive manner and allowing South Korea to control portions of the match. There were few real openings, with both goalkeepers standing tall to deny any that did arise, and when Lee Woon-jae was finally beaten, the referee's whistle came to his aid erroneously. Firstly, Iván Helguera had a header disallowed for alleged shirt-pulling in the penalty area, before Fernando Morientes headed home from close range for what seemed to be the golden goal, only for the referee to rule that the ball had gone out of play before the cross came into the box. Both decisions were debatable at best, with questions being raised about the standard of the officiating in matches involving the host nation. Paul Hayward, writing for the *Telegraph* after the match, opined that 'the records say that the Koreans knocked out Spain in a penalty shoot-out in Gwangju on Saturday. The records are a lie and this tournament has descended into farce'.

After their acrimonious exit from the 2002 World Cup was followed by a poor group stage exit from the European Championships in 2004, failing to qualify from a group containing Portugal, Russia and Greece, the Spanish football federation began their reform of the national set-up. The squads got younger, technically more proficient and the march to international domination was underway. Heading into Germany in 2006, expectations were not too high, but with a relatively easy group there was hope that there would be no group-stage exit and they might surprise a few people on their way through the tournament.

The biggest surprise for Spain was the exclusion of star striker Raúl from the starting line-up for the opening match against Ukraine. The Real Madrid forward had been the main attacking option for Spain alongside Morientes since making his debut in 1996, but new coach Luis Aragonés did not believe that he . was capable of performing as successfully in a possession-based system. Predictably, this decision proved unpopular prior to the tournament. As Graham Hunter summed up in *Spain: The Inside Story of La Roja's Historic Treble*, 'if some of Raúl's brilliance was based on what you might call speculative football, Aragonés wanted to move to control and security'. There was a clearly extraordinarily talented generation on the horizon, with Xavi, Andrés Iniesta, Fernando Torres and David Villa all beginning to feature prominently, and starlet Cesc Fàbregas emerging as a potential superstar. Raúl, for all his obvious talent, did not fit perfectly with this new style.

While Spain were undergoing a striker dilemma, their opponents had no such drama in that department. The only way that Ukraine were going to feature without their star striker was due to injury, as all their hopes rested squarely on the shoulders of Andriy Shevchenko. Having just moved from AC Milan to Chelsea before the tournament kicked off, everyone knew that for Ukraine to upset the odds in their first-ever independent appearance at the finals, Shevchenko would need to be firing on all cylinders. Although there was talent throughout the squad, with Shakhtar's Anatoliy Tymoshchuk and Bayer Leverkusen's Andriy Voronin, the new signing in West London was the undisputed star.

The match started under the Leipzig sun with Spain causing their opponents early problems. A 20-year-old Sergio Ramos, filling in at right-back rather than his usual central defence position, got forward early, producing a clever pull-back that Xavi could only roll wide. Torres weaved his way through the defence before watching his cross deflect behind for a corner, Luis García fired narrowly wide and Villarreal midfielder Marcos Senna, who was making just his fourth international appearance aged 29, saw a 30-yard effort well tipped over by the Ukraine goalkeeper, all within the opening 13 minutes.

Despite their new-found focus on intricate possession football, Spain's first goal came from a corner. Xavi drilled the corner in, where Xabi Alonso was unmarked in the box. He just had to stoop and nod the ball into the back of the net to give Spain a very well-deserved lead.

Matters nearly got worse for Ukraine just three minutes later when Andriy Rusol lunged into a challenge on Mariano Pernía. To describe the tackle at mistimed would almost be an injustice. The Dnipro Dnipropetrovsk midfielder was late, high and caught the defender on the knee with his studs. The ball was barely in the camera frame when he made contact. The referee brandished a yellow card but it could easily have been a red and perhaps would have been in the age of VAR. From the resulting free kick, David Villa sent a shot goalbound. It was hit well but looked to be easily within the reach of the diving Ukrainian goalkeeper. That was until the ball reached the wall and deflected off the head of Rusol, diverting it from its path and into the back of the net. Two goals ahead after just 17 minutes and Spain were into cruise control. It had been a rude awakening to tournament football for the Eastern Europeans.

Half-time came and Ukraine had managed to keep the score at just 2-0. It was a long road back to parity, but there was still some light at the end of the tunnel. However, that light was firmly extinguished just three minutes after the interval. Fernando Torres, who had been causing problems for the Ukrainian defence all afternoon, burst clean through down the middle and managed to scramble a shot away that was smothered by Shovkovskyi in the Ukraine goal. As he was running through, however, Torres was having his shorts pulled by Dynamo Kiev defender Vladyslav Vashchuk. Despite getting the shot away, the Swiss official ruled that the pull-back was enough to put the striker off and awarded a penalty. As Vashchuk was the last defender, there was little option but to send him off. Villa took the responsibility on his shoulders and fired a low, hard penalty to the keeper's right. Shovkovskyi guessed correctly and got fingertips to it but the shot was too powerful and the ball nestled securely into the corner of the goal. Three goals ahead and a one-man advantage. The opening match of Group H was over after just 48 minutes.

A fourth goal seemed just a matter of time for Spain and Villa almost completed his hat-trick just a few minutes later when he found himself free in the penalty area but could only shoot straight at the goalkeeper. With the result secure, there was even time for Raúl to get on the pitch and he nearly pounced in typical fashion, only for his header to be saved by the goalkeeper. Marcos Senna did manage to put the ball in the back of net but it was ruled out for a foul earlier in the build-up by Ramos, with suggestions that it may have been a leading elbow, but the referee only saw fit to award a free kick.

The fourth goal did eventually arrive and, when it did, it was a moment of true quality. A portent of the beautiful football that Spain would become famous for over the following years, the move was devastating and simple in equal measure. Barcelona captain Carles Puyol won the ball back just inside the Ukrainian half and burst forward, cleverly turning a challenge. The loose ball was diverted by Torres into the path of Arsenal youngster Cesc Fàbregas, who laid it back into Puyol's path. The central defender nodded the ball into space for Torres to run on to before rifling a powerful shot from the edge of the area into the bottom corner. It was no less than the Atlético Madrid striker deserved, as his running and movement had caused Ukraine problems. This was Torres at his best, the form that earned him the move to Liverpool where he was one of the best strikers in the world for a few years. His partnership with Villa would help catapult Spain to the forefront of international football and this tournament was evidence of a blossoming relationship emerging.

The final whistle was just a formality when it finally blew. The contest had been over since the opening exchanges of the second half, perhaps even after the second Spain goal in the 17th minute. Ukraine had simply not been able to lay a glove on their opponent. The greater international experience was on show for the Iberians, who seemed a step sharper, a step livelier and had laid down a marker for the other teams at the tournament that they were coming. Ukraine, as the lowest-ranked team in the group, knew that their hopes were hanging by a thread already. They faced Saudi Arabia in their second match, a nation in their fourth consecutive World Cup and one ranked 11 places higher in FIFA's rankings. An opening defeat is not the end of the world, but it certainly makes qualifying harder, and Ukraine now knew that they could not afford another slip-up or they would be heading home earlier than hoped.

With Ukraine comprehensively beaten by Spain, both Tunisia and Saudi Arabia knew that emerging from the opening contest with a victory would be a huge boost to their qualification hopes. Neither were highly fancied to cause any upsets heading into the tournament, with the two European nations favoured to progress, but both teams retained their own internal expectations. This would be Tunisia's fourth appearance in the finals and third consecutive showing. They boasted a good blend of experience and youth, with Radhi Jaïdi, Kaies Ghodhbane and captain Riadh Bouazizi all boasting over 80 caps, while Yassine Chikhaoui and Hamed Namouchi were talented youngsters who were hoping to provide the difference between simply making the finals and actually causing an upset. If everything clicked into place for the North Africans, then there was a genuine belief that they could finally progress beyond the group stages and, depending on the match-up they received in the second round, even reach the quarter-finals and match the best-ever result from an African nation at this point.

On the opposite side of the pitch, Saudi Arabia were hoping that they could match their best-ever World Cup appearance on debut in 1994 and make it out of the group. As was the case at every finals they had reached, Sami Al-Jaber was the key to the hopes of his nation. The Al-Hilal legend, having spent the majority of his 20-year career playing for the club, was perhaps past his best at 33, but his role as captain and impact sub could not be underestimated. His know-how and quality would be a valuable commodity in coming off the bench and helping to turn the momentum in their favour if the match was not going to plan. The Suadis boasted the fifth most experienced squad in the tournament. Al-Jaber was not even their most capped player. That honour fell to goalkeeper Mohamed Al-Deayea, who had 178 caps at the outset of the tournament, but had lost the gloves to Al-Ittihad's Mabrouk Zaid. Retiring after the tournament from internationals, Al-Deayea would finish his career for Saudi Arabia as the most-capped player for his country as well as being the most-capped male goalkeeper in international football, edging ahead of Gianluigi Buffon by just two caps.

The match started in a cagey manner, with both teams wary of making an early mistake. Tunisia's Karim Haggui headed wide from a corner before three Saudi corners all failed to produce a clear chance. Saudi Arabia were exerting a hint of control as the first 20 minutes ticked by, although they were struggling to actually create any openings.

As is often the case, the failure to create or convert a chance came back to haunt them as Tunisia took the lead against the run of play. A free kick from wide right was floated into the area and caused panic amid the Saudi defence. An attempted clearance from the head of a defender bounced off the back of his team-mate and landed perfectly at the feet of Ziad Jaziri, who smashed the ball into the roof of the net from ten yards out. It was the only real moment of quality in the first half as both teams attempted to settle in to the match. Redha Tukar did direct a free kick on target shortly before half-time, but it was well caught by the Tunisian goalkeeper.

While the opening 45 minutes may have been cagey, Saudi coach Marcos Paquetá clearly sent his team out for the second half with the intention of throwing everything at their opponents. It nearly paid immediate dividends when Noor managed to get behind the Tunisian back line and flick the ball beyond the goalkeeper, only to see it drop narrowly wide of the post. There was a renewed vigour about the Saudis throughout the second period and they eventually got their deserved equaliser. The goal came from a goal kick, with the ball being moved quickly from back to front. A clever through ball down the right-hand side from Ahmed Dokhi Al-Dosari freed Noor in behind once again, and his first-time cross perfectly found Al-Qahtani racing to the near post. The Al-Hilal striker beat his marker to the ball and smartly poked it above the goalkeeper at the near post and into the roof of the net. The speed of the movement seemed to catch Tunisia off guard and it was a goal that meant the scoreline better reflected the flow of the play.

With substitutes being introduced at regular intervals, the match lost any rhythm it had been developing and neither team seemed willing to push for an important winner. A draw was not a bad result for either team and would still provide a path to qualification for the knockout stages. That was until Paquetá summoned the ace up his sleeve and sent Al-Jaber into the action. It took just two minutes for the striker to make his mark. It was another simple but effective counter-attack, with fellow sub Malek Mouath slipping a ball beyond the last defender for Al-Jaber. One touch to control with his right foot and his second slotted the ball underneath the onrushing keeper and into the bottom corner. He had only been on the pitch for 90 seconds and had made his mark, further underlining his status as one of his country's footballing legends.

With just six minutes to go, Al-Jaber's goal appeared likely to be the winner. Tunisia had shown little attacking impetus and there seemed to be too little time left for them to up their levels and grab a barely deserved leveller. Ghodhbane shot over from 20 yards out before Sulaimani almost settled it for Saudi Arabia when his free kick was deflected but clipped the outside of the post and bounced clear. Throwing everything forward, Tunisia launched a hopeful ball into the box with just seconds remaining. Radhi Jaïdi managed to win the header and the ball fell to Jaziri on the right-hand side of the box. Having controlled the ball and drifted towards the byline, there was little option but to turn back on to his left foot and dink the ball back to the edge of the six-yard box for Jaïdi. The Bolton Wanderers defender powered over his marker and sent his header down into the ground at the feet of the goalkeeper, who could not react quickly enough to keep the ball out. Out of nowhere, Tunisia had drawn themselves level. It was a point they had hardly earned but one that was very welcome. Saudi Arabia's disappointment was clear to see as they had been moments away from an opening victory that would have increased their odds of qualification. As it stood, neither team was able to lay down the early marker and it meant that the battle for the second qualifying spot behind Spain was very much up for grabs between the these two and Ukraine.

* * *

As the second round of group fixtures commenced, both Saudi Arabia and Ukraine knew that no result in their match would clearly confirm their status. For The Blue and Yellow, though, a defeat would leave them hanging on by a thread. A draw would not be the worst outcome for them, but after the morale-sapping defeat in their opener against Spain, it was important that they showed that their pride was not fully broken and that they could express the quality that the team obviously possessed.

Oleg Blokhin rang the changes, making four alterations to the starting line-up, one enforced by the red card in the opener and three tactical switches, moving from a back four to a back three. The changes worked almost immediately as Ukraine started on the front foot. Rusol, perhaps fortunate to have not been sent off himself in the first match, made a clever run from a corner and arrived at the near post unmarked. His attempted header was not the cleanest and the ball ricocheted off of his knee, sneaking between the legs of the goalkeeper and into the back of the net. It was the dream start after just four minutes and allowed any nerves that the Ukrainians may have been feeling to drift away.

Saudi Arabia's vulnerability from set pieces nearly cost them a second goal not long after when Shevchenko had a free header from a corner, only for Al-Dohki to be in the right place on the goal line to get the ball clear. Whereas against Tunisia, the Saudis had been able to dictate terms and cause problems, they just could not get going against their European opponents. Ukraine were controlling everything, moving the ball around with ease. The biggest surprise was that it took so long for their second goal to arrive. With just under ten minutes left before the interval, Serhiy Rebrov received the ball with his back to goal and 35 yards or so out. The Dynamo Kyiv midfielder was given the freedom of the Hamburg pitch and turned, took a step towards goal and sent a shot goalbound. The ball flew off his right boot, swerving into the far corner of the goal, across and past the despairing dive of the Saudi keeper. Zaid slipped as he went to scramble across to attempt the save but he may have struggled to reach it even if he had not stumbled. It was a goal truly out of nothing and one that could easily have been avoided had a single Saudi put any pressure on Rebrov as he collected the ball.

A two-goal lead was the least that Ukraine deserved and the half-time whistle would have come as a blessing for Saudi Arabia. The intensity they had shown in their opening match had vanished and it was as if all the belief had been drained out of their players. The interval offered an opportunity for them to reset their game plan and figure out the best way to cause Ukraine problems. It seemed an unlikely task given their two-goal deficit and the evidence of the first half but football has a way of providing shocks and a fast start to the second period would give them hope that they could pull a result out of the hat.

That much-needed fast start came inside the first two minutes of the second half when a free kick from the left-hand side was whipped into the penalty area and the striker managed to find a yard of space in the penalty area to glance a header beyond the goalkeeper and into the goal. Unfortunately for Saudi Arabia, that goal came for Ukraine. Kalynychenko sent in the free kick and it was Shevchenko who found the free space in the area to score the header. It was clever movement from the elite striker in peeling slightly off the back of his marker to judge the flight of the ball so that all it required was a significant touch and the ball would fly in. However, it was another goal that Saudi Arabia would have been disappointed with. They had left one of the best finishers on the planet free in the penalty area and he had made no mistake. If they had any hope left, it had been firmly extinguished as Shevchenko opened his World Cup account. 3-0. Game over with most of the second half still to go.

Kalynychenko was proving too much to handle down the left-hand side and nearly added the fourth just before the hour mark when he rattled the crossbar with a brilliant effort from just outside the penalty area. Once the third goal had gone in, any Ukrainian tension had fully disappeared. There was never any doubt that they were going to run out winners, it was just a question of how aggressive they wanted to be in pushing for more goals. Having lost 4-0 in the opening match to Spain, equalling or bettering that result would have been a perfect antidote and would set them up with a great chance of reaching the knockout stages on debut. However, Blokhin's team seemed content to see the match out, perhaps conserving energy under the hot evening sun in Hamburg.

Everything was being played on Ukrainian terms. Having impressed in their opener, Saudi Arabia now seemed like the team that many had expected to see. It was more akin to the performance that saw them lose 8-0 to Germany in the group stage four years prior than the one from just a few days ago when they were unlucky to only draw. With just six minutes remaining, a challenge in midfield saw Shevchenko released into space down the left-hand side. There were three defenders between the new Chelsea striker and the goal but he managed to outpace two and, as the third came over to cover the angle towards goal, Shevchenko rolled the ball into space in the middle of the box. Completely unmarked was Kalynychenko, who had burst forwards from the halfway line when Shevchenko broke. Despite a desperate lunge from Saud Kariri, the Spartak Moscow midfielder smashed a first-time strike into the roof of the net. Kalynychenko almost added a fifth before the final whistle blew, creating space cleverly on the edge of the area but ultimately firing over the bar.

When Graham Poll called time, it was merely completing the formality of the outcome that had been certain since the second half was barely two minutes old. Ukraine had bounced back incredibly well from their opening defeat and had shown why so many people had fancied them to cause a shock during the tournament. Kalynychenko had caused problems for the defenders and Shevchenko had opened his goalscoring account, leading to hope that their star man could kick on and propel them on.

While Ukraine celebrated their first-ever World Cup finals victory, the Saudi Arabians knew that they had wasted a glorious opportunity. Had they avoided defeat they would have been in a good place to reach the second round and could have finally broken through the ceiling that they seemed to always reach. Little was ultimately expected of the nation, with the pre-tournament odds having them as one of the teams least likely to win, but this was an abject showing. Perhaps the best thing from the result was that it was only four goals conceded. Had Ukraine been feeling more adventurous, it could easily have been a result as bad as the 8-0 from 2002.

Spain knew that their task was simple. Beat Tunisia in Stuttgart and they would reach the knockout stages with a match to spare. After the impressive way in which his team dismantled Ukraine, it was no surprise to see Aragonés sticking with the same starting XI. On the other side, Tunisia went for two changes as they knew that, although a defeat would still leave their hopes of qualifying alive, should they pull off an upset and beat Spain, they would knock Saudi Arabia out and set up a thrilling final match, leaving themselves, Spain and Ukraine able to qualify.

Everything pointed towards a Spanish victory and, when David Villa ferociously shot into the side-netting inside the opening five minutes, it seemed that Tunisia were going to be in for a long evening. Yet nobody had provided the Tunisians with a copy of the expected script, as Jaziri found himself running in behind the Spanish defence after shrugging off the attempted challenge of Puyol. The Troyes striker bundled his way past three Spanish defenders, whose tackles were feeble at best, and laid the ball off to Mnari arriving at the edge of the box. His first-time effort was smartly saved by Casillas, who got down quickly, but the legendary shot-stopper could only parry the ball back into the danger zone, where it was Mnari who reacted quickest to convert the rebound. Eight minutes in and Tunisia had taken a shock lead.

As the old cliché goes, they may have scored too early. Leading so soon against a quality outfit like Spain simply meant they had longer to hold on and the natural temptation would be to drop deeper and defend that lead, an option that Tunisia seemed to choose. Time was on Spain's side, but drawing level quickly would ease any concerns of a potential upset. Xavi had a good chance just five minutes after the goal but the ball got stuck under his feet before he could get a shot away, Torres was an inch too short to get his head on a cross, and although Ramos did manage to get his head to a corner he could only send the ball wide of the goal. Everything was being dictated by Spain, with all the attacking play coming through them. The front three were causing problems, much like they had against Ukraine in the opener, but the clinical edge was missing. And unlike Ukraine, Tunisia were defending stoically.

Knowing their game plan would require a lot of defending, Roger Lemerre's team were well organised and offered little space to their opponents in the areas of the pitch that were most likely to cause problems. For all their dominance of the ball, Spain were not creating any clear openings. Torres embarked on a good run down the left but could not produce a cross to match the quality, and Luis García headed wide from a free kick, but anything Spain created was a half-chance at best.

Just before half-time, the rain began to fall. In a tournament of few upsets and played under the intense sun of the heatwave that enveloped Europe during the summer of 2006, both the rain falling and Tunisia leading Spain at in the interval were shocks that few would have predicted before kick-off.

There would have been no panicking in the dressing room at half-time as Aragonés delivered his team talk to inspire his team to a comeback but tactical changes were definitely needed. Raúl was introduced in place of García to keep a front three but the other big decision was the introduction of Fàbregas for Marcos Senna. The Arsenal teenager, who had featured briefly in the opener to become Spain's youngest-ever player at a World Cup, was a more attacking option than the Villarreal midfielder, and the faith shown in him by his manager underlined the talent that had been on show for the previous couple of seasons. Having left the Barcelona academy as a 16-year-old, fearing lack of first-team minutes, Fàbregas joined Arsenal in 2003. Sitting behind established midfielders Patrick Vieira and Gilberto Silva, his chances were limited immediately. Having missed out on a Premier League winner's medal in the Invincibles season, as he never played a single minute, his league opportunities came the following year when Vieira missed matches due to injury. Fàbregas took his chance, impressing during his time on the pitch and even becoming Arsenal's youngest-ever league goalscorer, an honour he held alongside being their youngest-ever first-team player and youngest-ever goalscorer in all competitions.

Despite being one of just 13 players under the age of 20 in the tournament, Fàbregas's inclusion was hardly a surprise. He was the only player of the under-20 contingent to start more than once and played nearly double the minutes of the next player, Togo's Assimiou Touré. Almost immediately off the bench, he was causing problems, finding space on the edge of the area and forcing a smart save from

Ali Boumnijel. Although Fàbregas was pulling the strings, Spain were still struggling to break down the stubborn Tunisian defence. Joaquín had been sent into the action in place of the misfiring Villa but could do little to alter the course of the match.

Eventually the three changes made by Aragonés proved the value of good strength in depth when a Joaquín cross was dummied by Torres and fell to Fàbregas at the edge of the area. The midfielder hit a first-time shot that Boumnijel could only parry back out into the danger area. In typical poacher fashion, Raúl was the fastest to react to the loose ball and held off his marker to smartly stick the ball into the top corner. Spain had finally drawn level with just 18 minutes remaining and the goal seemed to drain all the confidence out of the Tunisians.

Fàbregas almost gave Spain the lead just two minutes later when he burst into the box and fired a shot that was well saved by the keeper's legs, before he played a beautiful through ball in behind the defence for Torres to race on to. The Atlético forward reached the ball first, rounded the keeper and flicked the ball beyond the covering defender and into the goal. Two goals in four minutes and *La Roja* had fully turned the match on its head. It had begun to look as if they would fail in their task to come from behind but Spain had got the job done.

A few calm minutes would be needed for Spain to take advantage of their new-found momentum but Tunisia knew the value of a point and showed a brief glimmer of attacking intent. A free kick from near the halfway line was floated over the Spanish defensive line and found Ghodhbane completely free on the right-hand side. He played a brilliant first-time ball across for the box for a team-mate to tap home. Unfortunately, the assistant had raised his flag as soon as Ghodhbane moved towards the ball. The replays showed that it was an incredibly tight call and may have been called incorrectly.

As Tunisia committed to searching for an equaliser, space opened up and they became increasingly vulnerable to the counter-attack. Torres, still full of running, found himself through one-on-one with Boumnijel, who made amends for his rash decision in coming out for the second Spanish goal by holding Torres up and making a smart save from a tight angle.

As the match ticked into added time, Raúl dinked a cross into the area to try to find Torres. The striker was unable to reach the ball as he was being held back by a tired challenge from Alaeddine Yahia and the Brazilian referee pointed to the penalty spot. It was a soft call but one that falls into the category of 'seen them given'. Even if they did not manage to convert it, the time that would be taken over the spot kick would surely end the contest. Torres stepped up and dusted himself down to take the penalty, sending it low to the goalkeeper's right but quite close the middle of the goal. Boumnijel guessed the correct way and managed to get a hand to the ball but was unable to prevent it going in. A second goal of the match and third of the tournament moved Torres top of the goalscoring charts and showed that Spain were a team to be feared as they confirmed their place in the knockout stages. The result also meant that Tunisia were still in contention to qualify but it was out of their hands. Having come close to pulling off an incredible upset, they entered the final group fixtures needing Saudi Arabia to lose to Spain and for themselves to beat a now high-flying Ukraine.

* * *

With qualification assured, Aragonés opted for a completely different starting line-up to the opening two matches, giving game time to those on the fringes of the squad. There was a start for Fàbregas after his match-winning cameo against Tunisia, as well as Raúl and two talented 22-year-olds in Andrés Iniesta and

José Antonio Reyes. This represented a chance for those squad players to earn themselves a starting role in the knockout stages or at least make the choice more difficult for their manager. For Saudi Arabia, the equation was much more perilous. Anything other than a victory would see them knocked out, but even if they did manage to somehow beat Spain, they also needed Ukraine and Tunisia to draw or for Tunisia to win and hope that they beat Spain by three more goals than Tunisia won by.

Predictably, the Iberians kept possession in the match with ease, moving the ball well and settling into something more akin to the tiki-taka style that would dominate their philosophy in international football for years. Saudi Arabia could barely keep the ball long enough to remotely entertain the idea of causing an upset. It was all too simple for Spain, with both David Albelda and Joaquín forcing good saves from the Saudi goalkeeper in the first half an hour. Despite the scarcity of openings, it felt like only a matter of time before a goal came for Spain, and it arrived in an unlikely manner. Given their new preference for possession football, a simple free kick and header from Juanito was the source of the opener.

Two more chances came before half-time, both resulting in saves from Zaid in the Saudi goal, both efforts coming from Arsenal youngsters. Fàbregas had the first one before José Antonio Reyes nearly added to the two international goals he had scored in qualifying for the tournament. Much like Fàbregas, Reyes had left Spain to join Arsenal, but unlike his compatriot, he did not have to wait long to make his impact. Arriving at Highbury halfway through the 2003/04 season, Reyes was crucial in helping Arsenal to their unbeaten season. He netted in two of the final three matches of the season, including the equaliser away to Portsmouth that helped the unbeaten record remain intact. Alongside his Spanish colleague, they played a key role in pushing Arsenal to their first and only Champions League Final prior to this tournament. Despite Reyes ending his career having won the league title in both England and Spain, as well as five Europa League winners medals during his spells with Atlético and a second stint at Sevilla, Reyes' career always felt as if it was one of unfulfilled potential. Undoubtedly a footballer of incredible quality, he never quite lived up to the heights dreamed of after leaving Arsenal for Real Madrid after the Germany World Cup. His tragic death in a car crash aged just 35 brought about a degree of reflection on the talent he had to offer and the success his career actually was. During the summer of 2006, the world was at his feet and he played like it too.

The second half continued in the same vein as the first, with Spain totally dominating. Aragonés opted to use the second half to keep some of his key players sharp, with Villa, Xavi and Torres all getting runouts before the knockouts began. Antonio López had a low shot tipped wide before Joaquín could only poke an effort wide. With so much resting on the outcome of the match, the only Saudi Arabian who could perhaps come out of the opening 70 minutes with any credit was their goalkeeper. The plan may have been to hold Spain out for as long as possible then attack as the match ticked towards its conclusion. Being 1-0 down may have made that task nearly impossible, but with ten minutes to go Saudi Arabia finally started to push on in search of those all-important five goals.

A quick and clever free kick routine almost caught stand-in keeper Santiago Cañizares out at the near post but the ball did not find the back of the net. Saad Al-Harthi found himself presented with the best chance for Saudi Arabia with two minutes to go when he had the ball at his feet at the edge of the six-yard area. Lacking any composure, the striker blazed the ball clear over the crossbar. One final opening fell to Nawaf Al-Temyat but his half-shot, half-cross attempt drifted harmlessly wide. In truth, Saudi Arabia did not deserve to get anything out of the match. They knew that they needed to win by a convincing margin to have any chance of progressing, yet they opted to contain Spain for the majority of the match. Their efforts to salvage their tournament are best summarised by the phrase 'too little, too late'.

Spain, however, had certainly laid down a marker for the rest of the tournament. This match was not their best and the reserves had struggled to finish things off when it was there for the taking, but they had navigated their group with three wins from three. They were one of four teams to have a perfect record through the group stage, along with Germany, Portugal and Brazil, and they had done so in impressive fashion. Their dominant victory over Ukraine was followed by a great fightback against Tunisia. The only downside for Aragonés and his team was something out of their control. As France had performed below expectation in Group G, Spain would be facing the 1998 champions in the second round rather than an easier match-up against Switzerland. It was a harsh outcome for a team that had won all three matches, but if the performances so far had given anything to Spain, it should have been the optimism to take the challenge to an underperforming France and go on a run deep into the tournament.

With Spain securing top spot in the group and eliminating Saudi Arabia, the equation was simple in Berlin. Tunisia had to win to progress, while any other result would see Ukraine reach the knockout stages on their first-ever appearance in the competition. After solid performances in their previous matches, albeit with differing outcomes, neither coach opted to make any changes heading into their most important match of the tournament. Ukraine had been favoured by many to join Spain in qualifying from the group but Tunisia had always held the belief that they were a stronger team than predicted and certainly fancied their chances of progressing. Their opening match against the Saudis had been disappointing but the performance for 70 minutes against Spain was one of the most impressive in the competition and would have fostered the belief that should they get off to a fast start against their next European opponent, they would be able to carry that momentum to qualification.

The fast start nearly came, but it was for Ukraine rather than Tunisia. Bolton Wanderers defender Radhi Jaïdi attempted to be too clever when he was the last man and allowed Voronin to collect the ball. The Bayer Leverkusen striker could not take advantage, though, and played a poor ball to try to free Shevchenko. Tunisia managed to clear the danger. However, it was an early warning sign that Ukraine meant business. They continued to try to press home an early advantage, with Tymoshchuk driving into the penalty box only to fire his shot straight at the goalkeeper, who stood firm to block the effort. Despite the pressure Ukraine were exerting, Tunisia's defence was once more standing firm. Jaïdi and Haggui were both performing exceptionally well, and if Tunisia could start to click going forward, there was every chance they could win.

With half-time fast approaching, it seemed likely that both teams would be content to see the remaining time out and regroup at the break. Oleh Shelayev did try a speculative effort from range in added time that was well pushed over by Boumnijel. However, the referee, as opposed to just awarding the corner, had spotted a foul on Tymoshchuk in the build-up to the shot and went back to Ziad Jaziri to brandish the yellow card. Unfortunately for the Troyes midfielder, he had already been booked. Inside the first ten minutes, he had been shown a yellow card for a blatant dive and this latest transgression ended his participation in the contest early. The replays showed that the decision may have been harsh on the Tunisian, but it was also hard to argue that it was not a bookable offence. It fell firmly into the category of 'you can see why the referee has made that decision'.

Half-time came at the perfect time for Tunisia in that the whistle blew almost immediately after Jaziri's dismissal. It afforded Roger Lemerre the time to come up with a new plan to defeat Ukraine. His team needed a goal and could not afford to try to simply hold out for the remaining 45 minutes. No changes were made at half-time though, and Tunisia came out with a renewed sense of determination for the start of the second half. They showed a lot more intensity despite the man disadvantage and started to cause the Ukrainian back line problems. There was a strong appeal for a penalty too, when a Yari free kick was deflected over by Voronin. The Tunisians were convinced that the ball had deflected behind off the hand of the striker but the Paraguayan referee only saw fit to award a corner. The replay clearly showed that the ball did indeed hit the arm of the Ukrainian and his arm was certainly raised above his head and away from his body. In the era of VAR it would almost certainly have been given as a penalty but Ukraine got away with it. From the resulting corner, Haggui nearly made the lack of penalty award a moot point, but could only steer his header over the bar.

The failure to award Tunisia a penalty became even more controversial less than five minutes later when the referee pointed to the spot to award Ukraine a spot kick of their own. Shevchenko was driving into the six-yard box and attempting to squeeze through a gap between the goalkeeper and Haggui. There may have been slight contact between the defender and the striker but the replay suggested that Shevchenko actually tripped himself up rather than the crucial contact coming from any Tunisian player. From the angle the referee had of the incident, it is understandable why he felt that it was a penalty but, with the benefit of replay, it could easily be argued that he had to make two penalty calls in just four minutes and got both wrong.

The Chelsea striker picked himself and took charge of penalty-taking duties. His run-up was fairly simple and he calmly sent his penalty to the keeper's left, watching as Boumnijel dived in the opposite direction. The goal all but confirmed Ukraine's qualification as two quickfire Tunisian goals seemed unlikely with all 11 players on the pitch, let alone with ten.

Despite now throwing everything they had forward, Tunisia never seemed like getting the goals that they needed. Substitutes being introduced on both teams served to only disrupt any flow that the match was settling into and Ukraine were doing a near-perfect job of seeing the match out. Voronin did have a chance to put a stamp on the victory in the final minute of normal time but his close-range effort was straight down the throat of Boumnijel. However, there is usually one final big opportunity for a team chasing a goal in the final few minutes, and Tunisia saw that come and go when Francileudo Santos was the first to reach the ball in the box but could only send his header wide of the goal.

It was heartbreak for Tunisia when the final whistle finally blew as it confirmed their exit from the tournament. There could be few disappointments in their premature departure as they had failed to show much attacking intent during the competition. Their solitary point, the 2-2 draw with Saudi Arabia, came entirely against the run of play, and for all their endeavour against Spain, the final score was a 3-1 defeat that could have been more comfortable for the Spaniards. Even during this match their attempts to push for the victory that they knew they needed only came in the final exchanges when Ukraine had already taken a crucial lead.

Meanwhile, Blokhin's team had done it. Qualification from the group was seen as the minimum expectation but doubts will have undoubtedly crept in after their opening demolition at the hands of Spain. Their bounce back had been incredible and their star man Shevchenko was beginning to settle into the tournament. The better news for Ukraine was that, whereas Spain suffered the consequence of France's lack of form, they got to avoid the European giant. Instead it was Switzerland waiting for Ukraine in the Round of 16 and there was a very real chance that Ukraine could reach the quarter-finals on debut. It was an impressive turnaround, and now, playing without fear of not living up to expectations, the hope was for Ukraine to begin to show their attacking talents and step up their game to an even higher level and cause some shocks along the way.

3pm, 14 June 2006
Zentralstadion, Leipzig
Attendance: 43,000
Referee: Massimo Busacca (Switzerland)

Spain 4 (Alonso 13, Villa 17, 48 (p), Torres 81)
Ukraine 0

Spain: Iker Casillas (c), Sergio Ramos, Pablo, Carles Puyol, Mariano Pernía, Marcos Senna, Xabi Alonso (David Albelda 55), Xavi, David Villa (Raúl 55), Luis García (Cesc Fàbregas 77), Fernando Torres. **Manager:** Luis Aragonés.

Ukraine: Oleksandr Shovkovskyi, Volodymyr Yezerskiy, Vladyslav Vashchuk, Andriy Rusol, Andriy Nesmachnyi, Oleh Husyev (Oleh Shelayev 46), Anatoliy Tymoshchuk, Andriy Husin (Andriy Vorobey 46), Ruslan Rotan (Serhiy Rebrov 63), Andriy Voronin, Andriy Shevchenko (c). **Manager:** Oleg Blokhin.

Booked: Rusol (17), Yezerskiy (52)
Sent off: Vashchuk (47)

6pm, 14 June 2006
World Cup Stadium, Munich
Attendance: 66,000
Referee: Mark Shield (Australia)

Tunisia 2 (Jaziri 23, Jaïdi 90+2)
Saudi Arabia 2 (Al-Qahtani 57, Al-Jaber 84)

Tunisia: Ali Boumnijel, Hatem Trabelsi, Radhi Jaïdi, Karim Haggui, David Jemmali, Riadh Bouazizi (c) (Mehdi Nafti 55), Jawhar Mnari, Adel Chedli (Kaies Ghodhbane 69), Hamed Namouchi, Ziad Jaziri, Yassine Chikhaoui (Karim Essediri 82). **Manager:** Roger Lemerre.

Saudi Arabia: Mabrouk Zaid, Ahmed Dokhi, Redha Tukar, Hamad Al-Montashari, Hussein Sulaimani (c), Omar Al-Ghamdi, Khaled Aziz, Saud Kariri, Mohammed Noor (Mohammed Ameen 74), Nawaf Al-Temyat (Malek Mouath 67), Yasser Al-Qahtani (Sami Al-Jaber 82). **Manager:** Marcos Paquetá.

Booked: Haggui (35), Bouazizi (36), Chedli (65), Chikhaoui (79)

6pm, 19 June 2006
Volksparkstadion, Hamburg
Attendance: 50,000
Referee: Graham Poll (England)

Saudi Arabia 0
Ukraine 4 (Rusol 4, Rebrov 36, Shevchenko 46, Kalynychenko 84)

Saudi Arabia: Mabrouk Zaid, Ahmed Dokhi (Abdulaziz Khathran 55), Redha Tukar, Hamad Al-Montashari, Hussein Sulaimani (c), Omar Al-Ghamdi, Mohammed Ameen (Malek Mouath 55), Khaled Aziz, Mohammed Noor (Sami Al-Jaber 77), Saud Kariri, Yasser Al-Qahtani. **Manager:** Marcos Paquetá.

Ukraine: Oleksandr Shovkovskyi, Vyacheslav Sviderskyi, Andriy Rusol, Andriy Nesmachnyi, Oleh Husyev, Serhiy Rebrov (Ruslan Rotan 71), Anatoliy Tymoshchuk, Oleh Shelayev, Maksym Kalynychenko, Andriy Voronin (Andriy Husin 79), Andriy Shevchenko (c) (Artem Milevskyi 86). **Manager:** Oleg Blokhin.

Booked: Dokhi (41), Al-Ghamdi (57), Kariri (73); Nesmachnyi (22), Kalynychenko (77), Sviderskyi (89)

9pm, 19 June 2006
Gottlieb-Daimler-Stadion, Stuttgart
Attendance: 52,000
Referee: Carlos Simon (Brazil)

Spain 3 (Raúl 71, Torres 76, 90+1 (p))
Tunisia 1 (Mnari 8)

Spain: Iker Casillas (c), Sergio Ramos, Pablo, Carles Puyol, Mariano Pernía, Marcos Senna (Cesc Fàbregas 46), Xabi Alonso, Xavi, David Villa (Raúl 46), Luis García (Joaquín 57), Fernando Torres. **Manager:** Luis Aragonés.

Tunisia: Ali Boumnijel, Hatem Trabelsi, Radhi Jaïdi, Karim Haggui, Anis Ayari (Alaeddine Yahia 57), Riadh Bouazizi (c) (Kaies Ghodhbane 57), Hamed Namouchi, Mehdi Nafti, Jawhar Mnari, Adel Chedli (Haykel Guemamdia 80), Ziad Jaziri. **Manager:** Roger Lemerre.

Booked: Puyol (30), Fàbregas (89); Ayari (32), Trabelsi (40), Jaïdi (70), Guemamdia (81), Jaziri (85), Mnari (90+3)

4pm, 23 June 2006
Fritz-Walter-Stadion, Kaiserslautern
Attendance: 46,000
Referee: Coffi Codjia (Benin)

Saudi Arabia 0
Spain 1 (Juanito 36)

Saudi Arabia: Mabrouk Zaid, Ahmed Dokhi, Redha Tukar, Hamad Al-Montashari, Abdulaziz Khathran, Mohammed Noor, Saud Kariri, Khaled Aziz (Nawaf Al-Temyat 13), Hussein Sulaimani (Mohammad Massad 81), Saad Al-Harthi, Sami Al-Jaber (Malek Mouath 68). **Manager:** Marcos Paquetá.

Spain: Santiago Cañizares, Míchel Salgado, Juanito, Carlos Marchena, Antonio López, Cesc Fàbregas (Xavi 66), David Albelda, Andrés Iniesta, Joaquín, Raúl (c) (David Villa 46), José Antonio Reyes (Fernando Torres 70). **Manager:** Luis Aragonés.

Booked: Al-Jaber (27), Al-Temyat (77); Albelda (30), Reyes (35), Marchena (75)

4pm, 23 June 2006
Olympiastadion, Berlin
Attendance: 72,000
Referee: Carlos Amarilla (Paraguay)

Ukraine 1 (Shevchenko 70 (p))
Tunisia 0

Ukraine: Oleksandr Shovkovskyi, Vyacheslav Sviderskyi, Andriy Rusol, Andriy Nesmachnyi, Oleh Husyev, Serhiy Rebrov (Andriy Vorobey 55), Anatoliy Tymoshchuk, Oleh Shelayev, Maksym Kalynychenko (Andriy Husin 75), Andriy Voronin, Andriy Shevchenko (c) (Artem Milevskyi 88). **Manager:** Oleg Blokhin.

Tunisia: Ali Boumnijel, Hatem Trabelsi, Radhi Jaïdi, Karim Haggui, Anis Ayari, Riadh Bouazizi (c) (Francileudo Santos 79), Hamed Namouchi, Mehdi Nafti (Kaies Ghodhbane 90+1), Jawhar Mnari, Adel Chedli (Chaouki Ben Saada 79), Ziad Jaziri. **Manager:** Roger Lemerre.

Booked: Sviderskyi (18), Shelayev (47), Tymoshchuk (61), Rusol (65); Jaziri (9), Bouazizi (43), Jaïdi (90)
Sent off: Jaziri (45+1)

Group H	P	W	D	L	GF	GA	GD	PTS
SPAIN	3	3	0	0	8	1	+7	9
UKRAINE	3	2	0	1	5	4	+1	6
TUNISIA	3	0	1	2	3	6	-3	1
SAUDI ARABIA	3	0	1	2	2	7	-5	1

Spain and Ukraine qualified

Round of 16

KNOCKOUT FOOTBALL is a perilous journey as one wrong step will derail any progress. The best team quite often fails to win a tournament as one slightly below-par performance in the knockout stages leads to elimination. It creates an extra layer of jeopardy, one that some teams cope with and others do not. Five of the Round of 16 matches had favourites heading into them, while the other three were perhaps more of a coin flip as to who would win, but none of that mattered once the match kicked off. France, who had struggled to a bore draw with Switzerland in their opener, along with Ukraine and Ghana, who had both been comfortably beaten, knew that they could not afford another performance like those openers. This was the time for the cream to rise to the top. Not reaching top form in the groups was not a problem as long as you secured qualification, the key was timing the run into form. Teams that get better as the tournament progresses often end up winning it. Starting quickly and being a favourite after the group stages rarely translates into lifting the trophy. This was effectively a tournament within a tournament. The group stages and knockouts are two entirely different prospects and this was the time for the best in the world to showcase their talents.

There was no break in the action as Germany kicked off the Round of 16 against Sweden the day after the group stages had ended. It had been a promising group stage for the hosts as they made it through with a perfect record and had shown flashes of their new era beginning to take hold. The youngsters, Bayern duo Lahm and Schweinsteiger and FC Köln's Podolski had all been lively in the group matches, with the Bayern pair linking up particularly well down the left-hand side. The trio would all feature throughout Germany's ascension back to the top level of international football, culminating in their World Cup victory in 2014. Lahm, now playing in midfield after moving into a role just in front of the defence under Pep Guardiola at Bayern, and Schweinsteiger were key players, while Podolski was more of a squad player after the emergence of Thomas Müller. The other Germans who starred at both tournaments were Miroslav Klose and Per Mertesacker. Klose's inclusion, despite his age, was unsurprising as he represented the most natural goalscorer available to the Germans as evidenced by the fact that he became just the third player to score at four different World Cups and became the highest-ever World Cup goalscorer.

Their opponents Sweden were also trending in a positive direction, although perhaps not as upwardly mobile as their hosts. Having flattered to deceive against Trinidad and Tobago and Paraguay, there was a real show of life in the second half against England where they were unfortunate not to come away with all three points and top spot in the group. It was a group of players entering its best years, with key players Ibrahimović and Andreas Isaksson aged just 24, Kim Källström just 23 and Johan Elmander 25. Marcus Allbäck, Henrik Larsson and Niclas Alexandersson may have all been the other side of 30 but there was clearly a strong future ahead for the Swedes as they had a squad that could grow and thrive together as they all entered their primes. Zlatan was the only change in the Swedish team from that England match, with the striker coming back to replace Allbäck, who was perhaps unlucky to miss out on a starting spot.

It did not really matter who Lars Lagerbäck opted to lead the line alongside Larsson, as it was Germany that started on the front foot. It only took them four minutes to create the first opening when Torsten Frings lifted a ball over the defence that eventually came to the feet of Ballack via Podolski. The German captain played a clever ball in behind the Swedish defence for Klose to race on to but Isaksson was first to the ball and smothered at the feet of the striker. Unfortunately for the goalkeeper, he was unable to keep hold of the ball and it rolled dangerously to the waiting Podolski on the edge of the area. He kept his composure to fire the ball into the unguarded net under pressure from a desperate recovery lunge from Olof Mellberg. It was the dream start for the hosts, a goal ahead after just four minutes and a perfect way to calm any nerves that they may have been feeling.

It very nearly got even better just three minutes later when Podolski took aim from about 25 yards out, only for the ball to whistle narrowly over the crossbar. The near miss seemed to awaken Sweden from their lacklustre start as they nearly drew level straight away. A simple ball over the top found Larsson, who held off his defender brilliantly and turned to set himself free, running towards goal. The veteran striker had the angle against him, cutting in from the left-hand side of the area but would have still backed himself to test Lehmann. However, he could only drag his shot into the side-netting, with Ballack making a brilliant recovery to limit his shooting options, perhaps even getting a touch on the ball to help it wide, although a goal kick was given. It was the shot in the arm that Sweden desperately needed and Zlatan nearly drew them level when attempting a spectacular effort but his connection was unusually poor and the ball flew over the bar. Momentum was seemingly beginning to turn in the favour of the Scandinavians after a rocky opening, so it was almost predictable that Germany would double their lead just a minute after Zlatan's effort.

The front pairing of Klose and Podolski were again the scourge of the Swedes, with the Köln forward receiving the ball just inside the Swedish half and releasing it to Klose on the edge of the area. Klose drove to his left, taking his marker with him and clearing the space he had just been occupying. Three Swedish defenders converged on Klose to try to prevent him getting a shot away but nobody had tracked the run of Podolski. A simple ball took the three Swedes out of the equation and released Podolski in space just inside the box, and the youngster made no mistake, sweeping the ball home. It was a devastatingly simple goal and one that Sweden, notoriously hard to break down in defence, would have been incredibly frustrated to have conceded. With just 12 minutes gone Germany had already built a 2-0 lead and seemed to be riding a wave of confidence.

It was quickly turning into the perfect match for the Germans under Munich's evening sun. Chances were coming frequently, with Sweden seemingly unable to live with the movement of the German attacks. Ballack had the next opportunity, forcing a smart save from Isaksson with a powerful strike from the edge of the box, before Klose wasted a header he really should have hit the target with. However, for all Germany's attacking threat, not killing the game off left them vulnerable to counter-attacks, and Sweden were showing signs of life. Larsson again used his strength well to try to fashion a shooting chance but Christoph Metzelder defended the chance cleverly.

Bernd Schneider came close to adding to Germany's lead but could only drag a shot wide before Erik Edman was lucky to escape a booking for a mistimed challenge on Podolski. There was no malice in the tackle but it was late and could have caused injury.

Had they not been so profligate, Germany could easily have been five or six goals ahead before the interval. A brilliant run down the left by Lahm saw him reach the byline. His pull-back found Klose in a yard of space in the box. A quickfire effort was destined for the bottom corner before a remarkable save by Isaksson diverted it wide. The save was even better when considering the fact that the shot-stopper was originally moving in the opposite direction and had to adjust quickly. Frings and Schweinsteiger both tried their luck from 40 yards out, with Frings bringing another good save out of Isaksson and the Bayern midfielder's effort rippling the side-netting, causing premature celebrations from German fans.

Any faint, lingering hopes Sweden had of mounting a comeback seemed to be distinguished just 35 minutes into the contest when Teddy Lučić got too tight to Klose in the middle of the pitch. The attacker turned his marker and was running into space before Lučić grabbed a handful of his shirt and stopped his advance. It was as clear a yellow card as you will see but, unfortunately for Sweden, Lučić had already received a yellow card for an earlier infringement and was dismissed. There was no complaint from Lučić as he trudged from the pitch, knowing he may have just ended his nation's chance.

Surprisingly, the sending-off seemed to have the opposite effect on Sweden and their best spell of pressure came in the aftermath. Ibrahimović, finally making himself a presence in the match, collected possession of the ball just outside the six-yard box, turned and shot, forcing a smart save from Lehmann, who just about scrambled the ball behind for a corner. Then the Arsenal goalkeeper nearly cost his team a goal when he rushed out to gather a cross into the area but was beaten to the ball by Mattias Jonson. The ball rolled dangerously towards the goal line before a German defender managed to get back to clear it.

Half-time arrived and Germany were in seeming cruise control. A two-goal and one-man advantage represented the near-perfect half of football. The chances that they had afforded Sweden, especially in the immediate aftermath of the sending-off, would not have pleased Klinsmann as it highlighted the vulnerabilities in the defensive line that had been evident during their opener with Costa Rica, but the match was very much under his team's control and they just needed a calm second period to see it out.

One thing tournament football cannot be called, however, is calm. Just six minutes into the second half, a clever run down the left-hand side by Zlatan saw the ball reach Larsson in the middle. As the striker went to collect it, Metzelder stepped into him to try to retrieve the ball. Upon seeing the contact, the referee deemed that the central defender had been too forceful in his attempt and awarded Sweden a penalty kick and a lifeline. The replay showed that there was contact between the two but it was minimal, and had the Brazilian official not awarded the penalty, few people would have complained vociferously. The decision had been made, however, and Larsson took the responsibility on himself. A veteran of big matches, the Celtic cult hero was a world-renowned finisher, having scored 286 goals in 482 appearances in his club career as well as 36 in 92 to date for his nation. Looking composed while staring at the referee and waiting for the whistle to blow, Larsson stepped up to give his country a way back into the contest. He opted for power, aiming down the middle. Lehmann stood still but the ball sailed over his head. It also sailed over the crossbar as the Barcelona forward had gone with too much power and not enough accuracy. It was the perfect opportunity for Sweden to get themselves back into the match, but as the ball flew over the goal, Sweden's hopes may have gone with it.

Almost immediately Germany went in search of the clincher. Ballack cleverly worked some space for himself outside the area and curled an effort that hit the outside of the post and bounced clear. It was a near miss that on second viewing was actually a superb fingertip save by Isaksson, who was certainly showing his quality during this contest, impressing enough to earn a move to England with Manchester City after the conclusion of the tournament.

The match began to settle into a comfortable rhythm at this point as substitutions were made and the sweltering Munich heat started to take a toll on the energy levels of the players. Possession was the commodity that Germany wanted for the final half an hour and they retained it with comparative ease. They still managed to fashion a few chances, Ballack seeing a volley blocked, Schneider's deflected effort wrong-footing Isaksson but clipping the post and going wide, and Neuville's sharp effort being stopped again by the Swedish goalkeeper.

It had been a formality ever since Larsson's missed penalty but the final whistle confirmed Germany's passage into the quarter-finals. The disappointment was clear on the faces of the Swedish players as they left the pitch. They had been eliminated but they had also failed to show the quality that they evidently possessed. Isaksson aside, the Swedes had struggled to get to grips with the contest. Defensive mistakes had cost them two goals and set them on the back foot immediately. Lučić's rash decision to grab the shirt of Klose near the halfway line was borderline stupidity, and the usually reliable Larsson had wasted the perfect opportunity to offer some hope.

However, the biggest let-down was in the showing of Ibrahimović, who had entered the tournament with hopes of helping to inspire his nation to a good showing, but he failed to live up to that expectation. Injuries played a part in his underperformance, but had Zlatan shown his full capabilities then maybe Sweden could have caused an upset.

As far as World Cup knockout matches go, this was as routine a victory as possible. The two early goals settled any nerves that may have been lingering and more chances came at regular intervals. Perhaps the only negative for Klinsmann would have been the lack of cutting edge as his team wasted several chances to make the scoreline more comfortable. Against a higher calibre opposition, wasting as many opportunities as they had against Sweden could come back to haunt them. The only thing that would have been important for Germany was they were heading to Berlin to play in the quarter-finals with the complete backing of a home crowd that had thrown their entire support behind their nation in a way that had not been seen previously.

* * *

Awaiting Germany in the capital would be the winner of the clash between Argentina and Mexico. Leipzig was the host city for the second Round of 16 clash and, on paper at least, Argentina were the clear favourites. *La Albiceleste* had been the standout team of the group stages, playing some beautiful football at times and being unfortunate not to win all their matches, having been held by the Netherlands in a match that they dominated. Their zenith had been the 6-0 drubbing of Serbia and Montenegro when they had scored one of the most iconic goals in the history of the World Cup. José Pékerman had his team playing good football and had the squad depth that suggested that they would be force to be reckoned with. Their key players had been stepping up and they had the raw talent of Carlos Tevez and Lionel Messi to call upon from the bench should they need it. Seemingly, the only thing that would trip up Argentina's progress was themselves getting in their own way.

Hoping to cause that stumble earlier than anticipated was a Mexico team that had reached this stage at the previous three

World Cups, being eliminated each time. Their best-ever finish was two quarter-final appearances in 1970 and 1986 when they hosted the tournament. *El Tri* were a fixture of World Cups, only failing to reach the finals on five occasions, one of which was because of a FIFA-sanctioned ban. At a 1988 CONCACAF Under-20 tournament, Mexico were found guilty of using players that were over the age limit dictated in the rules. It was something that FIFA had warned against prior to the tournament as it was becoming a common practice for some teams to lie about the ages of their players in order to progress through these competitions. Mexican journalists eventually uncovered evidence showing that members of the Mexican squad were actually over the age limit and FIFA ultimately ruled that all Mexican teams were banned from competing in FIFA-sanctioned international tournaments for a two-year period. It was an incredibly harsh sentence handed down but it was designed to discourage teams from attempting similar in the future. Upon their return to international competitions, and with the hiring of famed Argentine coach César Luis Menotti, Mexican football had begun to become a constant presence on the world scene.

Both teams made extensive changes for the clash, with Argentina bringing back key players that they had rested for the final group fixture, meaning that Scaloni, Heinze, Sorin, Saviola and Crespo all returned. For Mexico, Ricardo La Volpe made four changes as he struggled to find the perfect balance to improve his team's mixed performances from the group stages.

As play got underway, there appeared to be nerves in the Argentina defence. An early clearance was panicky and hurriedly rushed behind for a corner, from which Jared Borgetti had a header on target, only for it to be deflected behind for another corner. It was a fast start from Mexico as they took the game to their more established opponents. Then their quick start became the dream start after just six minutes as a free kick from the right-hand side was glanced on by Méndez. The flick-on was the perfect weight to clear the Argentinian defence and reach captain Rafael Márquez, who had drifted into space at the back post. He was marked by Heinze, but the Manchester United defender had switched off and allowed him to get free. The Barcelona player made no mistake, catching the ball with his outstretched right boot and firing it past Abbondanzieri and into the net. Mexico could not have hoped to have started better and they were looking like a team fired up and ready to cause an upset.

An old cliché in football is that you are at your most vulnerable when you have just scored. Scoring brings about a lapse of concentration and the opponent is desperate to make amends immediately. It took Argentina only three minutes to gather their composure and draw themselves level. Riquelme was the provider, sending a corner into the Mexican penalty area for his team-mates to attack. Crespo was the Argentine challenging for the ball under pressure from Borgetti as he tried to volley home. The ball flew over the head of Oswaldo Sánchez, who could not react quickly enough to keep the ball out. Crespo wheeled away in celebration at having drawn his team level and the goal was awarded to him, but the replays seemed to suggest that the final touch actually came off the head of Borgetti as he tried to disrupt Crespo.

It had been a lightning start to the second match of the day and the contest developed into a brilliant back-and-forth one. Borgetti nearly made amends for his own goal just five minutes later when he was slipped in behind the Argentina defence but saw his shot blocked, before Crespo was released one-on-one with Sánchez and dinked the ball cleverly over the advancing keeper but could only send his shot beyond the far post. It seemed that there was an ongoing contest between the two strikers. Borgetti, who had only played for clubs outside of Mexico twice, while

Crespo, who was at Chelsea in between spells with both Milan clubs, were battling to see who was going to be the star, and the former Bolton Wanderers striker nearly restored Mexico's lead with a brilliant curling effort from 20 yards out, only for a flying save from Abbondanzieri to deny him.

As half-time approached, the match had begun to settle down as both teams took a breather. Argentina, seemingly content to get to the interval level and regroup, were keeping possession well, and their goalkeeper tried to play a simple ball out to Heinze in space. The defender, who was at fault for the Mexican goal, looked up to identify the next pass that he could make but in doing so completely lost track of the ball rolling into his path and could not control it. Francisco Fonseca, alive to the mistake, pounced on the loose ball and dinked it beyond the desperate lunge of Heinze, who made contact with the Mexican's leg. The referee immediately blew for the foul and brandished the yellow card. The replay showed that, although there was a defender back, he would have probably struggled to get round to cover before Fonseca could get his shot away, so Heinze was extremely fortunate to stay on the pitch. La Volpe was irate on the sideline and made sure the officials were aware of his displeasure at the decision, exacerbated by the fact that Márquez could only send the resulting free kick into the wall. It was the last meaningful action of a breathless first half and Mexico would certainly have been delighted with their performance and should have been in an even stronger position going into the second period.

Pékerman would have reinforced to his players at the break that they needed to step their game up if they were to progress into the next round, but they still seemed unsure of how to deal with Mexico at the start of the second half. The first opening again fell to Borgetti as he peeled free at the far post but his scruffy effort was palmed away by the keeper and then cleared away. It was a theme that had characterised Mexico's performances against Angola and Portugal in the group stage as they were capable of creating chances throughout but lacked a clinical finisher who could convert them. They had been fortunate to have a relatively easy group to navigate but should their wastefulness continue as the knockout matches progressed, they would struggle to keep up with those teams that could take the chances that fell their way.

Mexico's failure to take advantage of their pressure may have offered hope to Argentina that they could still win, and their key man Riquelme began to exert more influence over the play. The Villarreal midfielder saw his long-range effort blocked by Torrado, before his free kick found Maxi Rodríguez free at the back post, but his connection was not the best on the volley and the ball was tipped over the bar by the Mexican goalkeeper, albeit unconvincingly. The playmaker was again at the heart of Argentina's best moves when he drifted into space inside the Mexican half before playing a sublime through ball to free Saviola. The Barcelona striker was through one-on-one but his shot was too close to the keeper, whose strong hand diverted the ball behind. They may not have got their goal but Argentina were finally starting to play up to the hype that they had earned during the opening fixtures. Riquelme was dictating the tempo and Mexico were seemingly running out of ideas as to how to cause problems for their opponents.

Sensing the shift in momentum, Pékerman opted to go for the win. Tevez and Messi replaced Crespo and Saviola in like-for-like changes, but he also replaced the defensively minded Esteban Cambiasso with Pablo Aimar as he pushed for the winning goal in normal time. Tevez nearly provided an instant impact from the bench, but Sánchez was quickly off his line to prevent the goal. Argentina almost paid for their attacking gamble when

Fonseca outjumped the uncharacteristically poor Heinze with just two minutes remaining, but he made a poor connection with his header and could only send the ball well wide of the post. It was a warning sign that, despite their new-found momentum, Mexico were still capable of pinching the winner.

As extra time loomed, Argentina went forward one last time in search a winner. Once more it was Riquelme involved at the heart of the action, finding a pocket of space in a dangerous position and threading a perfect through ball for Maxi. The Atlético wide man was aware of his surroundings and played a simple square ball across the box to leave Lionel Messi with the simplest tap-in for what appeared to be the winner. The celebrations were surprisingly muted as the Argentines had already spotted that the assistant on the far side had raised his flag to indicate offside. There were barely any complaints from those in blue and white but the replays showed that they should have been incredibly aggrieved by the decision. Neither Maxi, who was played onside by a Mexican defender, nor Messi, who was behind Maxi when he played the ball across, were in offside positions and it should have been the match-winning goal.

With the disallowed goal, the match headed into extra time. This tournament was the first to see the removal of any attempts by FIFA to encourage more attacking football in extra time as neither a golden goal nor a silver goal was in operation. Designed as a way to encourage attacking football, the golden goal was simple in that if a team scored in extra time they automatically won the match. The silver goal, only in operation for two years, was even more of a failed experiment as it deemed that if either team was leading after the first 15-minute period ended they won the contest. Both rules made sense in theory as it rewarded those that were willing to push for a winner, but they had not seen any tangible increase in attacking play, so FIFA decided to remove them from the laws of the game, consigning golden or silver goal scorers to unique places in footballing history.

Even without the incentive of winning instantly, Mexico started extra time with a renewed vigour, moving the ball well and attempting to create space through clever movement. As players on both teams tired, the play became increasingly stretched and chances infrequent. It appeared that both teams were going to settle for a penalty shoot-out. However, with a little over five minutes to go in the first period of extra time, Argentina captain Juan Pablo Sorin collected the ball on the left-hand side and sent a brilliant cross-field ball to Maxi on the far right of the penalty area. What followed was the moment that young children dream of when playing on the street with their friends. His chest control was perfect, setting the ball away from his body and dropping for a beautifully hit volley. Stepping away from goal, Maxi unleashed the most perfect left-footed volley that saw the ball swerve across the goalkeeper and fly into the top corner of the net. The helpless outstretched dive of the keeper simply added to the aesthetic of the goal. It was easily one of the best World Cup goals ever scored and is worth watching more than once online to simply bask in the glory of the moment.

The remainder of the first period of extra time drifted away as everyone involved and watching was seemingly still in shock at the goal they had just witnessed. It was all or nothing time for Mexico now. Conceding a third goal made no difference so everything could be left on the pitch. Sinha did nearly produce a great moment, driving forwards into the Argentina half and curling a low shot that narrowly went wide of the post. Then Borgetti had perhaps the best chance for Mexico but his header was off target and was maybe a half-chance at best.

As the final whistle blew, those in blue and white were quick to race over to Maxi to celebrate his moment of genius. It had not been their best performance but sometimes those matches where you have to grind out a result can provide the most benefits. Pékerman had seen the character of his squad in the face of adversity and knew that they would battle for each other in search of their goal of winning the World Cup.

Contrasting the scenes of jubilation on the Argentina side was the heartbreak on the faces of the Mexicans. They had contributed enormously to the spectacle in what was one of the best matches of the tournament so far as both teams went for it. Had Heinze been sent off right at the end of the first half, who knows how different the result may have been. Being beaten by a truly special goal would have been scant consolation, and a fourth consecutive Round of 16 exit would have definitely hurt.

This run of Round of 16 defeats for Mexico remained unbroken until 2022, with losses to Argentina again in 2010, the Netherlands in 2014 and Brazil in 2018. However, the record breaker came in the opposite manner than many would have hoped, with Mexico failing to progress out of the group stage in Qatar. The Argentines would not have been worried about Mexico's dismal run though, they were more delighted to help continue it. Pékerman would have seen that he had work to do ahead of the Germany clash in the quarter-finals, but there was enough evidence that Argentina were going to be a force to be reckoned with in the latter stages.

* * *

With day one of the knockout producing no upsets, attention turned to Stuttgart where England were preparing to face Ecuador, and there is always a sense of an upset when England play in the knockout stages of a major tournament. Correctly or not, England always headed into international tournaments as one of the favourites to lift the trophy and they invariably always stumbled in pursuit of that goal. Four years earlier everything seemed to be aligning perfectly for them to win their second World Cup as shocks throughout served to create a seemingly easier route to the final. In the quarter-finals against Brazil, despite taking an early lead, England could not drag themselves to that next level and conceded two, including the infamous Ronaldinho free kick over the head of David Seaman, and Brazil would ultimately go on to win the competition.

Once again, England had entered the tournament as one of the favourites. The squad was well balanced and they had a superstar in Wayne Rooney working his way back to full fitness after injury. For the opening half of the first group match it had seemed like this time was going to be different. They had played well against Paraguay, moving the ball and creating chances, even if they had only taken one of them. After that, however, the momentum had seemed to stall. The rest of the group stage was more an akin to a marathon than a sprint as they just stumbled their way through with a narrow win over Trinidad and Tobago and a fortunate but entertaining draw with Sweden. The talent was clearly there and, if it clicked, England could certainly go deep into the tournament. Yet there just seemed to be an undercurrent in the air that something was going to go awry, there was going to be an infamous moment to match that of Seaman in 2002 and Beckham in 1998 to derail England's hopes. Sven-Göran Eriksson knew that the key to victory was controlling the tempo, so he brought back Gerrard and, in something of a shock, opted to replace Carragher as the right-back with Owen Hargreaves, bringing Michael Carrick in as the midfield shield in front of the defence. With Rooney the only striker, England were effectively playing with six midfielders spread across the pitch.

Hoping to facilitate their downfall was an Ecuador team that had been impressive in the group stage. Aside from the Germany match, when they took their foot off the accelerator as they had already qualified, they had looked like an incredibly solid team that would be hard to break down and that could attack well. Achieving qualification to the knockouts bettered their result on debut four years earlier and there was genuine belief in their ranks that they could beat England and produce the best result in their history. Having rested their key players during their final group match, the stars were back for Ecuador, especially the attacking duo of Carlos Tenorio and Agustín Delgado, who had impressed during the group stage with their clever link-up play and movement.

The opening exchanges may have vindicated Eriksson's decision as Carrick was a key influence on the match, keeping possession and helping his team to settle into the early flow. They were not creating any openings but everything seemed calm and composed, which was a positive sign, as chances were likely to come with the quality they had on the pitch. What could not be accounted for was a mistake by John Terry, whose attempted headed clearance simply bounced into the air behind him and allowed Tenorio a free run at goal. With Robinson setting himself to make a save and Tenorio fancying his chances, the Ecuadorian's shot was remarkably blocked by a lunging Ashley Cole, who had reacted perfectly to get back. His deflection sent the ball over Robinson and crashing against the crossbar. It was a perfect intervention by perhaps the best left-back in world football at the time.

It was the spark England needed to attempt to show some ambition of their own and Gerrard was the one who went the closest, curling a first-time effort just over the bar, but there was something lacking in England's performance. They had control of the midfield but Rooney was a completely isolated figure up front, not being supplied and unable to produce any of the magic that English fans had come to hope and expect. There was a lack of composure at the back as well with Terry compounding his earlier mistake by earning himself a booking for a high foot on Tenorio. The usually composed pairing of Terry and Ferdinand looked unsettled by the attacking duo of Ecuador, and England were struggling to create any positive momentum.

It was a match that was labouring, neither team able to fashion any chances as they were both seemingly more concerned about not making a mistake than pressing for the opening goal. That kind of match would have suited Ecuador more as England were perhaps more used to taking the initiative and dictating the tempo of the match. A cagey affair was the opposite of what was needed. Frank Lampard continued his tournament of missed chances when his 30-yard effort was easily stopped but it was at least a sign of positive intent from an English player. The next chance came from the boot of David Beckham. It had been a quiet tournament by his high standards but there was always the potential of him conjuring a moment of magic from nothing, which he nearly did when taking a free kick from 35 yards out that only just went wide of the post. The worrying thing for England was that his effort was one of their better chances in the opening period.

At the interval 0-0 was the predictable scoreline. England had controlled the tempo but all their efforts were long-range ones. The best chance had fallen to their opponents and the South Americans rarely seemed troubled against their more illustrious opposition. Something needed to change at half-time but Sven opted to leave things the same and trust his players on the pitch to turn things in their favour.

As the second half got underway, that faith seemed misplaced as nothing changed. Everything seemed like a chore and there was a lack of fluidity. A goal did not look likely, and even with half an hour remaining extra time seemed like the likely outcome. If a goal was to arrive, it was going to take a mistake or a moment of individual brilliance and, in Beckham, England had their talisman who was capable of producing that moment.

Having had a sighter in the first half, when England won a free kick 25 yards out and just to the left of centre, there was seemingly only one thought in Beckham's mind. He flighted the ball perfectly over the wall, the ball dipping low into the near corner, kissing the post as it crept into the back of the net. The Ecuadorian goalkeeper nearly got a hand to the ball, but it was so perfectly placed that it was tantalisingly out of reach. It was the moment of magic that England had so desperately needed and once again it was their captain that had stepped up to provide it. The reliance on Beckham in the biggest moments was perhaps a concern but there was still hope that as Rooney came back to full fitness the squad would continue to gel, becoming stronger and more fluid as the tournament progressed.

The goal did not change any aspect of England's performance, however. There was still a lack of intensity, the players struggling under the intense heat that was still present across Germany. The goal was a gift as it meant that there was less need for the players to over-exert themselves in search of that all-important goal. Lampard was again profligate in front of goal, dragging a shot wide and smashing one over the bar after some excellent work by Rooney down the left-hand side, his first real involvement in the match. But while England were struggling, they were hardly being tested either. Aside from the Tenorio chance at the beginning of the match, Ecuador were unable to create anything, barely keeping the ball long enough to threaten.

As the second half progressed and both managers began to make their changes, the play became even more disjointed. Neither team were creating any chances and the match was just passing everyone by as time ticked away. The most notable action of the last ten minutes or so was the unusual sight of Beckham throwing up on the pitch, with it revealed afterwards that he was struggling with heat exhaustion and dehydration. It was a match of few interesting moments, both teams failing to produce their best form and faltering under the intense sun that was baking the pitch in Stuttgart. For Ecuador there was probably a keen sense of regret as, had they played with a bit more intent and intensity, England would have been there for the taking and they could have quite easily claimed a historic victory for themselves.

On the opposite side of the table, the Three Lions would have been frustrated with the manner of their performance as it was nowhere near the quality that everyone knew they could produce, but there was still a sense of satisfaction at the completed job. Tournament football is often not about being the best team but the in-form team. Winning ugly and scraping through when not at your best is a hallmark of all the great teams and that could certainly summarise England so far. With Beckham producing a moment of quality and Rooney nearing full fitness for the first time during the summer, England were still a team to not be taken lightly. The hope was still there that this golden generation of English talent could finally take that next step, having fallen at the quarter-final stage in disappointing fashion four years earlier. England had reached their minimum expectation of the last eight and now needed to finally start showing why they had entered the tournament among the favourites to win it.

* * *

The origins of international footballing rivalries are usually easy to trace. They are often linked to old political or military tensions, such as England against both Germany and Argentina. Rivalries such as the one between Germany and the Netherlands, while starting through trauma from the Second World War, have been exacerbated by footballing history, especially with the Dutch being beaten in the 1974 World Cup Final by the Germans. History is often the biggest factor in creating animosity between nations when they meet on the football pitch. Egypt vs Algeria. Serbia vs Croatia. Brazil vs Argentina. These are all traditional and well-known rivalries and matches that could easily be expected to descend into chaotic scenes. One such match-up that seemed unlikely to produce any such drama was Portugal vs the Netherlands.

Relations between the Dutch and Portuguese have never been too problematic. Both were involved in overseas expeditions to other parts of the world, colonising nations that they came across and expanding their empires, but their paths rarely crossed. They were at war in their colonies during the 17th century with Dutch East and West India companies invading Portuguese territories in the Americas, leading to a conflict between the two. Aside from that, however, there was no lingering tensions between them and diplomatic relations remain strong to this day. Yet when their football teams met under the Nuremberg floodlights, anyone with no knowledge of the relationship between the two countries could be forgiven for thinking it was one that was filled with hatred.

Before the match began, the expectation was a close contest between two teams that had performed well during the group stages. Portugal, with an exciting blend of their two best generations, had won all three matches and looked a dangerous proposition under manager Scolari, while the Dutch, with two wins and a draw under their belt, had shown glimpses of quality and were being primarily led by their upcoming generation. This optimism for the future was perhaps evident in Van Basten's team selection, with Sneijder, Van Persie and Robben all included from the start and Ruud van Nistelrooy surprisingly dropped to the bench. Portugal's changes to their starting line-up were simply the return of the key players who had been rested for the group finale, with Deco,

Ronaldo and Pauleta all returning to hopefully inspire their nation on a run to the latter stages of an international tournament once again, having reached the European Championship Final two years earlier. The two teams had also met in the semi-final of that tournament, Portugal narrowly edging the contest 2-1. There was little animosity during that clash, certainly nothing to suggest what was about to occur in Germany.

As play got underway, the earliest sign suggested that the watching public was in for a treat. Inside the opening two minutes, Van Bommel fired a low shot from the edge of the area that narrowly went past the post. The Barcelona midfielder also managed to collect the first booking of the match within the same timeframe, cynically tripping Ronaldo as he attempted to burst free down the left-hand side. A narrow miss and a yellow card inside the first couple of minutes seemingly set things up for an enthralling contest but the mood soon began to shift with Khalid Boulahrouz picking up a booking for a nasty challenge on Ronaldo. The tackle was late and reckless, catching the Portuguese star on the thigh, studs first, and was perhaps a borderline red card challenge. Ronaldo was forced to the sidelines to receive some treatment and did not look comfortable when he re-joined the action.

The early intensity settled down after the frenetic start as both teams tried to figure out their best strategy for victory. The match managed to make it until the 20th minute before the next yellow card appeared, Maniche earning himself the caution for going through the back of Van Bommel. Despite a series of long-range sighters from the Dutch, highlights apart from bookings had been few and far between.

When Portugal managed to string a few passes together they looked capable of causing problems. Deco did well to get free down the right-hand side, playing a low cross into the area for Pauleta. The PSG striker laid it off for Maniche, who, after taking a couple of touches to release himself into space in the box, rifled a shot high into the roof of the net beyond the dive of Van der Sar. It was the first real moment of quality and it had led to the opening goal. It was the Chelsea midfielder's sixth international goal, the fourth scored in the finals of a major tournament and the second against the Dutch, having scored the winner at Euro 2004.

Despite the early setback for the Dutch, they continued to push on in search of the equaliser that they perhaps deserved on the balance of the early momentum. Almost immediately after conceding, a corner found Joris Mathijsen completely unmarked near the penalty spot. The central defender attempted to fire an audacious volley towards goal that flew harmlessly wide. Had it been his coach who had attempted it, maybe it would have flown into the back of the net, but the AZ Alkmaar defender lacked the same level of finesse as the legendary Van Basten. Everything the Dutch were trying was slightly off target. A long ball over the top of the Portuguese defence just evaded Dirk Kuyt, who would have been offside anyway. Then a wild slice at the ball from Costinha on the edge of his own area was not too far away from causing Ricardo a problem in goal.

While the Dutch continued to push forward, Portugal were threatening on the break. Maniche nearly added further misery when shooting narrowly over, and Deco's clever chipped effort never quite looked like dropping the right side of the bar for Scolari's team. The contest was levelled just after the half-hour mark, but unfortunately for the Dutch this was only in terms of bookings as Costinha added his name to the referee's notebook when he flew into a challenge on Philip Cocu. Mistimed rather than malicious but a clear yellow, especially in the context of the tone the Russian official had set early on.

The heavy challenges claimed their first victim of the night when Ronaldo, Portugal's great hope at inspiring them forwards on the international stage, was unable to shake off the knock he had picked up from the challenges of the opening five minutes. He was replaced by one of his predecessors in the lineage of tricky wingers produced by Sporting Club. Having been responsible for the development of Figo, the next one off the production line was arguably Simão. In a similar manner to Figo and Ronaldo, Simão was an out-and-out winger, hugging the touchline and taking players on with pace and skill. It was a key feature of the Portuguese set-up during this period as they had an unusually high number of incredible wingers in their national pool, evidenced by the fact that Ricardo Quaresma, the man who fitted between Simão and Ronaldo on the production line, was not even included in the squad.

With one young star now off the pitch, the Dutch were hopeful that their own talented youngsters could turn the tide in their favour. Van Persie was the man who nearly scored another in the long line of incredible Dutch World Cup goals. Picking up the ball on the right-hand side of the area, he cut back on to his favoured left foot, seemingly shaping to shoot. As two defenders dived to block the ball, he dragged it back beyond them, leaving both rooted to the floor. Rather than trying to shoot with his right, the Arsenal striker cut across the ball with the outside of his left, flashing the ball beyond the keeper but also wide of the far post. It was so nearly a beautiful goal for the youngster but he could not quite pull it off.

The first upping of the ante so to speak came with just five minutes left of the half. André Ooijer attempted to bring the ball out of the Dutch defence and was met by a strong challenge from Costinha. Having already been booked, it was a risky tackle to make, barely making contact with the ball and definitely catching the ankle of the marauding central defender. It was no better than previous challenges that had brought the card out of the referee's pocket, so the Portuguese midfielder was lucky to escape a second caution. The lack of a second card incensed the Dutch players, who quickly surrounded the Russian official, leading to some minor pushing and shoving from both sets of players.

Using their perceived injustice to spur them on, the Dutch nearly got in behind the disciplined Portugal defence, with Robben being flattened by a shoulder-high flying kick by Nuno Valente. Portugal were spared by the assistant's flag going up as Kuyt had been offside in the build-up, but the left-back was extremely lucky to avoid any reprimand as the challenge was extremely poor. Pauleta did manage to fire a snapshot away under pressure in the penalty area just after to almost add insult to injury for the Netherlands but Van der Sar made a smart save with his legs to deny the striker.

Costinha, perhaps agreeing with his opposition that some decisions had gone in Portugal's favour, decided to take matters into his own hands, literally. As the Dutch tried to progress on again, the midfielder inexplicably stuck out his arm and deflected the attempted pass away. Had the ball been heading through to a striker clear of the defence, the decision may have made sense. This, however, was a blatant handball for a pass that was maybe going to reach a midfielder just inside the Portuguese half. Left with little other option, the referee reached into his pocket once more and this time the red card followed the yellow.

Portugal managed to see out the final few seconds of the half but Costinha's rash decision had left the contest precariously balanced. A one-goal lead but a one-man disadvantage. Both teams would have been quietly confident at the interval. The Dutch now had one extra player and had been the better and more adventurous of the two teams, while Portugal had the lead and knew that, with Scolari leading them, they could see out the second half by making it a scrappier affair.

Having the one-player disadvantage meant Scolari needed to shuffle the pack around and set his team up to be more secure. Petit was a solid choice to come on and anchor the midfield but, perhaps surprisingly, Pauleta was the one sacrificed, all but confirming that Portugal's game plan was simply one of containment for the second period. The first involvement for the substitute was to deny Van Bommel from bursting forwards on the counter-attack and earning the next booking.

Van Bommel was at the centre of every action it seemed, crashing a close-range volley against the bar and seeing his long-range effort unconvincingly tipped behind by Ricardo, with the ball only just going wide after the goalkeeper's intervention. The Dutch were on top, predictably, and the introduction of another talented youngster in Rafael van der Vaart only cemented their superiority. The Hamburg midfielder almost drew his country level within two minutes of entering the play, unleashing a near-perfect effort from 30 yards out, only to see it smash into the post and eventually be cleared away.

The first real flashpoint came just at the hour mark, surprising given that there had been six yellows and one red already. Giovanni van Bronckhorst's lunging challenge on Deco was a clear free kick and yellow card, and everything seemed under control, with the defender helping Deco back to his feet, until there was some pushing and shoving and Van Bommel lay on the floor holding his face.

The replay showed Van Bommel and Figo squaring up to each other and the Portuguese captain headbutting the Dutch midfielder. There was minimal contact and the fall was dramatic and over the top, but it was a stupid decision from Figo and he was extremely fortunate to only receive a yellow card. The resulting

free kick by Simão went narrowly over the bar, clipping the top
of the net as it went over.

The number of players on each team was levelled up just after
Figo's headbutt when the winger was attempting to run down the
left and Boulahrouz stepped across him to attempt to shield the
ball. He used his left arm to help protect the ball but it caught
Figo in the face. If Van Bommel's reaction was pathetic when Figo
headbutted him, the Portuguese captain's was equally so when he
dropped to the floor. There was almost no contact but the Russian
ref saw fit to brandish another yellow card and the second red card
of the evening. The boiling point was well and truly reached in the
aftermath, with Joris Mathijsen getting agitated with the Portugal
players, believing, perhaps correctly, that they had influenced the
referee into evening up the numbers. It was not just on the pitch
that there was tension, with Scolari furiously protesting something
that may have happened in the ensuing melee.

When the players took a break from trying to kick each other,
there were openings falling for the Netherlands. Van Persie, the
shining light for his country, fired a dangerous ball across the box
that Ricardo left, but there was nobody waiting in the box for a
simple tap-in. Robben made good progress down the left, but
his cross was poor and cleared the heads of everyone in the area.
The Dutch were creating opportunities for themselves at regular
intervals and they should have done better with those chances that
they were carving out.

Another flashpoint came when substitute John Heitinga,
brought on to prevent Van Bommel becoming the third sending-
off, failed to give the ball back to Portugal when they believed he
should. Deco, acting more like his club team-mate Van Bommel
than his usual self, took matters into his own hands and hacked
the defender down as he charged forwards. An easy yellow for him
but, in the aftermath, Petit, who had been standing over Heitinga

voicing his displeasure, received a shove from both Sneijder and Van der Vaart, earning both Dutchmen a yellow card of their own.

Ricardo and Nuno Valente had their names added into the book for time-wasting and a clumsy challenge, respectively, before Deco became the third player to receive his marching orders. Having given away a free kick, he was wrestled to the ground by Cocu, who was trying to recover the ball to get play moving again. As the playmaker made his way back to his feet, he looked incredulous to see the referee brandishing a yellow and then a red at him. It was certainly a harsh decision but he had risked reprimand in delaying the match being restarted and the official was within the rules to issue the booking.

It was the shot in the arm the Dutch needed and their best chance came just two minutes later. Cocu made a perfect challenge on Figo just inside his own half and quickly released Kuyt in behind the Portuguese defence. The Feyenoord striker had the time to pick his spot as he was racing through but Ricardo was out quickly. A mix of good goalkeeping and poor finishing saw the shot saved and eventually cleared. It was the best opening that the Netherlands had created and it was hard to see a better one presenting itself.

Van Basten knew he had to roll the dice and go for it, so he brought off Cocu in favour of an extra striker. Bafflingly though, the forward he chose was Jan Vennegoor of Hesselink, who had scored 14 goals for PSV in all competitions the previous season, rather than Van Nistelrooy, who had scored 24 for Manchester United. It was an odd choice as Van Nistelrooy had already played during the tournament, while Vennegoor of Hesselink had not.

The Dutch knew their time was running out fast. Van der Vaart sent an acrobatic volley over, before Kuyt just missed tapping home a cross. But there was still time for one more moment of stupidity, bringing the 16th yellow card and fourth red of the match when Van Bronckhorst clipped the heel of Tiago. With the game seconds away from ending, it was one that the ref could have let go, but his previous decisions had set the tone and the red card was brought out again.

The Netherlands were unable to create that one last chance they needed to try to force extra time and Portugal edged through, setting up a match against England in the quarter-finals, Scolari's second tournament in a row meeting England at that stage. The match had been a very open and entertaining affair but has become infamous for the ridiculous number of cards shown. FIFA President Sepp Blatter said afterwards that Ivanov should have shown himself a yellow card, and the coaches felt that he had ruined the match. Retrospectively, that view is harsh. Ivanov's decision-making was well within the rules of the game and followed the protocol that the referees had been given prior to the tournament. He would not be chosen to officiate another match in the tournament but the reaction to his performance here was certainly overblown.

The match itself was a weird contest. There was no real animosity between both sets of players, despite all the cards. There were plenty of poor challenges and a few flashpoints but nothing that you would have expected from a match with four red cards. The Dutch would have been unhappy with their efforts as they arguably had the better chances but lacked a real cutting edge at the top of the pitch. They were never allowed to fully settle into a rhythm by a streetwise Portugal and, for that, Scolari would have been delighted. His team had shown that they would be stubborn, resolute and incredibly hard to break down. Nobody would have wanted to face this Portugal side, especially an England team that seemed to be lacking true confidence.

* * *

Sometimes a clear path opens up nicely during an international tournament for a team to progress. The luck of the draw and a shock result or two can completely alter the path to the final for one team, either clearing the route or adding more obstacles. For Italy in 2006 it was the former. France's slow start during the group stage meant that the Italians needed to beat Australia and then one of Switzerland or Ukraine to reach the semi-finals. Football is not a game played on paper but it was certainly opening up for Italy to reach the latter stages without too much trouble, should they perform to their capabilities. Lippi's team had done well so far, emerging from a tough group unbeaten, with only the USA managing to prevent them winning.

However, it had not been smooth sailing for Italy despite the positive results. Totti, included in the squad after impressively recovering from a broken ankle, was struggling to find his best form and was often drifting to the fringes of proceedings during their matches. His Roma team-mate Daniele De Rossi was now suspended until the final should Italy get that far, after having his ban for elbowing Brian McBride in that draw with the USA extended. Injuries had also begun to have an effect on the squad available, with Alessandro Nesta ruled out of the remainder of the tournament with a lower leg injury. There was plenty of depth within the squad with Materazzi and Gattuso being more than able deputies but Nesta and De Rossi were such integral parts of the system that Lippi had created, so their absences would certainly be felt.

They were perhaps aided by a slightly weaker draw than expected but their opponents Australia were one of the surprise packages of the tournament so far. Under experienced manager Guus Hiddink, the Socceroos had impressed in all their matches, with a stirring late comeback against Japan setting the tone, and they were unfortunate in their defeat to Brazil as they had arguably the better of the chances. The Dutchman was a seasoned campaigner, especially when it came to guiding teams to overachievement. He had led PSV to European Cup success in 1988 and he perhaps bettered that achievement in reaching the semi-finals of the Champions League with the same club in 2005, given the financial imbalance across European football. There was also another layer to the match-up of a Hiddink-coached team against Italy in the World Cup Round of 16 as he had been in charge of South Korea four years earlier in their infamous run to the semi-finals.

Italy were the obvious favourites prior to kick-off but Hiddink would have certainly had a quiet confidence in his team that it was not going to be the straightforward contest that many expected. The Italians were likely to have the majority of the possession but if Australia could keep it tight defensively, they could potentially steal the match on the counter.

The first chance did fall to Italy, with Luca Toni narrowly heading wide inside the opening three minutes, but there were few real openings as the match settled into its rhythm. It took 20 minutes for that rhythm to truly arrive but it was Italy who were the ones that looked the most likely to break the deadlock. Alberto Gilardino was benefitting from the hold-up play of his strike partner Toni, seeing two chances in two minutes well saved by Mark Schwarzer. However, Italy's early attacking play was unable to yield any positive results and it was exactly what Australia needed.

Having soaked up the early pressure, Hiddink's team began to venture forward themselves with a bit more confidence. Viduka had their first chance but could only direct his header straight at Buffon, before Chipperfield brought about a more difficult save but one that the Italian goalkeeper was a match for. Australia's forays showed a more positive intent but it may have simply spurred Italy into attack mode once again. Toni was at the centre of everything the *Azzurri* were doing well, being a nuisance with his physical presence and not allowing the Australian defenders time to settle. He saw a nice piece of chest control and volley blocked before his flick-on narrowly evaded Gilardino as he looked to link up with his strike partner.

Other than Craig Moore avoiding a booking for flattening Toni, the remainder of the first half passed by without any major incident. The Italians were in control, creating the better chances and keeping possession well but the openings that were being created were barely half-chances. Lippi would have been satisfied with some aspects of his team's performance but it was probably Hiddink who was the happier coach of the two. Australia had struggled going forward but that was unlikely to have been too problematic for Hiddink as, defensively, everything had been near perfect for his team. They were stifling the Italian attacks and limiting the influence that Pirlo could have over the match. With Viduka and Cahill lurking up front, if they could keep it secure at the back, Australia would have been fancying their chances of progressing if they could fashion one chance.

Half-time substitute Iaquinta almost proved his worth for Italy immediately after good play down the right in setting up Toni, who could only fire over the crossbar, but the match then seemed to switch in favour of the Australians just five minutes into the second period. A loose ball in the final third fell kindly for Mark Bresciano, who began to drive on towards the penalty area. Zambrotta was the covering defender from full-back but Materazzi dived recklessly into a challenge and missed the ball, bringing Bresciano down. It was a poor tackle but the majority of the contact was the central defender catching his team-mate's ankle as opposed to the Aussie forward. It was a clear foul and definitely a booking, but when the referee brought out the red card there was clear surprise among those watching.

The decision to send the Italian off was extremely harsh and would definitely have raised the hopes of the watching Australian public. Italy under Lippi, however, were an incredibly solid outfit and conceded rarely, with no opposition player finding the back of Buffon's net in the tournament so far. Lippi sacrificed Toni for Andrea Barzagli, the 25-year-old Palermo central defender, and hoped that the superior quality of player that they still possessed would be enough to allow them to keep control. Bresciano picked himself up and took charge of the free kick. His effort was good but was never really in danger of testing Buffon as it flashed wide.

The extra player was allowing Australia to properly gain a foothold in the contest for the first time and Chipperfield forced another save from Buffon with a low shot that the shot-stopper did well to palm away from danger. Even with the player advantage, Australia still seemed content to allow Italy to dictate the tempo and appeared happy to allow the match to drift towards extra time. Whether it was the new-found expectation on them, there was not much of a tempo increase and, against an Italian team even more likely to allow the play to come on to them, Australia needed to produce more of the showing that they had against Brazil. Instead, both teams settled into a cagey rhythm, no one willing to take a risk in producing the moment of quality that the match needed for fear of being the one who made the mistake that would cost their nation.

Even the introduction of Totti could do little to increase the tempo. Given 15 minutes to make a difference and finally stamp his mark on the tournament, the match was drifting away and the Roma captain still looked as if he lacked the fluidity and sharpness he had shown before his injury. Extra time was looming and there was literally just ten seconds left as Fabio Grosso drove down the left-hand side and into the Australian penalty area. As the full-back cut back inside on to his right foot, Lucas Neill lunged into the challenge to block the potential shot. With Neill prone on the floor, Grosso allowed himself to fall over the stricken defender. The Spanish referee, who was in the perfect position to see the action unfold, had no hesitation in pointing to the spot and awarding the penalty. The outrage of the Australian players and officials was predictable and perhaps justified as the contact was definitely initiated by the Italian, who took full advantage of Neill being on the ground. In his autobiography, *I Think Therefore I Play*, Andrea Pirlo describes it as 'a non-existent penalty', suggesting that even those in the blue of Italy knew that it was an incredibly harsh decision.

With the opportunity to avoid playing another 30 tiring minutes ahead of the quarter-finals, the pressure was placed on the shoulders of Totti to secure Italy's passage into the next round. Often the calmest player on the football pitch, Totti's recent autobiography, *Gladiator*, paints a different picture of the slow walk from picking the ball up and placing it down again on the spot. He describes the thought process of where he was going to put the penalty, debating whether or not to attempt an audacious Panenka. Six years earlier on Italy's run to the 2000 European Championship Final, their semi-final against the Netherlands had gone all the way to a penalty shoot-out. Totti was tasked with taking the third Italian penalty and he produced an iconic moment in Italian football history, dinking a penalty down the middle as Italy ultimately won the shoot-out. It was a moment of complete composure from one of the most stylish footballers and he clearly was thinking about doing it again against Australia.

However, he described Australian goalkeeper Mark Schwarzer as a smart keeper who would have studied the Italian penalty takers and he did not want to 'give him the chance to make him look clever, leaving me looking like an idiot'. Instead, Totti opted to aim for the top left, a spot where, if executed properly, it would leave the keeper with no chance of reaching it. Even though he had yet to show the true quality he was capable of during the tournament, there was little doubt among those watching that Totti would dispatch the spot kick and send Italy through, and that was exactly what he managed to do. Schwarzer guessed the right way but Totti's strike was too well placed and flew beyond the despairing dive of the goalkeeper. The relief among the Italians was evident immediately as all the players rushed to Totti, the emotion pouring out as they knew that they had booked their spot in the quarter-finals.

The result, or at least the manner of it, would have left a bitter taste in the Australians' mouths as the penalty was certainly harshly awarded. They had, however, benefitted from a soft dismissal of Materazzi and never looked like breaking down the Italians, even with the extra player. Everything seemed like it was a step too far for this iteration of the Australian team but their legacy definitely remained despite their exit. They had helped put football properly on the map within their nation, where sport was primarily dominated by rugby, cricket and hockey, and this team's progress was a key factor in the reason why more young children began to play the game in Australia.

Italy did not need to help grow the game in their country as they have always been one of the most passionate nations when it comes to football and that was clear based on the reaction of their players. They were the first to admit that they had not been at their best during the contest, perhaps even lucky to make it through at all, but they had progressed nevertheless, a key strength of any potential champion. It did not need to be pretty as long as it was effective, and the squad that Lippi had built was certainly that. With a theoretically easier quarter-final awaiting them no matter who won the other match-up, Italy were quietly making their way to the sharp end of the tournament and would be a team to be wary of for anyone coming up against them.

* * *

There are 64 matches during a 32-team World Cup. Some are instant classics, while others are fondly remembered in a retrospective review of the tournament as a whole. There are those that fail to live up to their hype and others that just fail to get going and are easier to forget. Yet, every so often, a match will occur that is almost impossible to forget, and not necessarily for good reasons. Unfortunately, the contest between Switzerland and Ukraine falls into that category.

Prior to the clash there was little to suggest what was to come. Both nations had entered the tournament expecting to qualify from their group but their performances had been more impressive than simply doing enough to qualify. The Swiss had done remarkably well during the group stages in beating France to the top spot and thus avoiding having to play Spain in the second round. They had been built around a solid defensive unit, led by Philippe Senderos, and they had emerged from the group without having conceded a goal. They had done enough to win their matches, except in a bore draw against France to open their campaign, but there was still a clear sense that they were a team that would prioritise keeping their opponents out before looking to hit on the counter-attack to steal their victories. The problem that potentially awaited, however, was that their star defender Senderos had damaged his shoulder ligaments during the final group match against South Korea and had been ruled out of the rest of the tournament, with his Arsenal team-mate Johan Djourou drafted in as his replacement.

For their opponents, Ukraine, it had been the worst possible start to their World Cup finals history when they were outclassed by Spain. Since that defeat, however, they had shown their true quality, winning both their remaining matches, including a comprehensive 4-0 victory over Saudi Arabia. Like their opponents, defensive solidity was a key component of their style as they were on a run of eight clean sheets in their previous nine outings, with only Spain getting the better of them. Led by star striker Andriy Shevchenko, Ukraine were a talented team with the potential to go on a deeper run than perhaps many predicted before the tournament, similar to Croatia's debut in 1998 when they reached the semi-finals. With a second-round clash against Switzerland rather than France, the opportunity for another shock at the sharp end of the tournament was very much alive. With both teams having matched their minimum expectations thus far, the hope was for a close encounter, one that would highlight the quality players of both teams that may so far have gone under the radar.

Perhaps both teams would have actually preferred to be playing against a clear favourite rather than a team they could realistically see themselves beating, as the pressure to take control of the match and dictate the tempo would have been lessened. For all the quality that they had shown so far, one characteristic that could not summarise the Swiss performances was attacking flair. Everything had been built on the defensive side of the game, keeping their opponents out and then hoping for moments of individual brilliance to snatch the victory. Despite this, they started the brighter of the two teams with two early long-range efforts. The first from Yakin was straight at the keeper and was easily caught, while the second from Wicky was more troublesome, with the keeper doing well to parry the ball behind for a corner.

The early Swiss opportunities were little more than half-chances and when the first clear opening came, it fell to the one player on the pitch that you expect to take it. A Ukraine free kick from the left-hand side was dangerously swiped into the penalty area by Kalynychenko, where it was met by a clever diving header from Shevchenko, who had beaten his marker Djourou to the ball. The new Chelsea striker made near-perfect connection, sending his header into the ground and up out of the reach of the Swiss goalkeeper, who was rooted to the spot. Unfortunately for the Ukrainians, the ball bounced off the crossbar and was cleared by a Swiss defender. It was the first real moment of quality that Ukraine had managed to produce in the match and it had almost led to the deadlock being broken.

Shevchenko's glorious chance threatened to spark the match into something resembling life as the Swiss produced their best opening immediately afterwards. Alexander Frei, the player that Switzerland's goalscoring hopes squarely rested with, took charge of a free kick nearly 30 yards from the goal. The Rennes striker whipped a beautiful shot on goal, getting the ball up and down over the wall and watching on in anguish as his shot crashed into the angle where the post meets the crossbar and deflected back out. His team-mate was unable to convert the rebound, wildly hacking an effort wide. Had the ball dropped an inch lower and nestled into the top corner for either of the star strikers on each team, the match may have gone a different way and we may have been treated to a more open and engaging game of football. Sadly, this was not to be and the match failed to get going.

The only other notable incident in the first half was the substitution of Djourou due to injury, a critical blow considering that Switzerland had already lost one defender to serious injury before this match. The half-time whistle came and there was an almost audible sigh of relief from those in the crowd that there was going to be a brief period of respite from the drudgery playing out on the Cologne pitch. Italian manager Annibale Frossi, coach of numerous Italian teams, including Napoli and Internazionale, once said that the perfect result of a game of football was 0-0 as it meant that every player, both attack and defence, must have done their job correctly. This 0-0 could not be said to fall into that category as it seemed that nobody was doing their job properly unless this was to allow time to expire without ever pushing forward properly in search of the breakthrough.

It was the Eastern Europeans who started the second half with a vague sense of intent, Voronin glancing a header wide just after the restart, but it was simply a case of more of the same from the first half. Tranquillo Barnetta picked up the only yellow card just before the hour mark and Cabanas somehow avoided one for himself after a poor challenge on Nesmachnyi. The match was very much in a lull and there was not even any needle to the tackles made, so there was no tension or drama for the watching public to get behind.

If either of the teams was going to be the one to make a breakthrough it was Ukraine, as they were the ones showing greater forward momentum and positivity. Shevchenko was the driving force behind his nation's good moments, cutting inside from the right-hand side and driving a fierce left-footed strike beyond the post. The striker also narrowly missed getting his head on another dangerous corner from Kalynychenko, although his team-mate Andriy Husin did manage to connect with the ball but could only send his header beyond the far post. It was a glancing header, there was pressure from defenders and the goalkeeper jumping at his back to try to punch clear, but he perhaps should have done better with the opportunity that presented itself. A poor Barnetta challenge for which he was lucky to avoid a second booking aside, the second half drifted harmlessly to a close with a goal never likely to arrive. Even FIFA's own match report struggled to find anything positive to say about the contest, describing it as a 'scrappy affair devoid of highlights', which was certainly an understatement.

Extra time is usually when a match can become cagey, with neither team wanting to make a mistake and the tiring players starting to struggle to positively influence the play. The last thing that this match needed was a decrease in tempo. Any slower and the match would have featured 22 statues. A few more substitutes, a couple of half-chances for the Swiss from Vogel and Streller that were saved and blocked, respectively, and then one brief moment of relief from the tedium provided by the interval during the extra period, before the inevitable end to the match was reached. The first penalty shoot-out of the tournament was here.

Strangely, just a few minutes before the shoot-out, the Swiss coach opted to take off Frei in favour of Mauro Lustrinelli, replacing a striker who would finish his career having scored 34 penalties with one who only scored 13. It was a strange decision and one that summed up the ludicrous nature of the match. That absurdity became all-conquering after the first round of penalties. Shevchenko took the first for Ukraine, sending his effort low to the goalkeeper's right, only for Zuberbühler to guess correctly and push it wide. Any advantage that the Swiss had was instantly given away when Marco Streller opted to go the same way as Shevchenko, with his effort nowhere near the corner and easily saved by the Ukrainian keeper. So far, 120 minutes and no goals; two penalties and no goals. It was a completely shambolic performance from both teams and the lack of goals even when taking penalties was the perfect summation of that.

The first moment of quality finally arrived with the third penalty as 21-year-old Artem Milevskyi executed the perfect Panenka, watching the ball nestle in the back of the net as the Swiss keeper dived out of the way. The pressure then flipped to Switzerland's 21-year-old Barnetta but the outcome was wildly different as he opted for power over precision, looking on in anguish as the ball rattled the crossbar and bounced clear. The early advantage had swung and was now in favour of Ukraine. That advantage was cemented further by Rebrov, whose penalty may not have been right in the corner but Zuberbühler had dived the wrong way and the Ukrainians had a 2-0 lead. A miss in their third penalty would not end Swiss hopes but would leave them hanging on by the barest of threads, and Cabanas was the one with the responsibility to keep the vague hope alive. Opting to aim down the middle and for the keeper to dive one way or the other is not the worst strategy for penalty taking but there usually needs to be some height on the ball so that if the trailing leg of the goalkeeper is still there, the ball will still go in. Cabanas had no height on his effort and that was the exact outcome as the Ukrainian goalkeeper managed to stop the ball.

With the knowledge that a successful spot kick would send his country through to the World Cup quarter-finals on their debut appearance, up stepped the Dynamo Kyiv midfielder Oleh Husyev. Belying what had gone before, Husyev was calm with his penalty, firing it hard and into the corner to the goalkeeper's right. Even had he dived the right way, it would have been a difficult penalty to save. Ukraine had triumphed 3-0 in the shoot-out. They were the victors but everyone watching was also a winner when Husyev scored as it meant that the match was finally over. There is a reason that this is routinely referred to as the dullest match in World Cup history and why the highlights package put on by British television opted to skip the entire 120 minutes and just show the penalties.

Despite the awfulness of the match, nothing can be taken away from the achievement of the Ukrainian players in reaching the next stage of the tournament. Reaching the quarter-finals of the World Cup is a good accomplishment for any nation, but to do it on debut made it even more special. With Italy awaiting them in the next round, the optimism may have been short-lived but Blokhin's team would have had a sense of confidence after seeing how the Italians had struggled to break down Australia earlier in the day.

As for the Swiss, they became the first nation to be eliminated from the World Cup without conceding a goal. An impressive if unwelcome achievement. This was certainly a talented Switzerland squad but with Barnetta, Djourou, Senderos and Behrami all aged 21 or under, there was certainly the hope that the best years were still to come for this generation of Swiss players, a nation that had continuously overachieved on the international stage and would have been hopeful of that trend continuing. However, despite an impressive win over eventual champions Spain to start their 2010 World Cup suggesting big things, they would only pick up one point in their next two matches and be eliminated at the group stages. Switzerland could always be counted on to reach major tournaments and upset a team or two, but for this generation the return was perhaps a little underwhelming.

* * *

With one of the most boring days in World Cup history out of the way, attention turned to the sport's usual entertainers to reignite the tournament's fire. Football is undoubtedly a better game to watch when Brazil are at the peak of their powers, the leading proponents of *joga bonito*, or playing beautifully. Think back to the best international teams ever to play the game and Brazil invariably appear on the list in multiple iterations. The 1958 World Cup-winning squad. The 1970 World Cup-winning squad. They do not need to even win anything to be revered throughout history. Just ask fans of a certain age about the 1982 World Cup team.

Even the pre-tournament adverts for 2006 knew that Brazil were the team most likely to produce football of a beautiful nature and be the entertainers. In a campaign fronted by Eric Cantona, Nike's adverts leading up to the tournament focused on encouraging the players to play the beautiful game in that way and not with theatrical dives and negative tactics that had become increasingly commonplace in football. The fifth advert of the group showed the Brazilian national team enjoying themselves on the way to a match, playing musical instruments and appearing entirely happy and relaxed. While in the changing room, Ronaldo, Adriano, Robinho and Ronaldinho, perhaps the most notable proponent of *joga bonito*, showed off their tricks and flicks, having some fun with huge grins on their faces. The entire advertising campaign aimed to showcase that football can truly be a beautiful game if its players were allowed to express themselves. If any team was going to provide a shot in the arm for the tournament after the previous day's action, then Brazil were definitely a good choice to take on that task.

Their opponents were also known for their attacking, entertaining football and had even been given the moniker of 'the Brazil of Africa' for their dominance over the continent in the 1960s while playing attractive football. This latest generation of Ghanaian football talent was beginning to reach its potential on the elite stage, having grown together as a squad since reaching the final of the 2001 FIFA World Youth Championship, with eight of that 18-player squad now featuring in the first team. The fact that this was Ghana's World Cup debut was surprising given their dominance during the 1960s and they would more than likely have been Africa's representative at the 1966 World Cup had it not been for a boycott of the tournament.

Ahead of that tournament held in England, FIFA decided that the 16 teams to participate in the event would be divided between ten European, four South American and one from the North American continent. The remaining place was to be contested between nations from Africa, Asia and Oceania. The Confederation of African Football (CAF) and 31 nations among their ranks decided to boycott the event to protest the lack of a guaranteed place for an African nation at any World Cup. CAF felt that this was grossly unfair to their nations, who they rightly believed should qualify directly for winning the African qualifiers. This meant that Ghana, who reached four consecutive finals between 1963 and 1970, winning in 1963 and 1965, would have more than likely been the African nation representing the confederation at least at the qualifier against the other continents, if not reaching the finals. Their protest and boycott ultimately paid dividends as, from 1970 onwards, African football was guaranteed a place in the finals, with the number slowly increasing to five for the 2022 World Cup and nine for the expanded 2026 tournament. The downside was that the wider world never got to see the brilliance of the Ghana team of the '60s, one consigned to history without ever getting their true recognition.

This Ghana generation came with high hopes of following in Senegal's footsteps from four years earlier and showcasing their talent on the global stage, and by qualifying through a considerably tough group, they were certainly showing that they could compete with the best the world had to offer. But Brazil would be a tougher challenge than they had faced so far. They would also have to face the reigning world champions without their star man Michael Essien, as the Chelsea midfielder had picked up a booking in the final group match and was suspended for this clash as it was his second of the tournament.

If Ghana were to have any chance of producing one of the biggest upsets in World Cup history, they needed to keep it tight for the opening exchanges and hope that frustration built among the Brazilian players. Sadly, it only took five minutes for the deadlock to be broken. However, the first chance nearly came inside the opening minute when Ronaldo received the ball in behind the Ghanaian defence but the offside flag went up before he could get a shot away, although the replay showed that it was a closer call than it initially appeared. The disappointment was short-lived for Brazil as Ronaldo again raced clear of the high line that Ghana were playing, fed by a through ball from Kaká, and was left one-on-one with the goalkeeper. A clever stepover and shimmy to the left gave him the open goal to tap the ball into to gave his nation the lead and to also claim a piece of personal history as that goal was the legendary striker's 15th in World Cup history, the most scored by a single player at that point.

The high defensive line that Ghana were choosing to operate was a high-risk, high-reward strategy but the risk was certainly outweighing the reward in the opening exchanges. Just eight minutes after conceding the opener, it was Adriano's turn to be completely free behind the defence with a straight run on goal. With Ronaldo alongside him, he opted to try to emulate his team-mate's goal by rounding the keeper and tapping into an empty net. This time, although the ball cleared Kingson, Adriano did not and initiated contact with the stricken goalkeeper to try to win a penalty. The Slovakian referee was not having any of it, however, and rather than award the penalty he booked the striker for diving. The yellow card seemed harsh but the lack of any meaningful protest from the Internazionale player suggested the referee made the right choice.

The Adriano chance seemed to spark Ghana into a bit of life and they began to try to assert themselves on their illustrious opponents. There seemed to be no fear in their ranks and they looked determined to be able to say that they had given the game a go, no matter the outcome, an admirable way of approaching the contest when it would have been easier to try to contain Brazil. Dramani had the first Ghanaian attempt with an ambitious effort from a long way out that Dida tipped over the bar, a good decision as the ball appeared to be destined for the back of the net. The decision to play two strikers was a bold call by the Ghanaian coach but it was working, as both Gyan and Matthew Amoah were creating problems for the Brazilian defence with clever movement and good hold-up play. Amoah had two chances in five minutes, the first when he was found in space on the edge of the area but could only drag his shot wide of the post, before bringing a routine save from Dida with another shot when found in space.

While Ghana were attacking in search of an equaliser, Brazil were still showing why they were the best team in the world heading into the tournament. Having been quiet so far, Ronaldinho was beginning to show flashes of the brilliance everyone knew he was capable of producing. The reigning Ballon d'Or winner had struggled to make an impact so far in the tournament but the quality was starting to shine through with some nice touches and flicks that created space for his team-mates. He nearly caught Kingson unawares in the Ghanaian goal with a clever effort to the near post that the keeper did well to claw away. After the lack of excitement the previous day, Brazil and Ghana were showing that football could still be played at high tempo in an attacking manner.

Openings kept coming for Ghana and they perhaps should have drawn themselves level in the first half. Gyan did well to get a shot away under pressure in the box but could only send his shot over the bar, then captain Appiah narrowly fired a free kick over the crossbar, before John Mensah had the best chance from a corner. The central defender was completely unmarked in the penalty area and aimed his header low to try to make it harder to deal with. Unfortunately for Ghana, the header was still too close to Dida, who did well to get his feet in the way and prevent the ball from reaching the back of the net. It was a flurry of chances that the Africans would regret not converting.

As Ghana pushed, space began to appear in their defensive third once again and right on the stroke of half-time Brazil punished their cavalier approach. Kaká picked up the ball inside the Ghanaian half and drove towards the box, feeding the overlapping Cafu down the right-hand side. The Brazilian captain fired a first-time cross into a dangerous area in between the goalkeeper and defenders for Adriano, who had drifted to the far post. It was not the cleanest contact, with the ball deflecting off his thigh after a touch from a desperate lunge by a defender, but the ball found its way into the roof of the net and doubled the lead for the reigning champions. On further inspection, as Cafu played the ball across, Adriano was clearly beyond the last Ghanaian defender and in an offside position. It was not a particularly close decision, with clear daylight between the two players, but the assistant referee obviously never saw it and the flag remained down. It was the last thing that Ghana wanted to happen right as the half ended as they were still in with a fighting chance at just one goal down, but coming back from two goals would present a more difficult challenge.

Despite the setback of the second goal, Ghana were undeterred in their attempts to show their quality. Brazil seemed to recognise the danger that their opponents were posing and brought on Gilberto Silva in an effort to gain control in the midfield battle but they never seemed truly comfortable in the match. There were opportunities for counter-attacks but Ghana were the more likely to grab the next goal and they fashioned several half-chances for themselves. Unfortunately, those remained half-chances as the quality was lacking in the final third, as either the final ball narrowly missed its intended target or the shot was saved or went wide. If they could only grab one goal back, there was every chance that they would get a second as Brazil seemed to be struggling to match their intensity. Gyan and Amoah both saw chances come and go, with the best falling to Gyan, who got a shot away that was brilliantly saved by a low dive from Dida, whose reactions were lightning fast to get back up and reach the ball before Amoah had a simple tap-in.

As the match ticked away into the final ten minutes, Ghana's hopes were fading. The chances had dried up as they became increasingly desperate to grab a goal, although Gyan did well to get free in the area but struck his well-hit shot straight at Dida. The Udinese striker was at the centre of all the quality that his nation produced and he nearly got free again after a through ball was played into the box and he tried to race clear of the final defender but fell to the floor. There was no contact at all with the Brazilian defender and the referee had little choice other than booking the striker for simulation. Unfortunately for Ghana, it was his second yellow, so he was shown the red card. In the three matches he played at the tournament, Gyan had managed to pick up four yellow cards and one red. The match was pretty much over before the dismissal but the sending-off certainly extinguished any faint hope of a remarkable fightback.

The seal was stamped on the result for Brazil with six minutes remaining when Ricardinho lofted the ball over the Ghanaian high line for Zé Roberto to race on to. Faced with the outrushing goalkeeper, the Bayern Munich midfielder calmly lifted the ball over his head and gave himself the simplest tap-in to add an undeserved third for Brazil. The goal was simple and effective and came from a prolonged Brazilian period of possession that involved 25 passes from start to finish. It was not as silky or memorable a goal as Cambiasso's team move for Argentina but it was definitely a reminder that Brazil were still a team of immense quality and would be a challenge for whoever they faced in the next round. They were beginning to click into gear. International football tournaments are often not won by the best team but the one with the most momentum, and Brazil, as well as being the best team in the tournament, were starting to gather the momentum that could see them retain their title.

Although the final result at first glance looks like a dominating performance by Brazil, the scoreline was definitely not an accurate reflection of the match. Despite the result, Ghana had well and truly announced their arrival on the international stage. This was a team that was very much on the rise with a generation of players that had come through the ranks together and seemed united. There was quality throughout, with many of their players playing at the top of the European game.

This tournament perhaps came a bit too soon but the 2010 World Cup had the potential to be a successful one and they bettered their achievements from their debut campaign. They progressed through their group in second place, before beating the USA in extra time in the first knockout round. Their quarter-final was against a Uruguay team who were undergoing a resurgence of their own led by Diego Forlán, Edinson Cavani and Luis Suárez. In another close match that went to extra time, Ghana were presented with the perfect opportunity to become the first African nation to ever reach the semi-finals of the World Cup when a goalbound header was pushed off the line by Suárez. As clear a handball as you could see, Suárez was sent off and Ghana had a penalty in the final minute of extra time to secure a victory. Gyan stepped up, having already scored two penalties at the tournament, and watched in anguish as his penalty cleared the crossbar. The striker then showed incredible courage to take the first penalty of the shoot-out and converted it, but two of his team-mates could not and Uruguay went through.

It was a heart-breaking end for Ghana, especially given the circumstances, and it was the peak for this generation of talent as they could only muster a solitary point in 2014 and failed to qualify for the finals of 2018. But this had been the beginning of an incredible period for Ghana, including reaching the semi-finals of AFCON for six consecutive tournaments between 2008 and 2017, although they failed to win any of them. Brazil were a step too far at this stage of this young generation's development but there were clear signs that Ghana were here to stay.

* * *

Of all the Round of 16 clashes, the meeting between Spain and France was maybe the most anticipated. Alongside Portugal and the Netherlands, this was a match between two teams that held realistic ambitions of reaching the latter stages of the tournament. It was an unlikely pairing as well, as France had struggled through their group and could only finish second behind Switzerland, meaning that they would have to face Spain rather than Ukraine and that they had now entered the side of the draw that featured Brazil. This was seen as the last hurrah for this incredible French squad, with Zidane retiring after the tournament for good, and they had made their journey to the final harder through their own sloppy play. Although he had not been at his best during the group stages, *Les Bleus* will have been relieved to have their talisman back for the knockout rounds as he was easily the one player on the pitch that could turn a match on its head in the blink of an eye.

While France were reaching the end of their best generation, Spain were at the opposite end of their journey. Only four players in the starting line-up for this match were over the age of 25, with nobody above 30, compared to France who only had one player under 25 and four over the age of 30. This was a Spain trending in the right direction and showing signs of the beautiful football that they would become synonymous with in the years to follow. They had a coach unafraid to make the big calls and upset the public and media in Aragonés, especially in the decision to effectively replace Raúl in favour of a strike partnership of Villa and Torres, although the Madrid captain would start against France. There was even a place for teenager Cesc Fàbregas in the starting line-up. He had evidently shown enough in his start in the final group fixture to earn a spot in the midfield trio for such a crucial match.

The worry for Spain was that they had yet to face an opponent of the quality of France and whether they would be able to compete against the elite of international football. In previous tournaments, Spain had flattered to deceive when the moment counted, often struggling to make an impact at the major events, with just a victory on home soil in the 1964 European Championships to show for all the incredible players that they had bestowed upon the game. There was always a sense of underachievement, with a fourth-place finish at the World Cup in 1950 their best finish outside of the victory in 1964. They had not arrived in Germany as one of the favourites to win the title but there was an increased optimism after their performance during the group stages and, should they beat France, the expectations for this promising generation would skyrocket.

Spain started on the front foot, trying to capitalise on any lack of confidence that the French may have had. Villa nearly breached the French back line inside the first three minutes but the through ball from Torres was slightly overhit and the Valencia forward could not quite reach it. It was a bright start from the Iberian nation and Pernía had a good opportunity from a free kick but could only send his effort over the bar. The match was going the way that the momentum from the group stages suggested it might, and France were struggling to contain the clever play of Spain. It was a clash of contrasting styles as Spain were keeping possession and playing more intricate football, while their opponents were playing in a more direct manner, attempting to exploit the pace of their front three of Henry, Ribéry and Malouda. Henry did have a chance when cutting inside from the left but it was weak and straight at Casillas; however, the best opening for France fell to Vieira when he was left free in the penalty area but was unable to poke the ball home as it was slightly out of the reach of his outstretched leg.

France were beginning to grow into the match and starting to push Spain back but they then failed to clear a corner properly and, as the ball was bouncing around in the area, Thuram trod on the heel of Pablo Ibáñez. The Italian referee was in the perfect position to see the incident and had no hesitation in pointing to the penalty spot. It was a clear penalty and only those cheering on the French could have argued differently. The responsibility was given to David Villa, perhaps surprisingly ahead of Xabi Alonso or Raúl, who had experience on their side, but the Valencia striker showed no signs of nerves, drilling the ball low and hard to the keeper's right, meaning that Barthez was unable to reach the ball even though he guessed the correct way to dive. Although France had begun to settle into the match, the goal was a deserved outcome for the early Spanish pressure and it put their struggling opponents on to the back foot once more.

The contest was only half an hour old so there was plenty of time for France to come back into it, but they needed to improve, and quickly. With half-time approaching, they finally broke through the Spanish resistance. The move started with Vieira picking up the ball inside the Spanish half and threatening to drive forward. As the defenders moved to close him down, he played a clever through ball for Ribéry, who had raced clear beyond the last defender. The young winger showed composure when faced with Casillas one-on-one and danced around the Real Madrid goalkeeper before rolling the ball into the unguarded net, beyond the despairing dive of two Spanish defenders. It was a simple but effective goal for the French and coming right on half-time was perhaps the momentum shift that they would need to finally start playing to the level that they knew they could reach.

There was still time for another Spanish appeal for a penalty when Fernando Torres drove into the French penalty area and was bundled to the ground under the challenge of Willy Sagnol. The striker was adamant that he had been helped to the ground in less than fair terms but the referee was unmoved by the protests. The replays showed that there was contact between the two players but not enough to warrant awarding a penalty. It was a warning sign for France that, although they had come back into the contest, Spain were still dangerous.

The second period started in the same manner as the first with Spain keeping the ball and patiently probing for an opening, while France relied on a more direct approach that almost paid dividends after just seven minutes, but Malouda's stabbed effort was well saved by a backpedalling Casillas. France were pushing on more consistently now, with Ribéry causing problems down the right-hand side. He cleverly ducked away from a tackle from Pernía but his cross could only find Puyol, who deflected the ball clear from danger. Spain responded by bringing on Joaquín and Luis García, and the latter almost made an immediate impact but Sagnol showed clever defensive awareness to get back and clear the ball before it could reach the forward.

Chances were coming and going without any ever really threatening either keeper but there was an intensity and physicality to the match that made it an entertaining watch. Vieira caught Torres with a flailing arm as he tried to shield the ball, and Abidal caught the back of Xavi's leg with a late and poorly timed challenge that he was lucky to avoid a booking for. Neither team could be accused of lacking courage for the challenge and the match seemed to be progressing towards a thrilling conclusion, whether a goal arrived or not. The substitutions made by Aragonés were almost proving to be inspired as the match wore on, with García seeing his header deflected wide before Joaquín did well cutting inside on to his left foot but could only drag his shot into the side-netting when he really should have been hitting the target.

However, the match was becoming disjointed, with a procession of niggly fouls breaking up any rhythm that the match had originally. The substitutes were having an impact on the play but it was Zidane who was gradually starting to wrestle some sense of control over the action and beginning to dictate the pace. With just seven minutes remaining, Henry was trying to burst beyond the Spanish defence but was met with Puyol in front of him. The Barcelona defender used his body to slow the momentum of the striker, although there was minimal contact between the two. The Arsenal striker fell to the floor holding his face and the referee felt that Puyol had been too forceful in denying Henry space, so awarded a free kick and booked the defender.

From the resulting set piece, Puyol was made to pay an even higher price. Zidane stood over the ball and floated it towards the penalty spot. It was actually an uncharacteristically poor delivery from the French talisman, only managing to pick out a Spanish head. Unfortunately for the Iberians, Alonso could only flick the ball on rather than clear it and it fell at the back post for a completely unmarked Vieira. It was the simplest of headers for the midfielder, who powered the ball to the near post, with it reaching the back of the net via a Spanish foot. It was a poor goal to concede as it was so simple to avoid had someone been marking Vieira, who was always a threat from set pieces. All the hard work that Spain had put in during the match was now undone and their tournament hopes were hanging by a thread.

Spain had yet to lose a game since Aragonés had taken over after their exit from Euro 2004 and they now pushed forwards with a renewed urgency in an attempt to salvage that record and their World Cup hopes. Their desperation was clear but it only served to make their play sloppy and predictable as they tried to force the equaliser. Sagnol was once again proving his defensive worth, being in the right place at the right time to deny Torres from receiving the ball in the area, but Spain just could not quite fashion another chance for themselves. Their profligacy from the early stages of the match was coming back to haunt them and the fears of them being unable to handle the step up in quality at the knockout stage were once again coming true.

As the match was ticking down and the play was becoming ragged, Zidane was still controlling France's effort. He was keeping the ball well and not allowing Spain to build any significant pressure on his team's defence. It was the first time all tournament that he was taking the game by the scruff of its neck and stamping his own mark over proceedings. The final nail in the Spanish coffin came two minutes into added time when France pinched the ball back on the halfway line and Wiltord flicked the ball through to Zidane, who was free to run at goal. Keeping his cool as Puyol came over to close down the angle, he danced inside and wrong-footed the defender before firing a low shot back towards the near post, deceiving his club team-mate Casillas and netting his first goal of the tournament.

It was not a vintage France performance but they had done enough to reach the quarter-finals. They had bettered their title defence of four years earlier simply by reaching the knockout stages but it was clear that they were still clicking into top gear. It would not have been all negative for Domenech in the changing room after the match, however. There had been positive signs as the match wore on and the re-emergence of the Zidane that had been one of the world's best players for a decade was a welcome sight for France and a worrying sight for the rest of the teams left in the tournament. If Zidane could play the way he had during the second half, then France would take some stopping, as he could turn a match on its head in a moment.

While France celebrated their progress, Spain would have been frustrated at their failure on the biggest stage once again. Losing to a France team of this quality is normally no disgrace but Spain had more than matched their opponents and had been the better team for the majority of the match. If anything, the match had come just a bit too early in the development of Aragones's Spain. The quality throughout the team was clear to see, with Torres and Villa particularly impressing as an attacking duo, and the future was clearly bright. So bright in fact that Spain would dominate world football for the next six years. They would add two European Championships, and the World Cup in 2010, as they won three international tournaments in a row and conquered any and all challengers they faced. With Barcelona's tiki-taka model taking shape on the international stage and Aragonés and his predecessor Vicente del Bosque managing to smooth the divide between those from Barcelona and Real Madrid, Spain finally achieved notable international success that matched their status as a leading footballing nation. Although 2006 may have been a tournament too early in Spain's development for them to add a trophy to their collection, it was clear that, while France were trying to win a title to end their golden generation, Spain were on the verge of entering theirs.

5pm, 24 June 2006
FIFA World Cup Stadium, Munich
Attendance: 66,000
Referee: Carlos Eugenio Simon (Brazil)

Germany 2 (Podolski 4, 12)
Sweden 0

Germany: Jens Lehmann, Arne Friedrich, Per Mertesacker, Christoph Metzelder, Philipp Lahm, Bernd Schneider, Torsten Frings (Sebastian Kehl 85), Michael Ballack (c), Bastian Schweinsteiger (Tim Borowski 72), Miroslav Klose, Lukas Podolski (Oliver Neuville 74). **Manager:** Jürgen Klinsmann.

Sweden: Andreas Isaksson, Niclas Alexandersson, Olof Mellberg (c), Teddy Lučić, Erik Edman, Tobias Linderoth, Mattias Jonson (Christian Wilhelmsson 52), Freddie Ljungberg, Kim Källström (Petter Hansson 39), Zlatan Ibrahimović, (Marcus Allback 72), Henrik Larsson. **Manager:** Lars Lagerbäck.

Booked: Frings (27); Lučić (28), Jonson (48), Allbäck (78)
Sent off: Lučić (35)

9pm, 24 June 2006
Zentralstadion, Leipzig
Attendance: 43,000
Referee: Massimo Busacca (Switzerland)

Argentina 2 (Crespo 10, Rodríguez 98)
Mexico 1 (Márquez 6)
After extra time

Argentina: Roberto Abbondanzieri, Lionel Scaloni, Roberto Ayala, Gabriel Heinze, Juan Pablo Sorin (c), Javier Mascherano, Esteban Cambiasso (Pablo Aimar 76), Maxi Rodríguez, Juan Román Riquelme, Javier Saviola (Lionel Messi 84), Hernán Crespo (Carlos Tevez 75). **Manager:** José Pékerman.

Mexico: Oswaldo Sánchez, Rafael Márquez (c), Ricardo Osorio, Carlos Salcido, Mario Méndez, Jose Antonio Castro, Pável Pardo (Gerard Torrado 38), Ramón Morales (Sinha 74), Andres Guardado (Gonzalo Pineda 66) , Francisco Fonseca, Jared Borgetti. **Manager:** Ricardo La Volpe.

Booked: Heinze (45+1), Sorin (112); Márquez (70), Castro (82), Torrado (118), Fonseca (119)

5pm, 25 June 2006
Gottlieb-Daimler-Stadion, Stuttgart
Attendance: 52,000
Referee: Frank De Bleeckere (Belgium)

England 1 (Beckham 60)
Ecuador 0

England: Paul Robinson, Owen Hargreaves, Rio Ferdinand, John Terry, Ashley Cole, Michael Carrick, David Beckham (c) (Aaron Lennon 87), Steven Gerrard (Stewart Downing 90+2), Frank Lampard, Joe Cole (Jamie Carragher 77), Wayne Rooney. **Manager:** Sven-Göran Eriksson.

Ecuador: Cristian Mora, Ulises de la Cruz, Iván Hurtado (c), Giovanny Espinoza, Néicer Reasco, Antonio Valencia, Segundo Castillo, Edwin Tenorio (Christian Lara 69), Édison Méndez, Carlos Tenorio (Iván Kaviedes 72), Agustín Delgado. **Manager:** Luis Fernando Suárez.

Booked: Terry (18), Robinson (78), Carragher (82); Valencia (24), C. Tenorio (37), de la Cruz (67)

9pm, 25 June 2006
Frankenstadion, Nuremburg
Attendance: 41,000
Referee: Valentin Ivanov (Russia)

Portugal 1 (Maniche 23)
Netherlands 0

Portugal: Ricardo, Miguel, Fernando Meira, Ricardo Carvalho, Nuno Valente, Costinha, Maniche, Luís Figo (c) (Tiago 84), Deco, Cristiano Ronaldo (Simão 34), Pauleta (Petit 46). **Manager:** Luis Felipe Scolari.

Netherlands: Edwin van der Sar (c), Khalid Boulahrouz, André Ooijer, Joris Mathijsen (Rafael van der Vaart 56), Giovanni van Bronckhorst, Mark van Bommel (John Heitinga 67), Wesley Sneijder, Philip Cocu (Jan Vennegoor of Hesselink 84), Robin van Persie, Dirk Kuyt, Arjen Robben. **Manager:** Marco van Basten.

Booked: Maniche (20), Costinha (31), Petit (50), Figo (60), Deco (73), Ricardo (76), Valente (76); Van Bommel (2), Boulahrouz (7), Van Bronckhorst (59), Sneijder (73), Van der Vaart (74)
Sent off: Costinha (45+1), Deco (78); Boulahrouz (63), Van Bronckhorst (90+5)

5pm, 26 June 2006
Fritz-Walter-Stadion, Kaiserslautern
Attendance: 46,000
Referee: Luis Medina Cantalejo (Spain)

Italy 1 (Totti 90+5 (p))
Australia 0

Italy: Gianluigi Buffon, Gianluca Zambrotta, Fabio Cannavaro (c), Marco Materazzi, Fabio Grosso, Simone Perrotta, Andrea Pirlo, Gennaro Gattuso, Alessandro Del Piero (Francesco Totti 75), Alberto Gilardino (Vincenzo Iaquinta 46), Luca Toni (Andrea Barzagli 56). **Manager:** Marcello Lippi.

Australia: Mark Schwarzer, Craig Moore, Lucas Neill, Scott Chipperfield, Jason Culina, Vince Grella, Luke Wilkshire,

Mile Sterjovski (John Aloisi 81), Tim Cahill, Mark Bresciano, Mark Viduka (c). **Manager:** Guus Hiddink.

Booked: Grosso (29), Gattuso (89), Zambrotta (90+1); Grella (23), Cahill (49), Wilkshire (61)
Sent off: Materazzi (50)

9pm, 26 June 2006
RheinEnergieStadion, Cologne
Attendance: 45,000
Referee: Benito Archundia (Mexico)

Switzerland 0
Ukraine 0
Ukraine won 3-0 on penalties after extra time
Shoot-out: Shevchenko saved, Streller saved, Milevskyi 1-0, Barnetta missed, Rebrov 2-0, Cabanas saved, Husyev 3-0

Switzerland: Pascal Zuberbühler, Philipp Degen, Johan Djourou (Stéphane Grichting 34), Patrick Müller, Ludovic Magnin, Johann Vogel (c), Tranquillo Barnetta, Raphaël Wicky, Ricardo Cabanas, Hakan Yakin (Marco Streller 64), Alexander Frei (Mauro Lustrinelli 117). **Manager:** Köbi Kuhn.

Ukraine: Oleksandr Shovkovskyi, Oleh Husyev, Vladyslav Vashchuk, Andriy Nesmachnyi, Oleh Shelayev, Andriy Husin, Anatoliy Tymoschuk, Andriy Vorobey (Serhiy Rebrov 94), Maksym Kalynychenko (Ruslan Rotan 75), Andriy Voronin (Artem Milevskyi 111), Andriy Shevchenko (c). **Manager:** Oleg Blokhin.

Booked: Barnetta (59)

5pm, 27 June 2006
Westfalenstadion, Dortmund
Attendance: 65,000
Referee: Ľuboš Micheľ (Slovakia)

Brazil 3 (Ronaldo 5, Adriano 45+1, Zé Roberto 84)
Ghana 0

Brazil: Dida, Cafu (c), Lúcio, Juan, Roberto Carlos, Emerson (Gilberto Silva 46), Zé Roberto, Kaká (Ricardinho 83), Ronaldinho, Adriano (Juninho 61), Ronaldo. **Manager:** Carlos Alberto Parreira.

Ghana: Richard Kingson, John Paintsil, John Mensah, Illiasu Shilla, Emmanuel Pappoe, Haminu Dramani, Eric Addo (Derek Boateng 60), Stephen Appiah (c), Sulley Muntari, Asamoah Gyan, Matthew Amoah (Alex Tachie-Mensah 70). **Manager:** Ratomir Dujković.

Booked: Adriano (13), Juan (44); Appiah (7), Muntari (11), Paintsil (29), Addo (38), Gyan (48)

Sent off: Gyan (81)

9pm, 27 June 2006
Niedersachsenstadion, Hanover
Attendance: 43,000
Referee: Roberto Rosetti (Italy)

Spain 1 (Villa 28 (p))
France 3 (Ribéry 41, Vieira 83, Zidane 90+2)

Spain: Iker Casillas, Sergio Ramos, Pablo, Carles Puyol, Mariano Pernía, Cesc Fàbregas, Xabi Alonso, Xavi (Marcos Senna 72), David Villa (Luis García 54), Fernando Torres, Raúl (c) (Joaquín 54). **Manager:** Luis Aragonés.

France: Fabien Barthez, Willy Sagnol, Lilian Thuram, William Gallas, Eric Abidal, Patrick Vieira, Claude Makélélé, Franck Ribéry,

Zinedine Zidane (c), Florent Malouda (Sidney Govou 74), Thierry Henry (Sylvain Wiltord 88). **Manager:** Raymond Domenech.

Booked: Puyol (82); Vieira (68), Ribéry (87), Zidane (90+1)

Quarter-Finals

AS THE quarter-finals approached, it was perhaps a welcome return to prominence for some of major nations. At the 2002 World Cup, the quarter-finals stage was littered with surprise appearances from the USA, Senegal, Turkey and South Korea. The semi-finals saw Turkey and South Korea both nearly reach their first World Cup Final. As exciting as upsets are, they led to a disjointed feel to the tournament and some of the excitement was diluted, especially due to some controversial decisions in favour of South Korea. In Germany the upsets had failed to materialise, with Ukraine as the only surprise entrant into the last eight. Every nation to have won a World Cup at this point was represented except for Uruguay, who had failed to qualify for the finals, and there were stars and incredible match-ups in every single match. The expectations for the tournament from here on in had skyrocketed and the first match, between Germany and Argentina, was certainly one to get peoples' mouths watering in anticipation.

It was a meeting between the hosts who had matched their minimum expectation, but had perhaps exceeded pre-tournament expectations in terms of performances, against the team that had shown the most quality and had entered the knockout stages with the favourites tag now applied to them. As expectations had risen for both teams, there was hope that the watching world was about to witness an all-time classic World Cup contest. These were two nations with a long history of World Cup contests, having met on four previous occasions, including two finals. Those two finals came in back-to-back tournaments in 1986 and 1990. The 1986 meeting was a brilliant match, with Argentina racing into a two-goal lead before Germany came back and levelled things up with just nine minutes remaining. There was still time for more drama as Jorge Burruchaga scored Argentina's winner just three minutes after Germany's equaliser, as the South Americans won their second World Cup title.

Four years later they met again in the final. Unlike 1986, the 1990 clash is not remembered fondly, often considered one of the worst finals in the tournament's history. The match was ill-tempered and Argentina earned not just the first but also the second red card in the history of the World Cup Final. The title was settled by a late Andreas Brehme penalty but it was not a final to showcase the tournament in the best way.

For the Munich clash in 2006, Klinsmann named the same starting line-up as he had against Sweden, keeping faith with his players and utilising their familiarity in the hope of another solid performance. Argentina, however, had been pushed hard by Mexico and had played the extra 30 minutes, so José Pékerman opted for three changes, including leaving out Cambiasso, who had provided a solid midfield base so far, and bringing in Carlos Tevez in favour of Javier Saviola, who had struggled to make a significant impact at the tournament.

The early tension was obvious. Mascherano complained about a late challenge on him going unpunished, while Klose and Riquelme exchanged words, followed by the German striker attempting a clumsy challenge on the Argentine. The Germans seemed intent on letting their opponents know they were in a contest from the start and certainly did not hold back when jumping into challenges. Podolski was the first to see the flash of the yellow card just three minutes in for a late clip of the heels on Heinze, who was quick to have words with Bernd Schneider, the German having jumped to his team-mate's defence, believing Heinze had gone down too easily. No openings were created in the first five minutes but the competitiveness was clear to see.

The first chance fell the way of the hosts from a free kick but Podolski's effort was gathered by the Argentina keeper, albeit uncomfortably at the second attempt. Within a minute of that effort, Argentina had won a set piece of their own but Sorin's header from the corner was well blocked and cleared. By now the initial brutal contest had faded away and the quality was starting to shine through. Riquelme was doing his best to dictate the tempo from the middle of the pitch, almost gliding across it in his typical style, while his German counterpart Ballack was perhaps the antithesis, all action and a traditional box-to-box powerhouse. It was the German captain who went the closest to opening the scoring, arriving in the penalty box to meet a Schweinsteiger cross with his head, steering it narrowly wide of the post.

The next chance fell to Mertesacker, perhaps the one player Germany would rather it had not dropped to. He managed to get a quickfire shot away on the turn at the edge of the penalty area but could not control his effort and simply smashed it over the crossbar. Despite the lack of true clear-cut chances, the match was end to end and being played at a high intensity. The contest in the middle of the pitch was intriguing as both were trying to wrestle some semblance of control. Everything that was being tried in the final third was just slightly off, with passes either overhit or being well intercepted by defenders.

At the end of the first period, the score was still 0-0 but it was certainly one of the more entertaining scoreless games of football. Both teams had had their moments and were occasionally threatening a breakthrough, yet the majority of the match had been a battle of attrition in the middle of the pitch. That kind of contest felt like it suited Germany more, with Frings and Ballack in the centre of their midfield, but with Mascherano highlighting his enormous quality in breaking up any German attacks, all Argentina needed to do was find a way to get Riquelme on the ball in space and the momentum could swing in their favour in an instant.

It was the South Americans who started the second period on the front foot and, with their first real chance on goal, they managed to take the lead. For all the incredible technical footballers on the pitch for Argentina, their opener came from a simple corner whipped in by Riquelme. Central defender Roberto Ayala was the first to reach the ball, powering his header low between Lehmann and Lahm, who was standing by the post. With Argentina having already scored two of the best goals in the tournament, Ayala's was much simpler and the nature of it will have frustrated the Germans.

The goal settled the nerves that Argentina had shown during the opening exchanges and they began to gain some control, keeping the ball and starting to limit German chances. If they could grab a second goal quickly while they were in the midst of this spell of dominance then it was hard to envisage a way back for Germany. They were probing and pushing but were unable to link the ball into Crespo or Tevez, who had both been quiet throughout the match, with Riquelme the one pulling all the strings.

Their inability to create or take another chance started to come back to haunt them just after the hour mark as Germany began to get back into the contest. Abbondanzieri caused panic in his penalty area when he came to gather a cross but flapped at the ball. The rebound dropped at the feet of Ballack, who saw his shot well deflected by Ayala. The Argentine keeper signalled that he had picked up a knock in coming for the ball, but he tried to carry on; however, he could only manage a further five minutes before needing to be replaced. Leo Franco was the back-up goalkeeper and was about to enter the World Cup at one of the most high-pressure moments imaginable. It was at this time that the match truly swung in favour of the Germans thanks to an Argentina substitution, although it was not the swapping of the goalkeeper that caused this.

Seeing Germany starting to gain a foothold in the contest again, Pékerman attempted to shore up his midfield and brought on Cambiasso. The surprise, however, was that he chose to take off Riquelme in order to bring the Internazionale player on. While Cambiasso would certainly help lock down the midfield with his presence, Riquelme was the one Argentina player that could dictate the tempo and was a vital cog in their playing style. As more of a luxury player with limited defensive responsibility, perhaps Pékerman simply just wanted more workmanlike players on the pitch but, should they not progress, it would be a decision that would be scrutinised heavily in the aftermath.

Pékerman then doubled down on his decision to try to hold the one-goal lead in sacrificing Crespo for Julio Cruz. The Internazionale player, while a striker like Crespo, offered more of a physical presence and would be a target for long balls rather than the more intricate style Argentina had been employing. As Jonathan Wilson wrote in his excellent book on Argentinian football history, *Angels with Dirty Faces*, the decision to swap Riquelme for Cambiasso was 'the moment at which the coach lost his nerve and with it the Word Cup'. Lionel Messi and Javier Saviola, both calm and talented on-the-ball footballers, had been left on the bench and it was up to those left on the pitch to try to hold out for the final 15 minutes. They lasted all of five.

Ballack managed to get space in the middle of the pitch to float a cross into the penalty area, where Borowski did well to flick the ball on. That deflection took the ball perfectly into the path of the late-arriving Klose, who beat Sorin to the ball and powered a perfect header back across the goalkeeper and into the corner of the net. It was a beautiful header and a typical Klose goal as he was in the right place at the right time to get himself on the scoresheet. The entire complexion of the match was now different as Pékerman had sacrificed his creative players in favour of more defensively minded ones, but now they needed a goal once again.

If Argentina were there for the taking, Klinsmann's team did not take advantage. The South Americans came storming back into the contest, with appeals for a penalty firmly dismissed by the Slovakian referee, who correctly booked Maxi Rodríguez for a dive instead. They almost pinched the result with just two minutes to go when substitute Cruz found himself free down the right-hand side and chipped a clever ball to the back post for Lucho González, who steered his header back the way the ball had come. It was destined for the far corner until a flying stop from Lehmann diverted the ball behind. It was a brilliant save from the German shot-stopper as he had to dive over Tevez to reach the ball and he was not to know that the flag would go up as the striker was in an offside position and interfering with play.

Neither team was able to fashion any further chances to book their ticket to the final four so, for the second round in a row, Argentina were faced with an extra half an hour to contend with. Having been more comfortable in their previous knockout match, Germany may have had the legs to take more risks during the extra period but, as often happens, both teams played risk-averse football as the fear of making the mistake that would cost their team was too high. Neither team created much, with Metzelder heading over from a corner and Tevez's shot being easily caught by Lehmann the only real highlights of extra time. Penalties appeared to be the only outcome once extra time began and that is exactly where the match ended up.

Both nations had perfect penalty shoot-out records ahead of this meeting, winning all three they had participated in. This was the opportunity for both goalkeepers to make themselves a hero for their nations. Leo Franco, having been brought into the action with just 20 minutes of normal time remaining, could now help Argentina take another step towards their third World Cup title. For Lehmann in the German goal, the pressure was maybe even higher. The doubts over whether or not he should have been the starter over Oliver Kahn had been lingering throughout the whole tournament, the rivalry between the two well-known and well-documented. Prior to the spot kicks, the television cameras caught the moment when the Bayern keeper went over to his counterpart and wished him luck and perhaps offered some advice ahead of the shoot-out. It was a moment that many thought they would never see between the two and showed the positivity that was flowing throughout the German squad at this point. They were a fully united front and buoyed by the home crowd.

Germany took the first penalty, with Oliver Neuville given the responsibility, and he showed all his experience to send his effort hard to the goalkeeper's left, beating him for pace. Fellow substitute Cruz was the first Argentine to step up and he executed an almost perfect spot kick, high and powerful to the goalkeeper's right, leaving Lehmann with no chance. Captain Ballack opted for sheer power and fired his effort straight down the middle, with Franco diving and unable to reach it. The first miss came when Ayala went low to Lehmann's left but the Arsenal stopper read the intention and made a smart save. Lehmann's power of prediction was explained by a note that he kept in his sock detailing the preferred penalty of the Argentina players, giving him the advantage of knowing what his opponents would do in a pressure situation.

Now holding the advantage, Podolski was Germany's third penalty taker and he delivered a perfect one, low and into the corner in the opposite direction of Franco's dive. Argentina could not afford any mistakes now, and Maxi followed Podolski's lead in sending his penalty low into the bottom corner. Lehmann, aided by his 'cheat sheet', dived the right way but was just unable to reach the effort. Borowski kept Germany's 100 per cent record intact, sending Franco in the wrong direction again, meaning that if Cambiasso did not score, Argentina were out.

The Internazionale midfielder kept his effort towards the middle of the goal, whether intentional or not, and it was at a nice height for Lehmann to stick out a hand and prevent the ball from crossing the line. As German celebrations began, words were exchanged between players and officials from opposing sides and a melee broke out on the pitch. It seemed to start during the shoot-out with Argentina players chatting to their German counterparts and Borowski shushing them after scoring his spot kick. After Cambiasso's miss, Coloccini appeared to approach Oliver Bierhoff, a member of the German backroom staff, and the altercation escalated from there. Cufré kicked out at Mertesacker, which earned him a red card, Maxi Rodríguez seemed to throw a punch at Schweinsteiger that went unpunished and Frings also threw a punch in the melee that was missed in the chaos, although he was later suspended for one match by FIFA, meaning he would miss the semi-final.

It was an unsavoury end to the competition for Argentina, who had entertained everyone so far and were perhaps the favourites once the knockout stages began. Their tournament could have been so different had Pékerman not gambled on holding on to the lead by bringing on more defensive-minded players. Everything had seemed set for Argentina to go all the way again, with a perfect blend of experienced international stars and rising talents. Yet their tournament was over at the quarter-final stage and their wait for a third World Cup title would go on.

The meeting in Munich in 2006 was the first World Cup contest between the two storied nations since 1990 and there have been a further two meetings since, including a third final, making this fixture the most played World Cup Final in history. They would meet at the quarter-final stage four years after this tournament, with Germany prevailing 4-0, before meeting again in 2014, although this time in the final. This was supposed to be the moment when Messi matched Maradona in winning the World Cup for his nation and it would have been in the backyard of their fierce rivals Brazil, making it an even more poetic victory. However, the match was a slow-burner and only settled late in extra time by Mario Götze's lovely finish that saw Germany take home another title, marking the pinnacle for a generation of talent that had been developing since their failures at the start of the century.

Argentina and Germany's respective fortunes went in opposite directions after the 2014 final, with Germany exiting the next two tournaments at the group stages, while Argentina lost to France in the Round of 16 in Russia 2018 before gaining their revenge in Qatar 2022, beating the same opposition in a truly remarkable final. Yet, in Germany in 2006, it was the hosts that were progressing and their South American opponents returning home earlier than desired.

* * *

In a quarter-final line-up filled with familiar names from the elite of international football, seeing Ukraine reach this stage on their tournament debut was a welcome addition. Usually, heading into a match against Italy, expectations would have been low for the Ukrainians. Yet, after Italy's struggle to beat Australia in the previous round, hopes of an upset had risen. Could they match Croatia's performance of 1998 and reach the World Cup semi-finals on their debut appearance as an independent nation?

For that to happen, they would need to beat an Italy that had not been at their best throughout the tournament so far but boasted plenty of winners and would undoubtedly provide the toughest test Ukraine had faced so far. Italy's problems in the centre of defence had continued to mount for Lippi as Materazzi was now suspended after his harsh dismissal against the Australians and, with Nesta still injured, it was the turn of Andrea Barzagli to step into the storied position of central defender in the Italian national team. Totti was also recalled in favour of Gilardino, and Camoranesi was brought in as Lippi switched to a 4-4-1-1 starting line-up rather than the 4-3-1-2 he had been favouring so far.

Lippi's tactical tinkering paid dividends almost immediately. The Argentina-born Camoranesi dragged an effort wide after just four minutes, before Zambrotta collected the ball on the right-hand side, drove forwards and cut inside on to his left foot. The Juventus full-back drilled a powerful left-footed strike towards goal that perhaps caught the goalkeeper unawares and flew into the back of the net. The ball was well hit but it was from a fair distance out and the keeper managed to get to the ball but was unable to produce a strong enough hand to prevent the opening goal. If Italy had laboured to their win in the previous round, this was the perfect start to settle any lingering nerves they may have had.

The early goal was ideal for Italy but did not help the match as a spectacle for the watching public. Ukraine were unable to lay a glove on their opponents as the Italians just retained possession with ease, probing without scoring a definitive second goal. The strings were being pulled by Totti, who, after his match-winning goal in the previous round, was finally making his mark on the tournament. It had been his clever back-heel that had released Zambrotta for the opening goal and the Roma playmaker was showing why Lippi had included him in the squad despite the doubts over his fitness. He was gliding around the pitch in complete control despite the close attentions of Sviderskyi, who had been given the unenviable task of man-marking him. Such was the joy that he was having that it took only 20 minutes for Blokhin to abandon his original plan, replacing the midfielder, who had barely been able to keep up with Totti's shadow.

The only negative for Italy in the opening half was that the scoreline was still only 1-0. For all their pressing and probing they had not created any further goalscoring chances and Ukraine had done a good job of stifling the Italian threat after their early tactical change. The problem for the Eastern Europeans was that they were unable to create any chances for themselves. Shevchenko was being kept quiet. He was well shadowed by the Italian central defenders, perhaps used to his style from his time playing for Milan. Without their talisman on form, the best Ukraine could muster were long-range efforts from distance.

Despite the Italians' dominance, Blokhin's team talk would have been positive. They were only one goal down, so a fast start to the second period could put the Italians on to the back foot and turn the momentum. That fast start came, as Buffon was called into action for the first time just five minutes in. Kalynychenko steered a header cleverly on target but the legendary goalkeeper produced a smart save, reacting quickly to reach his near post and palm the ball up and on to the post, with Cannavaro on hand to clear the rebound. Cannavaro was there again just a few moments later, making a vital interception with a brilliant header to stop the ball from reaching Kalynychenko.

It had been a great start for Ukraine and they should have drawn level with their third good opening inside 15 minutes. The right-back Husyev found himself free inside the penalty area after nice interplay and his powerful strike was well stopped by Buffon, although the ball was hit straight at him. The ball bounced off Cannavaro and fell into the path of Kalynychenko, once again in the right place. He managed to miss the diving Italian captain with his quick effort on goal and the ball was travelling towards the back of the net until a goal-line block from Zambrotta, who had positioned himself perfectly at the post. It was typical Italian defending and they celebrated it like they had scored a goal. Had Ukraine taken any of these chances, the final outcome may well have been different. Instead, it was only a minute after Zambrotta's block that Italy finally doubled their lead.

For the first time in the second half, Italy had broken forward and earned themselves a corner. It was played short to Totti, who floated a dangerous cross into the space between defenders and goalkeeper. It narrowly evaded the head of Cannavaro but landed perfectly for Luca Toni, who outmuscled his marker, steering his header across goal and into the far corner. It was a simple but pivotal goal. A one-goal deficit seemed possible to overturn but coming from two goals down would be a mountainous task.

The belief was still with the Ukrainian players though, and they almost halved their task straight away. A free kick from the right-hand touchline was whipped into the Italian penalty area and met by Husin at the far post. He produced a clever header back across goal that took Buffon out of play. Unfortunately for Husin, his header did not come down quickly enough, bouncing off the crossbar, to be volleyed clear by Zambrotta, in the right place once again.

Lippi, sensing the danger that Ukraine were posing in the second half, opted to make defensively minded changes now that they had the two-goal lead, bringing Oddo and Barone on for Camoranesi and Pirlo. The changes had barely been made when Italy worked a quick throw-in on the left to free Zambrotta into the penalty area. The full-back managed to get himself some space in the box and stab the ball across the goal despite the attention of two defenders and the outrushing goalkeeper. Waiting for the simplest goal of his career at the back post was Toni, who tapped home his second and Italy's third. If the second goal all but ended Ukraine's hopes of a shock result, the third confirmed their fate.

It had been a strange match. Italy had dominated the opening 20 minutes and looked like they could run away with it. Once Blokhin had made his tactical switch, his team grew back into the contest and more than matched Italy for periods of the match. Ukraine controlled the start of the second half and deserved to grab at least one goal. Yet it was Italy who had scored two more and the 3-0 scoreline seems more comfortable than it really was. Even at 3-0 down Ukraine still tried to get themselves on to the scoreboard. Shevchenko, who had still barely had a touch in the attacking third, finally found some space as he peeled off his markers and reached a cross at the far post but could not keep his header down to trouble Buffon.

Despite the trouble that they had been caused, Italy would only have cared about the final result and the fact that they had reached the semi-finals of the World Cup. They had not been one of the best teams in terms of attacking flair but their solidity had been exceptional. They had only conceded once so far in the entire tournament, and that was an own goal. With Cannavaro at the heart of their defence, they seemed almost impenetrable. Their reward for victory over Ukraine was a final-four match against their hosts Germany in Dortmund. A free-flowing forward-thinking German team against a resolute, experienced Italian one. But, for now at least, attention turned towards four other nations and who would be making up the other side of the semi-final line-up.

* * *

With Germany and Italy completing one side of the draw, all eyes turned to Gelsenkirchen to see who of England or Portugal would join them in the final four. Despite their struggles, England entered the match as slight favourites, especially with Deco suspended for Portugal and doubts over the fitness of Cristiano Ronaldo. This was supposed to be the crowning moment for England's golden generation and the expectations were high for them to gain revenge for their exit at the same stage of the European Championship to this opposition two years earlier and their defeat to a Scolari-coached team four years ago at the last World Cup. This felt like England's moment. The opportunity to finally regain the World Cup crown the nation believed it deserved. Some 40 years on from their win on home soil, this was the best squad they had taken to a tournament and represented the perfect opportunity.

They were aided by the fact that Portugal would be missing Costinha and Deco, both suspended after their red cards against the Netherlands, with Petit and Tiago their replacements, neither likely to replace the flair of the Barcelona playmaker Deco. While Portugal had made two enforced changes, England's one alteration was a welcome one, with Gary Neville returning to the starting line-up in place of Michael Carrick, and Hargreaves moving back into central midfield as Eriksson opted for control in the centre of the pitch by naming five in midfield and Rooney as the lone striker.

Unsurprisingly, it was a cagey opening as both teams feared making an early mistake. This tournament represented a great opportunity for both nations to finally make their mark on the international stage, Portugal for the first time, and only the second in England's case. Both were footballing nations of strong heritage but had always flattered to deceive when it truly mattered. With Argentina out and either Brazil or France being eliminated in the other quarter-final, this really was a superb opportunity.

Early long-range efforts from Manchester United team-mates Rooney and Ronaldo were easily caught by the opposing goalkeepers, before Tiago managed to find space in the area but the ball would not drop at his feet to allow him to get a shot away. The chances were being evenly distributed but it was England who were dominating possession and control over the contest. The extra player in midfield was certainly working as England were able to move the ball around the two occupying the Portuguese midfield and openings were being created on a regular basis. The problem was that none of those chances ever seemed like going in.

Rooney was cutting an isolated figure at the top of the pitch and did not look fully fit. The lingering doubts over his fitness were clearly proving to be a valid concern. Not only was the concern over broken metatarsal he suffered before the tournament hanging over England's head, but he later revealed that in training he had torn a muscle in his groin but, rather than alert the staff to the problem, he simply battled on. Bravery or stupidity? That surely depended on the outcome of the tournament. Should Rooney help lead England to World Cup glory then it would go down in English footballing folklore. If England lost, then perhaps he would be vilified for not allowing a fully fit option be called up in his place. Hindsight would always be the only way his decision-making could be viewed.

The contest was edgy and struggled to develop a proper rhythm. England were suffering with Rooney's isolation as a square ball found no one in the penalty area, before a Gerrard cross narrowly evaded Lampard. Ronaldo and Figo both countered for Portugal with efforts of their own but neither could steer their effort on target. As the half-time whistle approached, Lampard continued his underwhelming tournament as he wasted another chance and could only send his shot straight at the goalkeeper. Despite the scoreline, England would perhaps have been the happier of the two teams at the interval. They had controlled the play well for long periods, and if they could get their talisman involved with more than just the odd touch here and there, then perhaps they could reach the semi-finals for the first time since 1990.

Wanting to give themselves a lead to defend, England began the second half at a rapid pace. Just five minutes in they felt that they should have been awarded a penalty after Beckham's cross had deflected off the hand of Valente. The referee was unmoved and the replays did show that it hit the hand of the defender but the ball had come from such close range that it would have been almost impossible for him to get his arm out of the way. It would prove to be Beckham's final involvement as he pulled up with injury shortly after. Losing their captain was a difficult loss, especially due to his set-piece prowess, but his replacement Aaron Lennon was straight into the action and showing why there was such a hype around him at the early stages of his career.

Lennon was willing to run at his marker and try to take them on, an increasingly rare feat at this point. While Portugal operated with Figo and Ronaldo cutting inside from the wings, Lennon was a more traditional winger, beating his opponent through pace and skill. His direct running was causing problems in the Portuguese back line and he nearly set up a golden chance for Rooney. The Tottenham winger went past two of his challengers easily and, although it was more of a mis-control, he laid the ball perfectly into the path of Rooney. The striker could only slice his shot further across the box where it found Joe Cole on the stretch. He could not keep his effort down and the ball sailed harmlessly over the bar. This came just a few minutes after a Gerrard corner had found Lampard completely unmarked at the back post for a shot on target but, summing up his tournament so far, the Chelsea midfielder slipped and sent his volley into the ground and it cleared the crossbar comfortably.

If it was beginning to feel like it was not England's day, then everything became a lot worse just after the hour mark. A chipped ball upfield from Lampard was collected by Rooney under the close attention of Ricardo Carvalho, as had been the case all match. The striker did well to shield the ball from his marker as well as Petit, who had come over to help. It was a battling showing from Rooney, perhaps highlighting his frustration at his lack of involvement so far and the lack of protection he felt he was getting from the Argentine official. Just as the referee was awarding a Portuguese free kick, although the reason was a mystery, Rooney snapped and aimed a stamp at the groin of Carvalho. Had the referee not been directly on top of the incident, it may have been missed or seen as accidental contact, but it was clearly a deliberate action.

Both sets of players immediately surrounded the referee to argue their side of the debate, with Rooney's Manchester United team-mate Cristiano Ronaldo leading the Portuguese effort. The look of bewilderment on Rooney's face that his club-mate would do this was clear to see on the replays as he pushed him away in annoyance. The referee distanced himself from the chaos and summoned Rooney over, going to his pocket to produce a card. The English public watched in horror as the red card was brought out, although the replays showed it was the only option. It was a moment that rivalled his current captain Beckham's sending-off in 1998 against Argentina. It was a moment of pure stupidity borne out of frustration but it may have cost his nation a chance of progressing.

Rooney, despite the sending-off, was spared from the same vilification that Beckham received due to an incident picked up by the TV cameras in the aftermath. After Rooney had left the pitch, the camera caught a shot of Ronaldo walking towards the sideline and winking towards the Portuguese bench. Looking for any reason to deflect the attention away from their own player's lapse of judgement, the English media jumped immediately on to the fact that it was clear evidence that Ronaldo had instructed his team-mates to take advantage of Rooney's known short temper and try to wind him up. The wink was his way of saying job well done. Perhaps that was true. The Portuguese players did do a tight marking job on Rooney, and Ronaldo was also spotted nudging the back of Rooney's head prior to kick-off. There was no malice but also no love in the gesture, and he made sure Rooney knew who it had come from. But, if that was the tactic, then Rooney had fallen into the trap laid out for him. As he later admitted himself, it was a stupid act and the referee had made the correct decision.

With the player advantage now, Portugal began to grow into the contest and started fashioning chances for themselves. Figo was at the heart of most of their positive play and had the first opening after the red card but could only send his effort wildly over. The match was now being played primarily in England's half but the chances that came were never clear ones. Maniche fired over from 20 yards, Valente was denied by a strong challenge from Ferdinand, before a Viana shot was easily gathered by Robinson, although he did his best to fumble the ball. Despite the pressure, Portugal could not break England down, in large part thanks to the performance of Owen Hargreaves.

One of England's most underutilised players during this generation, Hargreaves suffered from the fact that he did not play in the top flight in England. At the 2002 World Cup he became just the sixth player in history to be selected for an England World Cup squad while not playing in either England or Scotland (Gerry Hitchens, Internazionale 1962; Tony Woodcock, FC Köln, 1982; Ray Wilkins and Mark Hateley, Milan, 1986; and Chris Waddle, Marseille 1990, were the others). The Bayern Munich midfielder was the perfect screen in front of his defenders, offering expert protection for them and stopping the opposition from threatening the goal. It was more than just a defensive performance though, as he was also a menace going in the other direction, producing a brilliant challenge to prevent a counter-attack before taking the ball back towards the Portugal goal, where his cross was not converted by either Ferdinand or Terry on separate occasions. This was his best time in an England shirt as he provided the energy to make up for the disparity in players on the pitch.

As the final ten minutes approached, England began to regain their composure and could sense the potential for a great result. Lampard sent a low free kick on goal that was well parried by Ricardo, who reacted brilliantly to dive at the feet of Lennon to deny him getting a shot away. Another brilliant Hargreaves cross narrowly missed all of his England team-mates in the centre, and if anyone looked like scoring the winning goal it was England. Scolari did try to change systems by bringing on Hélder Postiga as a second striker and surprised everyone by taking off his captain Figo, but Portugal still seemed like they would be content with taking the match all the way to a penalty shoot-out.

As extra time began, it seemed logical that England would start to tire and Portugal would be able to exploit the spaces left by England's player disadvantage. Yet it still seemed like it was Eriksson's team that was the one pushing for a winner and most likely to get it. Gerrard chipped a clever ball across the area, aiming for the head of Peter Crouch, on as a substitute to give England a presence up front after the red card, but Miguel did amazingly well to reach the ball first and head it clear. There was also a penalty shout just after the break in extra time as Lennon burst into the box and went down under the sliding challenge of Valente. The appeals came from the England bench but the replay showed the full-back's tackle to be inch-perfect and he got a toe on the ball.

With just ten minutes remaining, the ball finally found the back of the net as Postiga steered a beautiful header over Robinson and into the far corner. As the Portuguese bench began to celebrate what would surely be the winning goal, the assistant referee was raising his flag to signal that the striker had been offside when the ball had been played, a decision proven correct on replays. It was the last notable moment of the match as both teams tired and settled for the impending penalty shoot-out. It would be a repeat of two years earlier when the European Championship was decided by spot kicks, with Ricardo the Portuguese hero. A surprise England penalty taker then had been Darius Vassell, and Ricardo admitted that he had no knowledge of the striker's preferred option so took his gloves off before the penalty was taken to psyche his opponent out. It worked. He saved the spot kick before taking the next one himself and smashing Portugal into the semi-finals.

This time, Portugal won the coin toss and elected to take the first penalty, sending Simão up first. The substitute stepped up and sent his effort low to the keeper's right, giving Robinson no chance. The perfect start. In response, England sent Lampard up first. It was a safe choice as he regularly took penalties for Chelsea but his tournament form had been poor so far and the nerves were clear to see. He admitted in his autobiography, *Totally Frank*, that he allowed doubt to creep into his mind when taking the spot kick and his effort was a poor one to the goalkeepers left. Ricardo guessed right and pushed it away. Advantage Portugal.

Another Portuguese sub, Hugo Viana, was their second taker and he sent the goalkeeper the wrong way with his shot but committed the cardinal sin of penalty taking in missing the target entirely. The ball clipped the outside of the post and went wide. The pressure then fell on the shoulders of the player of the match Hargreaves, whose penalty, low to the goalkeeper's right, narrowly snuck in despite Ricardo getting a hand to it. The disappointment was clear on the keeper's face that he could not quite prevent the ball from going in but Portugal's early advantage had now been reset.

Petit followed in Simão's footsteps in sending his shot to Robinson's right-hand side but his effort was closer in quality to Viana's as he too missed the target completely, not even hitting the woodwork like his compatriot had done. With the opportunity to take the lead in the shoot-out, Liverpool's Gerrard was the third English taker. Much like Lampard, Gerrard was a regular penalty taker in club football and was usually a reliable option. There had not been vintage displays from the Liverpool captain but his confidence would still have been high. He opted to follow Lampard's lead, perhaps too literally, as his effort went the same way with the same outcome as Ricardo comfortably pushed it away. Now 1-1 after three penalties each, the pressure was ramping up.

Portugal continued to show faith in their substitutes as the third player brought on was called upon to take a penalty. Postiga showed little hesitation and smashed his effort to Robinson's right, hitting it with so much power that the keeper did not even move from the centre of his goal. Knowing a miss would give Portugal the opportunity to clinch the result with their next kick, the fourth taker for England was perhaps a surprising choice. Jamie Carragher, who had been brought on with just a minute remaining so he could take a penalty, had impressed enough in training to be considered one of the best five options to take a spot kick, especially with both Beckham and Rooney off the pitch. The Liverpool defender showed no nerves and smashed the ball home but the referee had not been set, so he ordered a retake. The second effort, to the goalkeeper's right, was met by the firm hands of Ricardo, who had guessed correctly on every spot kick and actually got a hand to each one. It was a known fact that he spent time researching his potential opposition from the spot so he knew their preferences and would have the edge over them when it mattered. It was a clever tactic that worked.

Ricardo's third save meant that Portugal just needed one more successful effort and they would be in the semi-finals for the first time since 1966. Who else to take it but their young star Ronaldo. At the centre of the controversial moment of the match, there was little doubt that he would be the one to break English hearts. He waited until Robinson had made it clear which way he was going to dive and expertly put his penalty into the top right corner. The pantomime villain in the English press after the tournament, it could only have been him. As Portugal celebrated, the English players sank to their knees. It was a missed opportunity and they knew it. The consensus in the years after the tournament was that a quarter-final exit was a major disappointment. Everyone, including the England camp, believed they were good enough to win the whole thing and the manner of exit was more frustrating.

Eriksson resigned afterwards, having failed to take this most-talented England squad beyond the quarter-finals of any tournament. The fallout of the Rooney-Ronaldo incident rumbled on until Ronaldo's first acrimonious exit from Manchester United, and some of the England squad still somehow believe the decision to send Rooney off was the incorrect one. It was the most disappointing exit as the quality was there in every position and those in English colours see this as the failed golden generation.

Portugal, however, could celebrate their gritty victory. They had the blend of experience and youth in their ranks, the mix of two talented generations of players, and knew that with Scolari at the helm they could more than match any team they faced. With only one match between them and the World Cup Final, could Portugal finally earn themselves an international success that they believed their footballing heritage deserved.

* * *

Whoever Portugal were to play in the semi-final would be considered to be the favourite to reach the final. Brazil, the holders and possessing elite talent, against France and the last hurrah for their ageing generation as well as the final matches of the glorious career of Zinedine Zidane. With the sun once again shining in Frankfurt, the smiles on the faces of Zidane, Ronaldo and Ronaldinho as they embraced at the start of the proceedings was one of the enduring images from the tournament. It was a picture of joy. The best players on the planet just enjoying representing their country on the highest stage and knowing that they were about to put on a memorable exhibition.

Despite the obvious quality on show, neither team had fully impressed as yet. Brazil had won all four matches they had played but it had never been as easy as it appeared by the scorelines. Against Ghana in the previous round they had been tested more than they expected and it had taken a controversial second goal and a late third to secure the result. They had fared better than France, however.

Having laboured through their group in second place, France were fortunate to come away from the Spain match with a positive result. They had been second-best for the majority of the time, with the match turning in the second half when Zidane began to wrestle control over proceedings. It was the arrival of Zidane at his best that had reignited French optimism and those flames were about to be fanned even higher.

It was an intriguing contest, not least because it was a rematch of the final in 1998 when Zidane had brought his nation their first World Cup title and Ronaldo had a match that he would like to forget and one shrouded in mystery. The Brazilian striker was initially left off the team sheet for the final, with no real explanation as to why. Shortly before kick-off, a modified team sheet was provided that now included Ronaldo from the start. The broadcasters were left scrambling for any sort of explanation but none was forthcoming. It was only some years later that it was revealed that he had suffered a convulsive fit and had spent three hours in hospital on the day of the match. Allegedly, it was Ronaldo who declared himself fit to play, although conspiracy theories abound, suggesting that sponsors Nike had pressurised Brazil into playing Ronaldo. It was the last time Brazil had failed to win at the World Cup, with seven wins from seven matches on route to victory in 2002 and four wins from four so far in Germany. This was supposed to be the revenge for Ronaldo and Brazil. An opportunity to right the wrongs of eight years earlier.

Brazil started like they had that point to prove. Two early chances fell to Ronaldo, who nearly found space in the area after a missed defensive header, before he then headed over. Despite these early chances, it was France that were in control of the match. In fact, it was Zidane alone that was in charge. Everything seemed easy for him. It was as if no Brazilian could get near to him. A master at work, Zidane evaded challenges, showed perfect close control and fancy trickery to escape any attention given him. He was the conductor and the World Cup was his orchestra. The only problem was that the rest of the ensemble for France was not quite at the same level as their leader. Ribéry had the best chance but his effort narrowly went over from 20 yards out and Vieira went down under challenge from Lúcio but the referee remained unmoved. There were few goalscoring opportunities but the match was being played at a high tempo and the midfield battle was entertaining as Zidane took Brazil on seemingly by himself.

As good as Zidane was, Brazil were poor. A tactical switch had brought greater midfield stability in favour of attacking options, with Gilberto Silva in place of Adriano. The result was not quite as intended as Zidane continued to find space between the lines and Ronaldo seemed isolated up front on his own. There was also the continued struggles of Kaká and Ronaldinho at the tournament, as neither seemed capable of replicating their club form on the international stage this time around.

As the second half began, France started to turn the screw and push for the opening goal. Henry, who had been relatively quiet all tournament so far, was drifting out wide into the left-hand channel and finding himself in space and threatening positions. Within the first ten minutes of the restart, he had created a chance for Vieira with a clever back-heel that the midfielder narrowly missed, and had put the ball in the back of the net himself only for the flag to go up for offside.

The French pressure finally told just 12 minutes into the second half. A free kick for the Europeans on the left-hand side was floated over to the far post by Zidane, where Henry was waiting, completely unmarked, to volley home over Dida. The quick taking of the set piece had caught Roberto Carlos out as he was tying the laces of his boots when Zidane took it and he was the one tasked with marking the Arsenal striker. Remarkably, this was the first time that Zidane had provided an assist for Henry during all their time playing for their national team. For some reason, the connection between two of the best players of their generation had never quite clicked but this was the perfect time for that relationship to finally produce.

The match had needed a goal and the hope was that Brazil would now start to show the quality that they were clearly capable of. Yet the flow was still in France's favour. Zidane was in control in the middle of the pitch and Henry and Ribéry were causing the Brazilian defence problems with their pace and running in behind. The Marseille winger could have doubled France's lead, having three great chances within ten minutes. First, after good skill to beat his marker, his cross was deflected by Juan but narrowly went wide of the far post after going beyond Dida. He showed his pace again as he burst forwards towards the box before being denied by a strong recovery challenge from Carlos, then his shot was saved by Dida to keep the deficit at one goal.

Perhaps realising the tactical gamble had not paid off, Brazilian coach Parreira reverted to his 'magic square', bringing on Adriano as the second striker. He also replaced the ineffective Kaká with Robinho in the hope that the youthful exuberance and flair of the midfielder would cause the French more problems than they had been given so far. It was not going to be a difficult challenge considering the fact that 70 minutes in Brazil had yet to have a shot on target. They were lacking any form of cutting edge and could not muster any semblance of control in the middle of the pitch. The first real chance that came their way was in the 81st minute when Robinho had space to shoot from the middle of the area, but his effort was wild and wayward.

Ronaldo, an isolated figure on the periphery so far, was still on the pitch and may only need a single chance to draw his nation level. However, for the first time since the opening minutes, he managed to shoot on goal but his effort was weak and dragged wide. The Real Madrid forward then earned his side a free kick in an excellent position just outside the penalty box with just two minutes remaining. With Juninho now off the pitch, the responsibility fell on the talented shoulders of Ronaldinho, whose free kick had won Brazil their quarter-final match against England four years earlier. His tournament had been one of frustration so far, with him unable to exert his usual influence over proceedings, but this was his moment to put all that aside and keep his country's hopes alive. Up stepped the Barcelona midfielder, who got his effort over the wall and back down again, but it did not dip enough and went the wrong side of the crossbar from Brazil's perspective.

Louis Saha, on as a sub for Henry, should have secured the result as France broke forwards on a three-on-three counter-attack but his effort was saved by Dida. As the play became stretched, France were looking to pick off their opponents on the counter with the fresh legs of their substitutes but Brazil were finally showing some desperation and, in the 91st minute, mustered their first shot on target. The chance fell to the one man on the pitch it should have fallen to but Ronaldo's effort was kept out by a smart save from Barthez, a spectator all evening, and his defenders came to his aid by reacting quickest to clear the loose ball from any potential danger.

That was the final action of the match and Brazil's World Cup dream was over. While everyone had been focused on the last opportunity for France's generation of talent, this was the end for a Brazilian group that were among their storied elite. This would mark the last time that Cafu, Roberto Carlos and Ronaldo would wear the gold of Brazil, except for one solitary appearance in a friendly in 2011 for Ronaldo. It was also, strangely, the final World Cup appearance for Ronaldinho, despite the fact he was just 26 years old and had been voted the best player on the planet just six months earlier. The fact that they had gone out with such a whimper would have been a source of pure disappointment. They had been unable to keep up with France, unable to lay a glove on their European counterparts. Once again Brazil had been undone by the elite performance of Zidane, the one player who would have fit into a Brazil squad of any generation.

There had been an aura of inevitability about Zidane's performances since the second half of the Spain match. It was as if he was playing a sport that only he knew how to play properly and everyone else was playing catch-up. This was his stage. His theatre. This World Cup was Zidane's 'last dance', the term used for the final season of Michael Jordan's incredible NBA career with the Chicago Bulls as they went in search of a sixth title in eight years. There was a gravitational pull towards the French maestro, an unseen force driving everything. Although there were still two tough matches to go before he would be a two-time world champion, it was increasingly clear that Zidane was going to exit the world stage while leaving his indelible mark on another international tournament. Few could have predicted, however, the manner in which that would be.

5pm, 30 June 2006
Olympiastadion, Berlin
Attendance: 72,000
Referee: Ľuboš Micheľ (Slovakia)

Germany 1 (Klose 80)
Argentina 1 (Ayala 49)
Germany won 4-2 on penalties after extra time
Shoot-out: Neuville 1-0, Cruz 1-1, Ballack 2-1, Ayala saved, Podolski 3-1, Rodríguez 3-2, Borowski 4-2, Cambiasso saved

Germany: Jens Lehmann, Arne Friedrich, Per Mertesacker, Christoph Metzelder, Philipp Lahm, Bernd Schneider (David Odonkor 62), Torsten Frings, Michael Ballack (c), Bastian Schweinsteiger (Tim Borowski 74), Miroslav Klose (Oliver Neuville 86), Lukas Podolski. **Manager:** Jürgen Klinsmann.

Argentina: Roberto Abbondanzieri (Leo Franco 71), Fabricio Coloccini, Roberto Ayala, Gabriel Heinze, Juan Pablo Sorin (c), Javier Mascherano, Maxi Rodríguez, Lucho González, Juan Román Riquelme (Esteban Cambiasso 72), Hernán Crespo (Julio Cruz 79), Carlos Tevez. **Manager:** José Pékerman.

Booked: Podolski (3), Odonkor (94), Friedrich (114); Sorin (46), Mascherano (60), Rodríguez (88), Cruz (95)
Sent off: Cufré (120)

9pm, 30 June 2006
Volksparkstadion, Hamburg
Attendance: 50,000
Referee: Frank De Bleeckere (Belgium)

Italy 3 (Zambrotta 6, Toni 59, 69)
Ukraine 0

Italy: Gianluigi Buffon, Gianluca Zambrotta, Fabio Cannavaro (c), Andrea Barzagli, Fabio Grosso, Mauro Camoranesi (Simone Barone 68), Andrea Pirlo (Massimo Oddo 68), Gennaro Gattuso (Cristian Zaccardo 77), Simone Perrotta, Francesco Totti, Luca Toni. **Manager:** Marcello Lippi.

Ukraine: Oleksandr Shovkovskyi, Oleh Husyev, Vyacheslav Sviderskyi (Andriy Vorobey 20), Andriy Rusol (Vladyslav Vashchuk 45+2), Andriy Nesmachnyi, Andriy Husin, Anatoliy Tymoschuk, Oleh Shelayev, Artem Milevskyi (Oleksiy Byelik 72), Andriy Shevchenko (c), Maksym Kalynychenko. **Manager:** Oleg Blokhin.

Booked: Sviderskyi (16), Kalynychenko (21), Milevskyi (67)

5pm, 1 July 2006
Arena AufSchalke, Gelsenkirchen
Attendance: 52,000
Referee: Horacio Elizondo (Argentina)

England 0
Portugal 0
Portugal won 3-1 on penalties after extra time
Shoot-out: Simão 1-0, Lampard saved, Viana missed, Hargreaves 1-1, Petit missed, Gerrard saved, Postiga 2-1, Carragher saved, Ronaldo 3-1

England: Paul Robinson, Gary Neville, Rio Ferdinand, John Terry, Ashley Cole, David Beckham (c) (Aaron Lennon 52 (Jamie Carragher 119)), Steven Gerrard, Owen Hargreaves, Frank Lampard, Joe Cole (Peter Crouch 65), Wayne Rooney. **Manager:** Sven-Göran Eriksson.

Portugal: Ricardo, Miguel, Fernando Meira, Ricardo Carvalho, Nuno Valente, Tiago (Hugo Viana 74), Petit, Maniche, Luís Figo (c) (Hélder Postiga 86), Cristiano Ronaldo, Pauleta (Simão 63). **Manager:** Luis Felipe Scolari.

Booked: Terry (30), Hargreaves 107); Petit (44), Carvalho (111)
Sent off: Rooney (62)

9pm, 1 July 2006
Waldstadion, Frankfurt
Attendance: 48,000
Referee: Luis Medina Cantalejo (Spain)

Brazil 0
France 1 (Henry 57)

Brazil: Dida, Cafu (c) (Cicinho 76), Lúcio, Juan, Roberto Carlos, Gilberto Silva, Kaká (Robinho 79), Juninho (Adriano 63), Zé Roberto, Ronaldinho, Ronaldo. **Manager:** Carlos Alberto Parreira.

France: Fabian Barthez, Willy Sagnol, Lilian Thuram, William Gallas, Eric Abidal, Patrick Vieira, Claude Makélélé, Franck Ribéry (Sidney Govou 77), Zinedine Zidane (c), Florent Malouda (Sylvain Wiltord 81), Thierry Henry (Louis Saha 86). **Manager:** Raymond Domenech.

Booked: Cafu (25), Juan (45), Ronaldo (45+2), Lúcio (75); Sagnol (74), Saha (87), Thuram (88)

Semi-Finals

THE FINAL four. The moment when those dreams of winning the World Cup for your nation seem realistic. The anticipation rises. The pressure mounts. The preparation and form go out of the window and all that is left is 22 players in each match and their ability to perform on the elite stage.

The first semi-final was a meeting of two unbroken records. Germany were hosting the match in Dortmund, a venue where they had never suffered a defeat, with 13 wins and a solitary draw against Wales coming from their 14 matches in the city prior to this meeting with Italy. On the other hand, while the Italians were on the back foot in terms of the record of their hosts in this stadium, they knew that the weight of history was on their side as Germany had never beaten them in a major tournament fixture in the previous six attempts. Italy had also thumped Klinsmann's team 4-1 in a March friendly in Florence that nearly left the manager's position untenable.

Often in high-pressure knockout matches, the start is cagey as both teams try to feel their way into the contest and avoid making any early mistakes to put them on the back foot. Here in Dortmund, however, that was not the case. It was a fast-paced start as both tried to find a quick breakthrough to turn things in their favour. It was full commitment from the first whistle, with the returning Materazzi taking out Klose with an old-fashioned 'reducer', a strong challenge designed to let the opposing striker know they are in for a tough match. It was a tone-setter for the contest.

Perrotta almost created a good opening with a ball played across the Germany penalty area but it was cleared away by Lahm. The Germans pushed back immediately. Podolski managed to get a quickfire shot away on the edge of the area that was well blocked by Cannavaro before the Italian captain reacted quickest to a loose ball in the penalty area to clear. There was an appeal for a handball against Pirlo that was waved away by the Mexican referee, then an Italian counter-attack broke down after a heavy touch by Perrotta allowed Lehmann to rush out and smother the ball. There was no suggestion that either team was going to try to sustain a period of possession and the match was stretched from the very start.

Amid all the chaos and energy, there was one man who was exuding calm and composure. This was Cannavaro's masterpiece. Following on from Zidane's mesmerising performance against Brazil, the Italian captain produced his own display of a world-class nature. With Nesta injured, Materazzi suspended for the quarter-finals and a rotation of the preferred full-backs, Cannavaro was the one constant in the Italian defence that had only conceded a solitary goal so far in the tournament. His performances throughout had been outstanding but this match against the hosts was on another level. It was as if he had watched the match the night before and knew how every ball would bounce, what the Germans' plan was before they knew it themselves. He was first to every ball, cleverly sweeping in behind his defensive partner for any dangerous passes that made it through. Despite only being 5ft 9in, unusually short for a central defender, every aspect of his game was simply impeccable during this match. He matched Klose's run, beat Ballack in the air, blocked every shot, and this was all inside the first 20 minutes. As everyone else around him was frenetic and sloppy, Cannavaro was the epitome of Italian class, the latest in the long lineage of elite Italian central defenders.

The tension in both sets of players was clear to see, especially among the Germans. After Podolski had volleyed over from the edge of the area, he urged the German supporters to make more noise despite the already incredible atmosphere. Germany were being drawn into the Italians' game, one dominated in the middle of the pitch where the Azzurri were strongest, with Pirlo, Gattuso and Totti making up perhaps the best midfield trio in the tournament. Germany were missing the presence of the suspended Torsten Frings in the middle of the pitch, his replacement Sebastian Kehl struggling to make any real impact. The Italians were on top and Materazzi should really have made more of a free header from a Pirlo free kick but could only glance his effort wide via a slight deflection. Another set piece from the Italian playmaker fashioned a good chance as he pulled a free kick from near the byline to the edge of the area for an unmarked Totti, but his first-time effort was well defended and blocked.

Italy had been unable to make their superiority over the opening half an hour count with a breakthrough and Germany began to exert their own pressure shortly after. Schneider, who had played well as the right-hand side midfielder for Germany all competition, started to have a growing influence, finding himself in space and able to get a shot on goal but he could not keep his effort under control. He almost had another chance just two minutes later but he was narrowly unable to reach a cross played into the area. There were positive signs for Germany though, as they had finally managed to peg the Italians back a little.

It was a first half played at a breathless pace, seeming to fly by without so much as a pause. It was a refreshing sight as the knockout stages had been cagey so far, with few matches being played in this manner. There was no holding back from either team here. Germany had played in a positive way all tournament but this was a change of pace from the Italians. Their cagey approach that had seen them progress this far had seemingly been left behind as they attempted to dominate their opponents on the front foot rather than counter-attacking.

Where Italy had been the more progressive of the two in the first half, Germany started the second half with renewed vigour. Kehl hit a left-footed volley from the edge of the area that drifted wide just a minute into the second period, before Klose's brilliant run into the penalty area was nullified by an onrushing Buffon. The restart had been cagey from Lippi's team, almost as if they had banked on being able to sit back and defend a lead for the second half rather than still needing to push forward. They had resorted to their typical style of holding out and attempting to pick their opponents off on the break, almost finding success as Grosso burst free, but he was offside and the ball well smothered by Lehmann in any case.

The match was still being played at what appeared to be an unsustainable pace, now being controlled by the Germans. Podolski was starting to become more influential in his second striker role, turning and shooting but seeing his effort well saved by Buffon, before nearly being played in by Borowski, who could only pick out an Italian defender with his attempted cross. An hour in and neither team had been able to find a breakthrough. The match had been competitive, even with only two yellow cards shown, although both Friedrich and Ballack were fortunate to avoid bookings for reckless challenges on Materazzi and Gattuso, respectively.

As the last ten minutes approached, a Cannavaro challenge on Podolski was awarded as a German free kick. The Italian captain had used the striker as leverage as he jumped to win a header.

The decision was incredibly harsh but, if the referee deemed it to be a foul, then it should have been a German spot kick as the offence clearly occurred inside the area. Instead, the official opted for a middle-ground of a free kick right on the edge of the area. Ballack, who had been a peripheral figure so far, stepped up to hopefully be his nation's hero once more but could not keep his effort down and the ball sailed over the crossbar.

Just a couple of minutes after the Germans could have been awarded a penalty, the Italians felt that one should have been given to them. Clever movement through the lines saw the ball played between Pirlo, Gilardino and Totti, who clipped a brilliant ball over the German defence for Perrotta to race on to. Lehmann, in his typical fashion, raced out of his goal to punch clear. In doing so he completely flattened the Italian winger with his body. His challenge was reckless and out of control. He got the ball with his fists first but goalkeepers seem to have a greater degree of leeway in what they can do when coming for the ball. Had had the referee awarded a foul then there could have been few complaints. While nowhere near as bad, there were shades of Harald Schumacher's infamous 'tackle' on Patrick Battiston in 1982.

Germany almost stole the victory in added time as Kehl flicked a Schweinsteiger free kick to the back post but the only players there were Italian defenders, who just let the ball go behind for a goal kick. It was the last action of an enthralling match and the extra 30 minutes was a gift to all watching. In a match that had been this free-flowing and entertaining, it is perhaps strange to use a quote from a proponent of the catenaccio style of football. Yet, when Annibale Frossi said that the perfect match would end 0-0 because it meant nobody made any mistakes and there was balance in the game, this contest could be shown as the perfect example of that notion. No goals had been scored but you would have been hard pressed to find anybody that wanted the match to end or was not on the edge of their seat. Both teams had created a spectacle, a World Cup classic, despite the lack of impression on the scoresheet.

Italy had begun to look understandably tired as the 90 minutes ended, but Lippi's team talk prior to extra time clearly drew some last reserves of energy from somewhere as they pressed their opponents like it was the first minute of the season. In the opening minute of the extra period, Gilardino drove to the edge of the pitch before cutting back inside Ballack on to his left foot. Surprising most in the stadium, he snuck a left-footed shot to the near post, creeping under the despairing dive of Lehmann before hitting the post and rolling clear of the goal, with no Italian on hand to tap home. Undeterred, Italy continued to push up, earning themselves a corner that Pirlo whipped into the area. It was unconvincingly cleared by the Germans and fell to Zambrotta on the edge of the box. He took a touch on to his right foot and smashed a fierce effort that flew beyond Lehmann but crashed against the top of the crossbar and over.

Perhaps it was the fear of facing the Germans in a penalty shoot-out, but Lippi was not going to settle for that outcome, even sending on another attacker in Del Piero in place of one of his wide midfielders. Italy's intention was clear. They would try to avoid penalties at all costs. It was a risky strategy that almost backfired as a David Odonkor cross picked out Podolski completely unmarked in the area. It was the perfect chance but his connection with the ball was all wrong and it sailed wide. Had it been Klose, maybe Germany would have been heading into the break ahead but instead it was still 0-0. After 105 minutes of high-octane football, the obvious expectation was that both teams would be exhausted and the tempo would finally drop but, if anything, it only increased in the second half of extra time.

Chances were exchanged straight away as Iaquinta tried to find a team-mate in support but did well to earn a corner, before Lahm curled an effort over the crossbar after being found by another Odonkor cross. It was essentially a basketball match at this point as the play kept flowing from one end to the other. A clever dinked ball over the top would not settle for Del Piero to get a shot away, then Zambrotta's strike was blocked, leading to a German counter that saw Buffon produce an outstanding save to tip Podolski's goalbound effort over the bar for a corner. The next opening fell to Del Piero after Iaquinta was played in over the top and Lehmann rushed out rashly. The Italian striker played a clever back-heel to Gilardino who layed it into the path of the Juventus striker, but he could only drag his shot wide.

As the match approached the final two minutes, Pirlo picked up a beautiful position in space around 25 yards out. He turned towards goal, saw nothing on and decided to shoot with his left foot. His effort was almost perfect. It was flying into the top right-hand corner of the goal before a diving Lehmann got a strong hand behind the ball and diverted it behind for a corner. It seemed as if we were destined to not get any goals. But Italy had other ideas.

From the resulting corner, Del Piero's delivery was poorly cleared and found Pirlo in space at the edge of the area. Resisting the urge to take another shot at goal, the Milan playmaker kept his composure and took an extra touch towards the right-hand side. As three German defenders stepped towards him, he slipped the ball into the area for the now unmarked Fabio Grosso. The Palermo full-back, who had been playing in the second tier of Italian football just two years earlier, curled a first-time left-footed shot across the goal, bending perfectly into the far corner of the net. In the 119th minute the deadlock had finally been broken. Channelling his inner Marco Tardelli, Grosso ran away, almost shaking his head in disbelief at his moment, screaming 'Non ci credo' (I don't believe it). This was his moment. His nation's moment. There was still time on the clock but the looks on the faces of the German players said they knew it was over. Italy had earned their reward for taking the game on in the extra period and not settling for the penalty shoot-out.

Despite the limited time remaining, Germany poured forwards desperately. Another Cannavaro clearing header fell to Ballack on the edge of the area but he could only shoot wide. And it was the Italian captain who beat Podolski to a bouncing ball, winning the second ball after having won an initial header inside the area. He started to bring the ball out but Totti took over, playing Gilardino through on goal. Knowing he lacked the pace to beat his marker, he delayed his run and allowed the support to arrive. He played the ball under his shoulder for the bursting run from the fresh Del Piero, who produced a perfectly weighted shot over Lehmann and into the top corner. Two goals in three minutes and Italy had earned their place in the World Cup Final. This was the their moment. Becoming the first team to beat Germany in Dortmund had earned them their opportunity to win sporting immortality. Led by the magnificent Cannavaro, they seemed unbreachable.

All the attention was focused on the Italian victory but this had been a match made by both teams. Germany had pushed and pressed and had continued their attacking style that had been evident all tournament. It was a heartbreak for Klinsmann and his players, especially the manner in which it ended, but the positives massively outweighed the disappointment once the dust settled. They had restored pride and hope in the national team, uniting their nation behind them and being incredible hosts for an exceptional tournament.

This was the end of Germany's World Cup but not their journey. Klinsmann left after the defeat, replaced by his assistant

Joachim Löw. With Löw in charge and Lahm, Schweinsteiger, Mertesacker, Podolski and Klose still playing, Germany would reach the semi-finals of the next four major international tournaments, losing the Euro 2008 final 1-0 to Spain before winning the World Cup in 2014. The early stages of the rebuild that the German footballing culture underwent to reach that stage were felt in 2006 with Klinsmann's team, and Germany had been brilliant hosts.

* * *

After Italy's dramatic victory over the hosts, the other semi-final saw two teams trending in opposite directions going head-to-head. Portugal's journey to their first World Cup semi-final appearance since 1966 had been one of battling rather than elegant performances. They had outfought the Netherlands, almost literally, and had outlasted England despite having a man advantage for half an hour of regular time and the whole of extra time. France, on the other hand, had finally begun to show the quality that everyone knew was littered throughout their squad, with Zidane carrying his nation on his back with one of the greatest World Cup performances in their quarter-final against Brazil. Understandably, Domenech retained faith in the starting line-up from that Brazil encounter, while Scolari made two changes, bringing Costinha and Deco straight back into the starting XI after serving their suspensions.

France created the first opening inside the first minute as Florent Malouda got free in behind the Portuguese defence but could only drag his shot wide. Despite that, it was the Iberian nation that made the majority of the running in the opening exchanges. The returning Deco had a low shot well tipped away by Barthez with Sagnol doing well to deny a Portugal player getting to the rebound first, before Maniche struck a fierce shot that narrowly flew over Barthez's goal. Luís Figo got himself into the action as well with a cross deflected behind and a powerful effort that was well gathered by Barthez, although the Portugal captain had to be stretchered off the pitch after being clattered by Vieira in the aftermath of that effort. He did return to the action and it was crucial that he did as his team was winning the wide battle.

Portugal had a long history of producing tricky wide players, and the latest, Ronaldo and Figo, had been crucial to Portugal's chances in this tournament. During the opening half an hour Ronaldo was giving Sagnol no rest, even causing problems when Ribéry tracked back to try to nullify him, while Figo was easily winning his one-on-one battle with Abidal. Unfortunately, although Portugal had wingers to deliver the ball into the penalty area, their striking options left something to be desired, Pauleta struggling to convert any of those chances. It was partly a poor showing by him but also what was quickly turning into an excellent one by Thuram, who had intercepted three dangerous balls inside 20 minutes, meaning that Portugal were unable to make their early pressure count.

Having ridden out the early storm, France started to show their own quality. Henry, drifting out towards his preferred left-hand side, was giving Miguel trouble, turning him in the wrong direction before he could only send his cross straight into the arms of Ricardo. Shortly after the half-hour mark, Henry received the ball more centrally with his back to goal. He took one touch to control and then a second to flick the ball away from his marker, Carvalho. The Chelsea defender desperately lunged out a leg to try to nick the ball but could only catch the French forward, who went to ground. Henry definitely left his leg there to be caught but it was a clumsy challenge and the Uruguayan official had little choice but to award a penalty to France.

There was only ever one option to take the penalty. Up stepped captain Zidane. Against Ricardo the outcome was not as clear as it usually was when Zidane took a penalty. Over the past couple of international tournaments, Ricardo had proven his worth as an elite penalty saver through preparation and mind games. As Zidane took the ball to set it on the penalty spot, he seemed completely calm. His iconic gold predator boots almost shone under the floodlights and he only needed a simple two-step run-up, drilling the penalty low to Ricardo's right. The goalkeeper dived the right way but the penalty was perfectly placed in the bottom corner and the ball nestled firmly in the back of the net. France had taken the lead and Zidane was once again his country's hero.

Portugal immediately bounced back in search of an immediate reply but Maniche's long-range effort was brought under control at the second attempt by Barthez. They appealed for a penalty of their own after Ronaldo went to ground while jumping for a header but the replay showed clearly that he was already diving towards the ground without any contact from Sagnol's challenge. As the half-time whistle blew, Scolari would have been disappointed but not disheartened. Although they were behind, Portugal had been the better and more positive team. With their wingers causing problems for the French full-backs, and Deco picking up clever spaces in between the lines, Portugal would have still been hopeful that they could create enough chances to get themselves back into the match.

Hoping to start the second half and kill the match off early, France began to push straight away. Henry did brilliantly in the box to get his shot away when surrounded by three defenders but was denied by a good save by Ricardo, although he was fortunate that the ball squirmed wide of the goalpost. The Portuguese keeper then produced another save to keep out Ribéry's effort. It was the most sustained spell of French pressure so far as they looked to play more proactively and take the game to their opponents rather than adopting the passive approach of the opening period. Their positivity almost was undone, however, when Pauleta found himself in space in the area but, continuing his ineffective tournament, he could only shoot into the side-netting.

As the second half drew on, the play settled into a predictable rhythm with France allowing Portugal the ball but keeping them at arm's length from their goal. The substitutions made to freshen up the teams simply served to disrupt the action and prevent either team from being able to sustain a period of pressure on their opposing goal. Raymond Domenech was clever with his changes, introducing them at steady intervals to cause the most interruption to the Portuguese efforts of finding an equaliser. Everything Scolari's team tried failed to work. Crosses were blocked, shots were fired in from distance that barely troubled Barthez even if on target and, as the match wore on, Ronaldo and Figo became increasingly ineffectual, hampered by injury and tiredness, respectively.

Even with time fast running out, Portugal's desperation could not inspire them into that extra gear they needed. Miguel and Hélder Postiga both felt they were impeded, drawing angry appeals from the Portuguese bench and players, but neither were fouls as Miguel tripped over his own feet and Postiga simply fell over when he felt the slightest touch from Gallas at his back. They did have one opportunity with just over ten minutes to go when Ronaldo took a free kick from 30 yards out that Barthez couldn't hold. It was a poor effort at stopping the ball when he really should have caught it. The loose ball was met by the head of Figo, who could not control his effort and his header looped agonisingly on to the roof of the net rather than dropping under the crossbar. Even if it had been dropping in, Gallas was back on to the line and would have headed it clear.

As time ticked away, Portugal began lumping the ball forwards in hope rather than creating any chances through clever football. Meanwhile, France, through Zidane, were taking the sting out of the match. This was less exceptional than the Brazil match but he was controlling everything and dragging his team upfield and away from danger with ease.

Challenges were starting to fly in at this stage as Portugal desperately tried to win the ball back. Carvalho's challenge on Wiltord was a borderline sending-off offence and Figo caught Saha with a possible stamp as the French striker lunged in for a tackle, with Saha picking up the caution.

In close matches like this, there is always one last good opportunity. It came from a simple punt upfield that was won by Postiga. As the ball bounced on the edge of the area, Fernando Meira, the central defender now playing as an auxiliary striker as Portugal pushed forward, let the ball bounce before attempting a first-time half-volley. He hit it with power but no accuracy and the ball flew harmlessly over the crossbar. The look of anguish on his face showed that he knew that it was the chance that his nation needed. By falling to him, it had probably fallen to the last player in the Portuguese squad that their fans would have hoped. However, Portugal did manage to get the ball into the back of the net in the fifth minute of added time when Deco clipped the ball over the stranded keeper after he had denied Ronaldo, who was through one-on-one, but the offside flag had gone up as the Manchester United winger had been walking back from an offside position as the ball was played through to him.

There was no more time for Portugal to create anything and France had hung on to reach their second World Cup Final in three tournaments. This was an incredible achievement for their ageing squad, their last chance at glory still alive thanks to the Herculean effort of their captain and talisman, who had put the nation on his back once again, carrying them through the knockout stage all the way to the final. His last-ever match would be the World Cup Final. It would be a fitting end for maybe the best player of his generation and the opportunity to firmly cement his legacy on the international stage.

Portugal's greatest generation of players at this stage had failed to support their captain in the manner the French had Zidane. This was Figo's final tournament for his country, his last cap would be the third-place play-off rather than the final. This was the changing of the guard to the key player that Portugal would hang their hopes on in future. With Figo retiring, Ronaldo would become the centre point for his country's attempt to win their first major international honour. That finally came in 2016 when they defeated France 1-0 after extra time to win the European Championship, although Ronaldo was again ineffective and spent the majority of the final cheerleading from the sidelines after picking up a knock. There was hope that their World Cup duck could be broken in 2022 but they again crashed out unconvincingly, beaten in the quarter-finals by Morocco, with Ronaldo having been dropped due to his attitude after being substituted. This was amid his decline and fallout with Manchester United, which led to him being released from his contract.

There was a feeling of a major missed opportunity for Portugal after this exit, as France had not outplayed them. Portugal perhaps edged the contest. They were just lacking a goalscorer to take the chances they were creating. They had not scored since their first-half goal against the Netherlands in the Round of 16 – 277 minutes of goalless action. They had only conceded once in that time, Zidane's penalty, so they only needed one player up front to take a chance to give them that cutting edge they so desperately needed. With Figo, Deco and Ronaldo all in the same team, this really should have been the Portugal generation that went one step further than Eusébio had managed to bring international glory to the Iberian nation.

9pm, 4 July 2006
Westfalenstadion, Dortmund
Attendance: 65,000
Referee: Benito Archundia (Mexico)

Germany 0
Italy 2 (Grosso 119, Del Piero 120+1)
After extra time

Germany: Jens Lehmann, Arne Friedrich, Per Mertesacker, Christoph Metzelder, Philipp Lahm, Bernd Schneider (David Odonkor 83), Michael Ballack (c), Sebastian Kehl, Tim Borowski (Bastian Schweinsteiger 73), Miroslav Klose (Oliver Neuville 111), Lukas Podolski. **Manager**: Jürgen Klinsmann.

Italy: Gianluigi Buffon, Gianluca Zambrotta, Fabio Cannavaro (c), Marco Materazzi, Fabio Grosso, Mauro Camoranesi (Vincenzo Iaquinta 91), Andrea Pirlo, Gennaro Gattuso, Simone Perrotta (Alessandro Del Piero 104), Francesco Totti, Luca Toni (Alberto Gilardino 74). **Manager**: Marcello Lippi.

Booked: Borowski (40), Metzelder (56); Camoranesi (90)

9pm, 5 July 2006
World Cup Stadium, Munich
Attendance: 66,000
Referee: Jorge Larrionda (Uruguay)

Portugal 0
France 1 (Zidane 33 (p))

323

Portugal: Ricardo, Miguel (Paulo Ferreira 62), Fernando Meira, Ricardo Carvalho, Nuno Valente, Costinha (Hélder Postiga 75), Maniche, Luís Figo (c), Deco, Cristiano Ronaldo, Pauleta (Simão 68). **Manager**: Luis Felipe Scolari.

France: Fabien Barthez, Willy Sagnol, Lilian Thuram, William Gallas, Eric Abidal, Patrick Vieira, Claude Makélélé, Franck Ribéry (Sidney Govou 72), Zinedine Zidane (c), Florent Malouda (Sylvain Wiltord 69), Thierry Henry (Louis Saha 85). **Manager**: Raymond Domenech.

Booked: Carvalho (83); Saha (87)

Third-Place Play-off

THE SEVENTH match of a 32-team World Cup is either the greatest high of a player's career or perhaps the biggest let-down. From the potential of lining up for your nation in the World Cup Final to the lacklustre feeling of having to appear in the third-place play-off. The disappointment that Figo must have felt after the semi-final defeat would have been compounded by the fact that Scolari decided not to start him in this match, his final international appearance for Portugal, bringing Simão in instead. Changes are common in this fixture as both coaches tend to use it as an opportunity to give minutes to those players who had not featured as much as they would have hoped, but leaving your captain, the country's all-time leading appearance-maker on the bench for their final match was an interesting decision.

Klinsmann also opted to ring the changes, bringing Frings back in place of Ballack, who was given a rest, and starting Oliver Kahn in goal ahead of Lehmann. The decision to start the Arsenal keeper over Kahn had been one of the biggest controversies heading into the tournament but Lehmann had proved his worth and there was almost unity between the two ahead of the penalty shoot-out in the quarter-final. This would prove to be the last appearance for the legendary German goalkeeper, Kahn, an 89th cap for his country and one final World Cup appearance meaning that his last appearance would not be the infamous 2002 final when he had been Germany's star all tournament but made a horrific mistake that allowed Ronaldo to open the scoring on the way to a 2-0 victory for Brazil.

Despite this being a match that nobody wants to play, it can often produce some of the best football in a tournament. With both teams freed from the pressure of the outcome and an opportunity for those fringe players to make a point to their coach for future squad selections, the third-place play-off can often make for an interesting contest. In 2002 and 2010 it finished 3-2 in entertaining contests as the teams took the match seriously. For Germany, this was an opportunity to thank their fans for the support they had received as the hosts and to end their tournament on a relative high.

As they had all tournament, Germany started with high intensity, with a Kehl volley deflected behind and appeals for a handball being waved away. The returning Schweinsteiger did well to play Klose in behind but he ended up going slightly wider than he ideally wanted and could only shoot into the side-netting, unable to extend his lead in the race for the golden boot.

Portugal grew into the match after Germany's early flurry of chances, with Pauleta being released in behind before shooting straight at Kahn, continuing his tournament trend of wasting good chances. Deco was starting to exert his influence over proceedings, with the majority of the Portuguese chances being orchestrated by him and he also saw his own shot well blocked. The play was becoming increasingly stretched as both teams took the contest seriously, Podolski seeing his well-struck free kick saved, before Deco curled another effort narrowly wide at the other end.

The surprise at the break was that it was still 0-0 despite the intensity in which the match was being played. Neither team seemed to be settling for a 'whatever' outcome and both seemed desperate to emerge victorious. For both it was the same story that had been there throughout the tournament as Germany pressed and harried, while Portugal looked defensively solid but any chances they did create were not being taken, as they lacked a proper goalscorer.

It was Pauleta again who had the first chance of the second half but, after clever work to cut inside his marker on to his left foot, his shot was poor and bobbled harmlessly into the arms of Kahn. Ronaldo then went down in the box looking for a penalty after running into Jansen but the referee was in a good position and rightfully waved play on.

Portugal were made to rue Pauleta's missed chance just a few minutes later when Schweinsteiger collected the ball in space on the right-hand side. He cut inside both Ferreira and Petit before shooting. His effort was powerful and swerved late as it headed on target, wrong-footing Ricardo, who had already started moving the other way. The Portuguese keeper reacted well and nearly got a hand on it but there was too much pace on the shot and it nestled into the roof of the net. It was a deserved goal for the Bayern Munich midfielder, who had performed well without much end product all tournament and was perhaps harshly left out of the starting line-up in the semi-final.

It was Schweinsteiger who was causing the Portugal defence the majority of their problems and it was he that created the second goal. A simple free kick from the left-hand side was drilled low into the penalty area and, under no real pressure, Petit stuck out his leg and could only deflect the ball into his own goal. Portugal had conceded as many goals in this match as they had done all tournament and it seemed like their energy levels had dropped and their desire to win had all but evaporated. They did nearly get a goal back instantly as Deco picked up the ball on the edge of the area and fired a clever near-post effort but Kahn was there to tip the ball behind and maintain his clean sheet.

The contest was decided with just ten minutes to go as Schweinsteiger repeated the trick from his first goal, driving forwards on the left, cutting on to his right foot and hitting a swerving effort across goal. Once again Ricardo was caught out by the movement of the ball and had already taken a step to his right before having to dive back across, but he was unlikely to have reached it either way as the ball was perfectly placed in the side-netting. Three goals and all created by the Bayern midfielder. This was his moment to announce himself on the global stage and he would go on to become an integral part of the future German success. Klinsmann responded to the third goal by bringing on Thomas Hitzlsperger in his place and the reception the departing Schweinsteiger received from the crowd gathered in Stuttgart showed that they knew that he was becoming a key player.

Portugal, to their credit, still went forward in search of a consolation goal, with a Ronaldo free kick causing Kahn problems as it swerved erratically on its way towards goal, but the experienced keeper managed to do enough to push the ball clear from danger. They did manage to finally score again, ending their run of 365 minutes without a goal, when Figo, introduced as a substitute, whipped in a perfect cross that evaded the German defenders and goalkeeper to find Nuno Gomes free at the far post. He planted a diving header firmly into the back of the net. It was a goal that they definitely deserved as they had played their part in an absorbing contest but the result was entirely fair. As had been the case all tournament, Portugal simply could not convert enough of their chances.

All focus after the match was on Germany, however. They had ended the competition on a high, albeit not the one they were hoping for. They had entertained throughout, being one of the few teams committed to playing in a positive manner, and had been excellent hosts. The team had united the country, introducing a level of patriotism that had not been seen since the end of the Second World War. With great weather all summer, a strong performance from their own country and the introduction of the fan zones throughout the host cities designed to welcome people into the country and create a party-like atmosphere, there can be no doubt that Germany had been an excellent host nation. The tournament motto had been 'A Time to Make Friends', and Germany certainly filled that remit.

9pm, 8 July 2006
Gottlieb-Daimler-Stadion, Stuttgart
Attendance: 52,000
Referee: Toru Kamikawa (Japan)

Germany 3 (Schweinsteiger 56, 78, Petit 60 (o.g.))
Portugal 1 (Nuno Gomes 88)

Germany: Oliver Kahn (c), Philipp Lahm, Jens Nowotny, Christoph Metzelder, Marcell Jansen, Bernd Schneider, Sebastian Kehl, Torsten Frings, Bastian Schweinsteiger (Thomas Hitzlsperger 79), Miroslav Klose (Oliver Neuville 65), Lukas Podolski (Mike Hanke 71). **Manager:** Jürgen Klinsmann.

Portugal: Ricardo, Paulo Ferreira, Fernando Meira, Ricardo Costa, Nuno Valente (Nuno Gomes 69), Costinha (Petit 46), Maniche, Cristiano Ronaldo, Deco, Simão, Pauleta (c) (Luís Figo 77). **Manager:** Luis Felipe Scolari.

Booked: Frings (7), Schweinsteiger (78); Costa (24), Costinha (33), Ferreira (60)

Final

SO, IT all came down to this – 32 teams, 63 matches and 145 goals so far and now just two teams and one match remained. Italy vs France, to win the greatest honour that a footballer can achieve. As the footballing world, along with the high-profile celebrities that always seem to populate these major sporting events at the expense of actual fans, descended on Berlin, the players would have been feeling the nerves and anticipation ahead of the final. Well, most of them. In his autobiography, *I Think Therefore I Play*, Andrea Pirlo described his routine before the biggest match of his career: 'I spent the afternoon of Sunday, 9 July, 2006 in Berlin sleeping and playing the PlayStation.' While Pirlo may not have been feeling the nerves, his team-mates must surely have been, and that was perhaps where the advantage could lie for the French. Domenech could call upon players who had won the World Cup before, with six of his squad victorious in 1998, and his starting line-up having three from that final in Barthez, Thuram and Zidane, as well as Vieira who came off the bench in that final.

If there were any doubts about the competitive nature of the match, an early challenge from Cannavaro on Henry certainly belied those thoughts. The Italian captain caught the Arsenal striker with his arm, completely accidentally, but it left Henry stricken on the floor and looking rather shaky as the medical team tended to him. With the improved concussion protocols in place now, perhaps he would have been removed from the match, but he came back on to the pitch and carried on, however fit he may have been. There was certainly no holding back by the Italians, as Zambrotta dived into a wild challenge on Vieira on the edge of the French penalty area as he tried to bring the ball clear and was maybe fortunate that the challenge occurred so early that the Argentine referee only gave a yellow card.

From that free kick, Barthez launched the ball upfield, where Henry won his header, flicking the ball on for Malouda, who found space in between Cannavaro and Materazzi to race into. As he was bearing down on goal and heading into the area but Materazzi came over to challenge and clipped the heels of the winger, who went down under the contact. The referee had little hesitation and immediately pointed to the penalty spot. The replay was inconclusive, showing that there was a little bit of contact between the two but Materazzi had been trying to jump clear of making a challenge and it was the flailing heel of Malouda that had initiated contact. Whether or not it should have been awarded, it had been, and France had the perfect opportunity to take an early lead.

Predictably, it was Zidane who took the responsibility on his shoulders. He was the reason that France had made it to this stage, playing a key role in each knockout round, including scoring a penalty against Portugal last time out. He also knew what it took to score in a World Cup Final, having scored twice in 1998 in a man-of-the match performance. Facing his former Juventus team-mate, Zidane replicated his short run-up. In a way that maybe only he could, he strode towards the ball with purpose, appearing to line up a powerful strike but, at the last second, he slowed down and dinked a Panenka. So named after Antonín Panenka, the Czechoslovakian midfielder who was the first to delicately chip his effort down the middle, it was a risky strategy, because if the keeper did not move, it would be the easiest save they could make. However, Buffon dived to his right, but Zidane had put more power into his chip than he would have liked and the ball sailed towards the top of the goal. It bounced off the underside of the crossbar, down behind the goal line, up against the bar again and then was grabbed by Buffon. Zidane wheeled away with his arm aloft, knowing it had crossed the line and the referee agreed, awarding the goal. It was a moment of sheer brilliance and stupidity all in one. Had it bounced differently, it would be remembered as a ridiculous decision but this was almost a more fitting a way for Zidane to score. The confidence of a player to take a Panenka in the World Cup Final in their final-ever match and to see it clip the crossbar and bounce in. It was the dream start for France, who had the early lead.

The breakthrough forced the Italians to change their game plan as they now had to go on the attack. They took a few minutes to regroup before mounting their fightback, with Grosso getting into space on the left but wasting the crossing opportunity with a poor effort. Focusing down the flanks had been a key aspect of Italy's play all tournament and France had struggled against the Portuguese wide players in their previous match, so it made sense that the positive play from the Azzurri was down the wings, with Grosso and Zambrotta causing problems.

Camoranesi did well to win a corner from Abidal on the right-hand side. Pirlo's delivery was predictably perfect. It found Materazzi in perfect stride, the central defender rising higher than Vieira to power a header on target. It sailed over the head of Barthez and Ribéry on the line and drew Italy level. Two goals in the first 20 minutes, one from a predictable goalscorer, the other less so. This, however, was not the link between Zidane and Materazzi that this final would be forever remembered for.

Having dragged themselves back into the contest, Italy continued to push forwards to try to take control. They were playing with the same intensity that had seen them prevail over Germany in the semi-final, and France were struggling to cope. Another Pirlo corner found the head of Materazzi again. His header was on target but was cleared off the line. France did fashion a chance of their own when Malouda shot weakly at Buffon but that was very much against the run of play. The Italian midfield had total dominance over their French counterparts, Gattuso doing an incredible job of nullifying the threat that Zidane posed, and he almost created a goal for his team when bulldozing his way forwards through sheer force of will. The ball fell loose to Toni, who got a shot away but was denied by a brilliant challenge from Thuram. The resulting corner again caused problems for the French defence, with Toni winning the ball and watching in agony as his header crashed against the crossbar and went over. Every set piece for Italy was creating a goalscoring opportunity and it seemed to be their best route to goal.

France did manage to create another chance before the break, with Henry nearly getting the better of Cannavaro, but the Italian captain continued his remarkable tournament with another excellent challenge. It was the last meaningful action of the first half, which had been a half played at an incredible pace. The early penalty for France was exactly what the final needed as it forced Italy out of their shell, and even after their equaliser they did not retreat into it. Pirlo's delivery from free kicks and corners was causing problems and France looked unable to cope.

Buoyed by whatever Domenech said to them at the break, France started the second half with intensity. Inside the opening minute Henry did brilliantly to dribble beyond three Italian defenders but could only shoot straight at Buffon, before repeating the trick a few minutes later, watching on as his cross was cleared behind by Zambrotta. The French striker was becoming the most dangerous player on the pitch, with everything good for France coming through him. He nearly got a shot away in the area before his clever control on halfway released Ribéry on the right-hand side. He drove forward before dropping the ball inside for Zidane, who laid it off for Malouda on the left. As Malouda made his way into the box, Zambrotta came to tackle him and produced a clumsy challenge that did not get the ball. The referee awarded a goal kick for Italy but it could easily have been a second French penalty as it was a silly tackle to make. Malouda got to the byline again just a minute later but his cross was narrowly behind Ribéry as France continued their impressive start to the second period.

The first concern for France in the second half came just before the hour mark when Vieira pulled up with what looked like a pulled hamstring. Domenech made a surprising choice as his replacement, bringing on Lens midfielder Alou Diarra for just his tenth international cap and his first minutes of the tournament. Lippi responded with changes of his own, Iaquinta replacing Perrotta in an attacking move and De Rossi coming on for his Roma team-mate Totti to try to wrestle back control over the middle of the pitch. It was De Rossi's first appearance since being suspended for an elbow on USA's McBride during the group stage, so he would have certainly been coming on with a point to prove.

Just two minutes after those changes, Italy thought they had taken the lead when Toni produced a brilliant glancing header from a free kick that nestled into the bottom corner, but he had broken the line too soon and the assistant rightfully raised his flag for offside.

After great work from Makélélé in the middle of the pitch, he freed Henry one-on-one with Cannavaro. For the first time all tournament, someone got the better of the central defender as Henry manoeuvred the ball on to his right foot, creating enough space to get a shot away. Unfortunately for France, Buffon was still there as the last line of defence, and he produced a strong save to palm the ball away.

The tempo now seemed to be catching up with the players, understandable at the very end of a competitive tournament, and the chances had started to dry up. A Pirlo free kick went narrowly wide, then Henry nearly picked out Zidane in the box, but the ball was cleared well by Materazzi. There was a moment of worry for the French captain when he went down holding his shoulder and seemed to be indicating to the French bench that he would need to be taken off, but he continued, determined to not let his career end on that note.

As the final whistle blew, thoughts turned back to the final of the European Championships in 2000 when France beat Italy in extra time thanks to a David Trezeguet golden goal. There would not be a winner in that manner this time as FIFA had removed the rule after Euro 2004, but France hoped for a similar moment. Trezeguet even came on to the pitch just before the break in extra time as Domenech attempted to recreate history, but it was almost Zidane that produced a déjà vu moment. Both of Zidane's goals in 1998 had come from headers and he almost headed France to victory once more. He started the move, playing a simple pass wide right for Sagnol. As the full-back prepared to cross, Zidane drifted unmarked into the penalty area, leaving Pirlo at the edge of the area and ghosting in behind Gattuso. The cross was perfect. It floated over the head of Gattuso and on to the head of the arriving Zidane, who powered a header just under the crossbar. It was nearly the perfect moment for Zidane's career to end on. Denying him that moment was Buffon, who reacted with cat-like reflexes and produced a magnificent fingertip stop to turn the ball over the crossbar. The more often the save was shown on replay, the better it looked.

The momentum was firmly in France's favour now, with Italy looking tired. With Henry replaced by Wiltord, all French eyes were on Zidane to produce for his nation one last time. With just ten minutes remaining, a Malouda cross into the area was easily repelled by an Italian defender and they tried to burst upfield. A physical contest between Del Piero and Makélélé was ruled to be a foul by the striker and, as France tried to go forward again, the referee called a halt to the play. Watching on television, it was unclear why. Argentine referee Horacio Elizondo walked towards the Italian area as Materazzi lay prone on the floor. The broadcast cut to a replay of the Italian defender and Zidane walking away from the box in conversation. The two were clearly exchanging words and Zidane began to jog in front of his marker. Something clearly irked the French playmaker, as he stopped, turned back towards Materazzi, inexplicably reared back and launched a headbutt squarely into the middle of his chest. Describing it as a headbutt really does not do it justice. As James Horncastle wrote in a piece for *The Athletic*, it more closely resembled a rutting ram than a headbutt. It was perfect contact, a similar connection to that he had made on the ball just five minutes earlier.

The camera had not been on the incident at the time but the replay was conclusive. Yet this was in the days before VAR and the referee had been focused on the Italian break, so he had not seen the act unfold. He asked for help from his team, with both assistants saying they had not seen it. The Spanish fourth official, Luis Medina Cantalejo, offered a saving grace. He alerted Elizondo to the fact that Zidane had produced a headbutt. There was controversy as the French claimed that he had only seen it on a replay monitor at the side of the pitch rather than witnessing it himself, a claim he strongly denied. As referees were prohibited from using technology to aid them at this time, had he not seen it live then Zidane would have been free to carry on. As such, Elizondo had the information he needed and produced the only possible outcome. A red card. In a single moment of chaos, Zidane had ended his career in an almost unthinkable manner.

The speculation was immediate. What had been said between the two to cause such a violent outburst. There was a rumour that it had been a comment made about Zidane's mother, an accusation strongly refuted by Materazzi, eventually leading to him winning a libel case against the British tabloid press. The silence from both in the aftermath fuelled speculation further. It was only years later that what was said emerged into public knowledge. As Materazzi had been marking Zidane tightly in the area before the cross came in, the French playmaker walked away telling his opponent that he could have his shirt after the match if he was so desperate for it. The defender produced a classic childlike insult, telling him he would rather have his sister. The comment, as throwaway as it was, struck a nerve and led to one of the most iconic moments in footballing history. It created two of the most recognisable images, one of Materazzi collapsing to the ground and then of Zidane walking forlornly past the World Cup trophy. This was supposed to be his crowning achievement, his graceful way of saying goodbye to the game he loved. It had ended on his terms, just not terms anybody would have expected.

While the watching world came to terms with what they had witnessed, those on the pitch still had a match to finish. Understandably, the atmosphere among the players had gone flat, with most still reeling from what they had seen. The final ten minutes drifted away without any real action as both teams seemed to settle for penalties. That outcome historically favoured the French, who had won two out of the three shoot-outs they had contested, while Italy had lost all three of theirs, including to France in 1998. The best penalty taker for France was now off the pitch though. Only once before had a World Cup Final been decided on penalties, back in 1994 when Italy lost to Brazil, and Roberto Baggio, usually a reliable penalty taker, had missed the target completely.

Italy won the coin toss and opted to take the first penalty, sending up their best taker in Andrea Pirlo. Some teams have a habit of saving their best penalty takers for the fifth penalty, a gamble, as the shoot-out may already have been decided by that stage. But not Lippi. Pirlo was the tone-setter. The little maestro was the calmest man in the stadium, shooting high and straight as Barthez dived to his right. Wiltord followed and sent his effort right into the left-hand corner of Buffon's goal, a shot that would have been almost impossible to save even if the Italian had guessed correctly.

Then came the turn of the pantomime villain of the night in French eyes. The scorer of the equaliser and the man they believed conspired to have Zidane sent off. If Materazzi was feeling any sort of pressure, he did not show it. His spot kick was perfect, low and into the corner, giving Barthez zero chance of saving it even though he guessed right. The second French taker was that man Trezeguet, who had broken Italian hearts six years earlier. He, like his captain, went for height but chose a powerful strike rather than a delicate one. His penalty crashed into the crossbar and bounced down and away from goal. The advantage was now with Italy.

De Rossi was given the responsibility to press home that advantage, hoping to make amends for missing most of the tournament through suspension. Many would have preferred his Roma team-mate Totti, but the midfield anchor was inch-perfect with his effort, showing Trezeguet how to do it as his effort went to the same spot the Frenchman had aimed for but settled into the top corner rather than hitting the bar. Barthez did guess correctly but was given no chance by the pace and accuracy. Penalties are heavily weighted in the favour of the takers, but the goalkeepers were being given no chance with any of them so far. However, Abidal bucked that trend, leaving his effort at a saveable height for Buffon. Fortunately for France, Buffon had gambled wrong and was diving in the other direction.

All the Italians had to do was hold their nerve and they would win. They had the edge and just needed to cement it. Del Piero was the man tasked with that job and he confidently smashed his spot kick to Barthez's right, the goalkeeper having dived in the other direction. At 4-2 to Italy it was now sudden death for France. If Willy Sagnol missed his penalty, Italy were world champions for a fourth time. Not many would have predicted that it would be the right-back carrying that pressure on his shoulders, but he managed it well. He drilled his effort hard to the keeper's right, watching relieved as it hit the back of the net, Buffon may not have saved it even if he guessed correctly.

So, all eyes turned to Italy's left-back Fabio Grosso. The unexpected match-winner in the semi-final was stepping up once again to further etch his name into Italian football folklore. His run-up was central, not offering much clue as to his intention. He struck the ball hard and true with his left foot to Barthez's left as he dived right. The French keeper looked on helplessly, hoping the ball rose high enough to hit the woodwork and bounce clear. The French had no such luck. Grosso had produced a picture-perfect penalty. The ball crashed into the top corner, leaving the Palermo defender to sprint across the Berlin turf in sheer joy and disbelief. He was mobbed by his team-mates, half celebrating with him and half rushing to Buffon. The joy was clear. The despair on Barthez's face equally so as he crouched by his goalpost, staring into the distance.

The Italian celebrations were joyous, a bright end to a miserable year for Italian football under the cloud of the Calciopoli scandal. Those allegations and the repeated criticism from the world media had fuelled a siege mentality among those in the squad, creating a team that would not be denied. Their celebrations were deserved and Cannavaro's trophy lift among the best in World Cup history, the picture becoming an iconic symbol of this tournament.

But all attention was seemingly on Zidane. It was scarcely believable at the time. It is still unfathomable now. Zidane had taken a tournament littered with moments and brushed them all aside. This was forever his tournament. He was named player of the tournament, an honour that should maybe have gone to Cannavaro, but this was his legacy. When thinking about Zidane at World Cups, the first memory that jumps to mind is this final, this use of his head, rather than the match-winning uses from 1998. It is hard to find the words to summarise what happened that night in Berlin, but it left a hole in Zidane's legacy. This is not how he wanted his time with France to end. He wanted to leave as a champion, and he maintains he has unfinished business. His goal is clear: to lead France to glory once again, this time as their coach. Whether or not that happens remains to be seen, but one thing is clear: whenever Zidane reaches a World Cup Final, expect drama, one way or another.

9pm, 9 July 2006
Olympiastadion, Berlin
Attendance: 69,000
Referee: Horacio Elizondo (Argentina)

Italy 1 (Materazzi 19)
France 1 (Zidane 7 (p))
Italy won 5-3 on penalties after extra time

Shoot-out: Pirlo 1-0, Wiltord 1-1, Materazzi 2-1, Trezeguet missed, De Rossi 3-1, Abidal 3-2, Del Piero 4-2, Sagnol 4-3, Grosso 5-3

Italy: Gianluigi Buffon, Gianluca Zambrotta, Fabio Cannavaro (c), Marco Materazzi, Fabio Grosso, Mauro Camoranesi (Alessandro Del Piero 86), Gennaro Gattuso, Andrea Pirlo, Simone Perrotta (Vincenzo Iaquinta 61), Francesco Totti (Daniele De Rossi 61), Luca Toni. **Manager:** Marcello Lippi.

France: Fabien Barthez, Willy Sagnol, Lilian Thuram, William Gallas, Eric Abidal, Patrick Vieira (Alou Diarra 56), Claude Makélélé, Franck Ribéry (David Trezeguet 100), Zinedine Zidane (c), Florent Malouda, Thierry Henry (Sylvain Wiltord 107). **Manager:** Raymond Domenech.

Booked: Zambrotta (5); Sagnol (12), Makélélé (76), Malouda (111) Sent off: Zidane (110)

Legacy

IN ZIDANE'S headbutt, the tournament had been given its iconic moment. Its moment that would live on forever. Yet to remember it entirely for that is unfair. It had been an exciting tournament throughout, played by a myriad of the generation's greatest talents at the end of their career, some at the start in Ronaldo, Messi and Modrić, and was played under scorching sun with amicable hosts.

A party atmosphere had enveloped the entire country, leading to new-found positive associations with German nationalism. As mentioned in *Das Reboot*, fans were flying German flags from their houses and cars, outwardly expressing a pride in their nation that had rarely been seen in the preceding decades. As Uli Hesse wrote in an article for *FourFourTwo* magazine in 2014, Germany was not a nation that was comfortable with expressions of national pride, primarily due to the horrific events of the 20th century. Perhaps there was unease at the reception they would get in welcoming the world inside its borders once more, but they cannot be seen as anything other than perfect hosts. FIFA's creation of fan zones had been an enormous success. Introduced to encourage people without tickets to visit the country and spend their money at FIFA-sanctioned events, they were a greater success than any may have imagined. Rather than treating fans without tickets as a security risk, they were welcomed with open arms by the host cities, contributing to the positive atmosphere throughout the tournament and country. The German National Tourist Board estimated that the fan fests brought 21 million visitors. The fan zones were so popular that they had to be expanded during the tournament in some cities. Their success can be seen in the fact that they have been implemented at every World Cup since and other confederations have copied and brought in their own version for their tournaments. FIFA President Sepp Blatter declared that Germany were the best hosts in the history of the World Cup and it would be hard to argue with that assessment.

On the pitch, the tournament did not disappoint. Germany performed better than expected, reaching the semi-finals while playing an attacking brand of football. The positivity of the team on the pitch helped contribute to the good atmosphere being experienced off it as Germans could get behind the entertaining nature of their team. The emergence of a generation of young talent, primarily Lahm, Schweinsteiger and Podolski, offered hope for a brighter future and Klinsmann had sown the seeds of a more proactive approach in the German national team. It worked in the immediate and long term, as few felt a sense of disappointment that they could not edge past Italy and earn themselves a spot in the final. The groundwork laid here was key to Germany's run to becoming world champions in 2014. This team had reunited a nation and its love for its national team; it is hard to think of a better legacy than that.

Away from the hosts, there was still plenty to enjoy. Sure, there were cagey matches, some poor ones and one particularly dreadful one. That happens at every tournament. There were storylines throughout, with very few matches being lopsided or foregone conclusions. There were eight debutant nations, depending on definition. Eight countries entered for the first time as sovereign nations, although the records have the Czech Republic and Serbia and Montenegro as the continuation of Czechoslovakia and the Kingdom of Yugoslavia. Even if only six are counted, it was still the highest number of new nations since 1934 and there have only been four debutants since 2006.

The entertainers in Argentina and Brazil shone brightly but burned out quickly. Dark horses either fell at the group stages (Ivory Coast, Czech Republic, Serbia and Montenegro) or performed well (Ukraine, Ghana) but the major nations rose to the task. The final eight contained all but one of the winners of the previous World Cups, with just Uruguay missing. With maybe Ukraine as the exception, the final eight had the strongest nations in the tournament. England showed promise but ultimately fell short on penalties, again. Portugal nearly got over their struggles at the sharp end of major international tournaments but were a quality goalscorer short of upsetting France.

Both finalists flattered to deceive but found themselves competing for the biggest honour in football. This was the end for France's best-ever generation of footballing talent, although the current one might argue differently. Zidane was leaving football for good. Makélélé and Thuram were likely to retire from internationals again. This was also the zenith for Italy. Cannavaro was the best defender on the planet. Serie A was a world-leading league still, although Calciopoli was tearing Juventus and the country apart.

The victory was a healing moment for Italian football. Their league had been torn apart and there had been pre-tournament calls for the national team to be kicked out. The siege mentality fostered in the Italian camp was played upon by Lippi, used as a motivating tactic to inspire his team, and it clearly worked as Italy showed every trick possible. There were tough matches, narrowly beating Australia in the first knockout round, yet they took part in one of the best matches in World Cup history, playing a classic in the semi-final against Germany, even though the score was 0-0 after 90 minutes.

Individually, the tournament was its usual success. As always, players were given the platform to express themselves and earn a move to a new club. Javier Mascherano and Carlos Tevez both departed Corinthians for West Ham United, Yaya Touré earned himself a move to from Olympiakos to Monaco, despite his nation's struggles, before excelling at both Barcelona and Manchester City, and the Netherlands' Dirk Kuyt showed enough to earn himself a switch from Feyenoord to Liverpool, where he would become a cult hero and stay for six seasons. This was the tournament of established stars rather than the unknowns. The squads were all littered with household names, with the debutant nations bringing their own stars. Ukraine had Andriy Shevchenko, Ghana had Michael Essien and the Ivory Coast were led by Didier Drogba, and those are just the ones who plied their trade in West London for Chelsea.

It also marked the end for some of the best players of their time. The tournament was the last time that Cafu and Roberto Carlos played for their nation, the last competitive match for Ronaldo, who only appeared in Brazil yellow again for a friendly against Romania, and, perhaps most surprisingly, the last World Cup appearance for Ronaldinho, who was only 26. Mauricio Solís, Sami Al-Jaber, Ali Daei, Karel Poborský, Phillip Cocu, Claudio Reyna and Luís Figo all earned the last of their 100-plus caps for their respective nations while in Germany. These finals were the only World Cup appearances during the glittering careers of Andriy Shevchenko, Karel Poborský and Pavel Nedvěd, among others. The cast list for the tournament was unlike any other and it marked the end of an era, with Cristiano Ronaldo and Lionel Messi dominating football headlines from this point on.

Any retrospective look at sporting events highlights the problems rather than the positives. The lens we are viewing through is different than it was when first viewed. We are more cynical, more world-weary and the flaws that may have been glossed over at a younger age are increasingly prevalent now. Yet the 2006 World Cup still evokes positive memories and feelings. The atmosphere it was played in was one of the best ever seen as Germany hosted with perfection. Both on and off the pitch, the tournament excelled. Wonder goals from the very beginning, close groups and cagey knockout matches. It was the perfect modern tournament played by 'golden generations' for most competing nations.

Bibliography

Books:

Foot, J., *Calcio: A History of Italian Football* (Great Britain: Fourth Estate, 2006)

Hesse, U., *Tor! The Story of German Football* (Edinburgh: Polaris Publishing Ltd, 2022)

Honigstein, R., *Das Reboot: How German Football Reinvented Itself and Conquered the World* (Great Britain: Yellow Jersey Press, 2015)

Hubbard, R., *From Partition to Solidarity: The First 100 Years of Polish Football* (Leicester: RAH, 2019)

Hunter, G., *Spain: The Inside Story of La Roja's Historic Treble* (United Kingdom: BackPage Press, 2013)

Lampard, F., *Totally Frank: The Autobiography of Frank Lampard* (United Kingdom: HarperCollins Publishers, 2006)

Mustapha, I., *No Longer Naïve: African Football's Growing Impact at the World Cup* (Sussex: Pitch Publishing, 2021)

Pirlo, A. and Alciato, A., *I Think Therefore I Play* (Milan: BackPage Press, 2014)

Spiro, M., *Sacré Bleu: From Zidane to Mbappé – A Football Journey* (Great Britain: Biteback Publishing Ltd, 2021)

Totti, F., *Gladiator* (Liverpool: deCoubertin Books, 2021)

Wilson, J., *Angels with Dirty Faces: The Footballing History of Argentina* (London: Weidenfeld & Nicolson, 2016)

Wilson, J., *Inverting the Pyramid: The History of Football Tactics* (United Kingdom: Orion, 2008)

Magazines:
FourFourTwo

Websites:
spiegel.de
thesefootballtimes.com
theguardian.com
bbc.co.uk/sport
transfermarkt.co.uk
footballia.net

YouTube Channels:
FIFATV